BECOMING A WRITER

BY DOROTHEA BRANDE

ON BECO... LIST

BY JOH...

ONE WRITER'S BEGINNINGS

BY EUDORA WELTY

BECOMING A WRITER

BY DOROTHEA BRANDE

ON BECOMING A NOVELIST

BY JOHN GARDNER

ONE WRITER'S BEGINNINGS

BY EUDORA WELTY

QUALITY PAPERBACK BOOK CLUB
NEW YORK

Becoming a Writer

by Dorothea Brande

Foreword by John Gardner

For Two Josephines

Contents

🐦

Foreword

It's an astonishing thing that Dorothea Brande's *Becoming a Writer* should ever have fallen out of print, and a lucky thing it is now back in the light where it belongs. The root problems of the writer, whether the writer is young or old, just starting out or much published, are no different today than in 1934, when *Becoming a Writer* was first published. They do not have to do with "the techniques of writing fiction" — the subject matter of all creative writing courses — and insofar as the root problems never get mentioned, almost all creative writing courses are for most people most of the time failures. The root problems of the writer are personality problems: He or she cannot get started, or starts a story well then gets lost or loses heart, or writes very well some of the time, badly the rest of the time, or writes brilliantly but after one superb story or novel cannot write again, or writes brilliantly while the creative writing course lasts but after it is over can no longer write. The root problems, in other words, are problems of confidence, self-respect, freedom: The writer's demon is imprisoned by the various ghosts in the unconscious.

Ms. Brande points out — with the delightful wit we find everywhere in her book — that for the writer suffering from uncertainty and self-doubt, writing teachers and books about writing, not to mention symposia of famous authors, do to the young (or old) struggling writer just about the worst thing they could do: "In the opening lecture, within the first few pages of his book, within a sentence or two of his authors' symposium, he will be told rather shortly that 'genius cannot be taught'; and there goes his hope glimmering. For whether he knows it or not, he is in search of the very thing that is denied him in that dismissive sentence." Ms. Brande's purpose in *Becoming a Writer* is to make available to the writer the very thing usually denied.

She is right that genius can be taught (once the secret emptiness of that phrase is understood) because in fact genius is as common as old shoes. Everybody has it, some more than others, perhaps; but that hardly matters, since no one can hope to use up more than a very small portion of his or her native gift. Every nightmare (and even dogs have them) hints at the secret reserves of imaginative power in the human mind. What the stalled or not-yet-started writer needs is some magic for getting in touch with himself, some key. The writer needs to know what kinds of habits of thought and action impede progress, what unnoticed forces undermine confidence, and so on. These problems are special for the writer, she points out. Writing teachers and how-to-write books are peculiarly pessimistic. "Books written for painters do not imply that the chances are that the reader can never be anything but a conceited dauber, nor do textbooks on engineering start out by warning the student that because he has been able to make a grasshopper out of two rubber bands and a matchstick he is not to think he is likely ever to be an honor to his chosen profession." Ms. Brande knows and exposes the reasons for this mistaken pessimism in the field of writing. For one thing, most successful writers (and writing teachers) are not conscious themselves of how they got past the root problems; and having learned by experience that they cannot help others past them (in fact not fully understanding that the problems are there to get past), they give warning in advance of their limitation, unfortunately laying the blame on the student and thereby incidentally intensifying the student's problems.

There are various other reasons for this pessimism, this widespread error, even among writing teachers, that "writing cannot be taught." Ms. Brande comments on the workaday world's stereotypic idea about writers — how they're childlike, undisciplined people, possibly witches, since when writers are very good at what they do they seem to know more than a decent person ought to know. How writers, more than other artists, have no visible proof of their specialness once they've achieved it. Visual artists, carrying around their leather-enclosed portfolios, and musicians, bringing complicated and persuasive noise out of tubing or pieces of string and wood, have cumbersome physical evidence that they are not like other mortals. Writers only use words, as even parrots do. The defensiveness writers feel in the beginning and often feel even after they've achieved success (since to write at all is to lay oneself open to attack, even scorn) can take shape, in the older writer or writing teacher, as a kind of arrogant exclusiveness: Though he takes your money for the creative-writing course, he would not have you believe you are even in potential as clever as he is. Ms. Brande says, "You are likely to hear that your desire to write is perhaps only an infantile exhibitionism, or to be warned that because your friends think you are a great writer (as if they ever did!) the world cannot be expected to share that fond opinion. And so on, most tiresomely."

Ms. Brande's purpose, then, is to lay the ghosts — by specific advice and exercises lead the writer into close touch with his-her unconscious, help the writer to develop healthy habits (there are reasons most writers smoke too much and drink too much coffee, if not gin), and guide the writer to freedom from all forms of writer's block. (Her approach, I might mention, is wonderfully forward looking: Though TM was unknown, I think, at the time she wrote, she gives ingenious and subtle exercises in meditation, even speaks of what we would call mantras.) Her whole focus, and a very valuable focus indeed, is on the writer's mind and heart. Except incidentally and in passing, she has nothing to say about writing technique. She would perhaps argue, if one could raise the question with her, that technique lies outside the specific concern of this book, which is the root problems; but here and there she betrays a real and, based on her own experience, apparently justified distrust of writing classes. At one point she mentions the possibility that if the student did not suffer the psychological ailments she is out to eradicate, he would probably not be in a writing course at all. At various points she shows a touch of impatience with classes on "story form," and she mentions that all of the creative-writing classes she herself attended were, like most books on writing, disappointing. She speaks of the tendency of workshop writers to go after one another's stories "tooth and fang"; and she again and again urges (rightly) that true original-ity can come only from within.

It is certainly true that very few creative-writing courses get at the root problems — Ms. Brande's book makes me see that I myself have never seen or taught one that did — but I do not share Ms. Brande's low opinion of creative-writing classes. I do not mention this to suggest reservations about the work she does here but only to point out that the root psychological prob-lems are not the only problems a writer must deal with. I cannot remember, myself, ever suffering any form of writer's block, and I've had, I think, a number of students who could say the same. Al-most no one would argue, surely, that Cezanne's painting students, or the piano students of Cortot, would have been better off with a smart psychi-atrist, or that what the young engineer really needs is a wise guru from Bombay. Though these days it is fashionable in some quarters to attack creative-writing classes, it seems to me obvious that, for the student lucky enough not to be plagued by psychological root problems, or for the student who has somehow overcome those problems, such classes serve an invaluable function. I can think of only a handful of well-known American writers who have not taken creative-writing courses, and usually not one course but several. What Ms. Brande's book suggests to me is not that creative-writing courses do not do their job well, but that they do it well only for the lucky few, turning away or turning off those whose problems are anterior to the matter of the course. It is easy for writing teachers to become so fixed on high standards of writing (it is his or her own implacable will to write well or not at all that has made the teacher worthy of the role), and to become so impatient with those who, presumably from laziness or bad character or stupidity, do not do their work, that teachers dismiss a majority of those they work with as "not really writers" or downright nincompoops, failing to notice where the nincompoopery really lies. If student writers go after one another "tooth and fang," or anyway if they try it more than once, the fault is the teacher's — he or she has failed to set the proper tone.

No one can write successfully without some measure of technical mastery and an ability to analyze truthfully and usefully the virtues and defects in his own work or the work of others. Those are the things one learns in a good creative-writing course. Ms. Brande's book brilliantly lays the foundation for such a course. Until the root problems have been confronted and dealt with, the student of creative writing is the victim of an unwitting mean trick. And until the teacher has recognized his or her responsibility to deal with those root human problems, as well as with those problems more dear to our hearts, the teacher belongs not in the classroom but in somebody's army — preferably far away. I speak of such teachers, you will have noticed, with great scorn. One often takes that tone when one feels guilty. I mean to improve myself (pray for me), so that when Ms. Brande sees me trudging toward Heaven she will not use her influence and cunning wit and have the gate locked.

John Gardner
Susquehanna, Pa.
October 25, 1980

In Introduction

For most of my adult life I have been engaged in the writing, the editing, or the criticizing of fiction. I took, and I still take, the writing of fiction seriously. The importance of novels and short stories in our society is great. Fiction supplies the only philosophy that many readers know; it establishes their ethical, social, and material standards; it confirms them in their prejudices or opens their minds to a wider world. The influence of any widely read book can hardly be overestimated. If it is sensational, shoddy, or vulgar our lives are the poorer for the cheap ideals which it sets in circulation; if, as so rarely happens, it is a thoroughly good book, honestly conceived and honestly executed, we are all indebted to it. The movies have not undermined the influence of fiction. On the contrary, they have extended its field, carrying the ideas which are already current among readers to those too young, too impatient, or too uneducated to read.

So I make no apology for writing seriously about the problems of fiction writers; but until two years ago I should have felt apologetic about adding another volume to the writer's working library. During the period of my own apprenticeship—and, I confess, long after that apprenticeship should have been over—I read every book on the technique of fiction, the constructing of plots, the handling of characters, that I could lay my hands on. I sat at the feet of teachers of various schools: I have heard the writing of fiction analyzed by a neo-Freudian; I submitted myself to an enthusiast who saw in the glandular theory of personality determination an inexhaustible mine for writers in search of characters; I underwent instruction from one who drew diagrams and from another who started with a synopsis and slowly inflated it into a completed story. I have lived in a literary "colony" and talked to practicing writers who regarded their calling variously as a trade, a profession, and (rather sheepishly) as an art. In short, I have had firsthand experience with almost every current "approach" to the problems of writing, and my bookshelves overflow with the works of other instructors whom I have not seen in the flesh.

But two years ago—after still more years

spent in reading for publishers, choosing the fiction for a magazine of national circulation, writing articles, stories, reviews and more extended criticism, conferring informally with editors and with authors of all ages about their work—I began, myself, to teach a class in fiction writing. Nothing was further from my mind, on the evening of my first lecture, than adding to the top-heavy literature on the subject. Although I had been considerably disappointed in most of the books I had read and all the classes I had attended, it was not until I joined the ranks of instructors that I realized the true basis of my discontent.

That basis of discontent was that the difficulties of the average student or amateur writer begin long before he has come to the place where he can benefit by technical instruction in story writing. He himself is in no position to suspect that truth. If he were able to discover for himself the reasons for his aridity the chances are that he would never be found enrolled in any class at all. But he only vaguely knows that successful writers have overcome the difficulties which seem almost insuperable to him; he believes that accepted authors have some magic, or at the very lowest, some trade secret, which, if he is alert and attentive, he may surprise. He suspects, further, that the teacher who offers his services knows that magic, and may drop a word about it which will prove an Open Sesame to him. In the hope of hearing it, or surprising it, he will sit doggedly through a series of instructions in story types and plot forming and technical problems which have no relation to his own dilemma. He will buy or borrow every book with "fiction" in the title; he will read any symposium by authors in which they tell their methods of work.

In almost every case he will be disappointed. In the opening lecture, within the first few pages of his book, within a sentence or two of his authors' symposium, he will be told rather shortly that "genius cannot be taught"; and there goes his hope glimmering. For whether he knows it or not, he is in search of the very thing that is denied him in that dismissive sentence. He may never presume to call the obscure impulse to set down his picture of the world in words by the name of "genius," he may never dare to bracket himself for a moment with the immortals of writing, but the disclaimer that genius cannot be taught, which most teachers and authors seem to feel must be stated as early and as abruptly as possible, is the death knell of his real hope. He had longed to hear that there *was* some magic about writing, and to be initiated into the brotherhood of authors.

This book, I believe, will be unique; for I think he is right. I think there is such a magic, and that it is teachable. This book is all about the writer's magic.

One

❧

The Four Difficulties

So, having made my apologies, and stated my belief, I am going, from now on, to address myself solely to those who hope to write.

There is a sort of writer's magic. There is a procedure which many an author has come upon by happy accident or has worked out for himself which can, in part, be taught. To be ready to learn it you will have to go by a rather roundabout way, first considering the main difficulties which you will meet, then embarking on simple, but stringently self-enforced, exercises to overcome those difficulties. Last of all you must have the faith, or the curiosity, to take one odd piece of advice which will be unlike any of the exhortations that have come your way in classrooms or in text-books.

In one other way, beside the admission that there is an initiate's knowledge in writing, I am going to depart from the usual procedure of those who offer handbooks for young authors. Open book after book devoted to the writer's problems: in nine cases out of ten you will find, well toward the front of the volume, some very gloomy paragraphs warning you that you may be no writer at all, that you probably lack taste, judgment, imagination, and every trace of the special abilities necessary to turn yourself from an aspirant into an artist, or even into a passable craftsman. You are likely to hear that your desire to write is perhaps only an infantile exhibitionism, or to be warned that because your friends think you a great writer (as if they ever did!) the world cannot be expected to share that fond opinion. And so on, most tiresomely. The reasons for this pessimism about young writers are dark to me. Books written for painters do not imply that the chances are that the reader can never be anything but a conceited dauber, nor do textbooks on engineering start out by warning the student that because he has been able to make a grasshopper out of two rubber bands and a matchstick he is not to think that he is likely ever to be an honor to his chosen profession.

Perhaps it is true that self-delusion most often takes the form of a belief that one can write; as to that I cannot say. My own experience has been that there is no field where one who is in earnest about learning to do good work can make such enormous strides in so short a time. So I am going to write this book for those who are fully in earnest, trusting to their good sense and their intelligence to see to it that they learn the elements of sentence and paragraph structure, that they already see that when they have chosen to write they have assumed an obligation toward their reader to write as well as they are able, that they will have taken (and are still taking) every opportunity to study the masters of English prose writing, and that they have set up an exigent standard for themselves which they work without intermission to attain.

It may be that it is only my extraordinary good fortune that I have met more writers of whom these things are true than deluded imbecile scribblers. But tragically enough I have met a number of sensitive young men and women who have very nearly been persuaded, because they had come up against one of the obstacles to writing which we are shortly going to consider, that they were unfit to write at all. Sometimes the desire to write overcame the humiliation they had had to undergo; but others dropped back into a life with no creative outlet, unhappy, thwarted, and restless. I hope this book persuades some who are hesitating on the verge of abandoning writing to make a different decision.

In my experience four difficulties have turned up again and again. I am consulted about them far oftener than I am asked for help in story structure or character delineation. I suspect that every teacher hears the same complaints, but that, being seldom a practicing author, he tends to dismiss them as out of his field, or to see in them evidence that the troubled student has not the true vocation. Yet it is the very pupils who are most obviously gifted who suffer from these disabilities, and the more sensitively organized they are the higher the hazard seems to them. Your embryo journalist or hack writer seldom asks for help of any sort; he is off after agents and editors while his more serious brother-in-arms is suffering the torments of the damned because of his insufficiencies. Yet instruction in writing is oftenest aimed at the oblivious tradesman of fiction, and the troubles of the artist are dismissed or overlooked.

The Difficulty of Writing at All

First there is the difficulty of writing *at all*. The full, abundant flow that must be established if the writer is to be heard from simply will not begin. The stupid conclusion that if he cannot write easily he has mistaken his career is sheer nonsense. There are a dozen reasons for the difficulty which should be canvassed before the teacher is entitled to say that he can see no signs of hope for this pupil.

It may be that the root of the trouble is youth and humility. Sometimes it is self-consciousness that stems the flow. Often it is the result of misapprehensions about writing, or it arises from an embarrassment of scruples: the beginner may be waiting for the divine fire of which he has heard to glow unmistakably, and may believe that it can only be lighted by a fortuitous spark from above. The particular point to be noted just here is that this difficulty is *anterior* to any problems about story structure or plot building, and that unless the writer can be helped past it there is very likely to be no need for technical instruction at all.

The "One-Book Author"

Second, and far more often than the layman would believe, there is the writer who has had an early success but is unable to repeat it. Here again there is a cant explanation which is offered whenever this difficulty is met: this type of

writer, we are assured, is a "one-book author"; he
has written a fragment of autobiography, has un-
burdened himself of his animus against his parents and his background, and, being relieved,
cannot repeat his tour de force. But obviously
he does not consider himself a one-book author,
or we should hear nothing more from him.
Moreover, all fiction is, in the sense used here,
autobiographical, and yet there are fortunate
authors who go on shaping, recombining, and ob-
jectifying the items of their experience into a long
series of satisfactory books or stories. No; he is
right in considering the sudden stoppage of his
gift a morbid symptom, and right, usually, in
thinking it can be relieved.

It is evident, if this writer had a deserved success, that he already knows something, presumably a great deal, of the technical end of his art. His
trouble is not there, and, except by happy accident, no amount of counsel and advice about
technique will break the deadlock. He is, in some
ways, more fortunate than the beginner who cannot learn to write fluently, for at least he has given
evidence of his ability to set down words in impressive order. But his first impatience at being
unable to repeat his success can pass into discouragement and go on to actual despair; and an
excellent author may be lost in consequence.

The Occasional Writer

The third difficulty is a sort of combination of the first two: there are writers who can, at wearisomely long intervals, write with great effectiveness. I have had a pupil whose output was one excellent short story each year—hardly enough to satisfy either body or spirit. The sterile periods were torture to her; the world, till she could write again, a desert waste. Each time she found herself unable to work she was certain she could never repeat her success, and, on first acquaintance, she very nearly persuaded me of it. But when the cycle was lived through from start to finish she always wrote again, and wrote well.

Here again no technical instruction can touch the difficulty. Those who suffer from these silences in which not one idea seems to arise, not one sentence to come irresistibly to the mind's surface, may write like artists and craftsmen when they have once broken the spell. The teacher-consultant must form a definite idea of the root of the trouble and give counsel accordingly. It may be, again, that some notion of waiting for the lightning of inspiration to strike is behind the matter. Often it is the result of such ideals of perfection as can hardly bear the light of day. Sometimes, but rarely, a kind of touchy vanity is at work, which will not risk any rebuff and so will not allow anything to be undertaken which is not assured in advance of acceptance.

The Uneven Writer

The fourth difficulty actually has a technical aspect: it is the inability to carry a story, vividly but imperfectly apprehended, to a successful conclusion. Writers who complain of this are often able to start a story well, but find it out of control after a few pages. Or they will write a good story so drily and sparely that all its virtues are lost. Occasionally they cannot motivate their central action adequately, and the story carries no conviction.

It is quite true that those who find themselves in this pass can be greatly helped by learning about structure, about the various forms which the story may take, of the innocuous "tricks of the trade" which will help a story over the stile. But even here the real difficulty has set in long before the story *form* is in question. The author has not the self-confidence necessary to present his idea well, or he is too inexperienced to know how his characters would act in real life, or he is too shy to write as fully and emotionally as he needs to write if his story is to come to life. The writer who turns out one weak, embarrassed, or abruptly told story after another obviously needs something more than to have his individual manuscripts criticized for him. As soon as possible he must learn to trust his own feeling for the story, and to relax in the telling, until he has learned to use the sure, deft stroke of the man who is master of his medium. So even this dilemma comes down, after all, to being a trouble in the writer's personality rather than a defect in his technical equipment.

The Difficulties Not in Technical Equipment

Those are the four difficulties oftenest met at the outset of an author's writing life. Almost everyone who buys books on fiction writing, or takes classes in the art of the short story, suffers from one or another of these troubles, and until they have been overcome he is able to get very little benefit from the technical training which will be so valuable to him later. Occasionally writers are stimulated enough by the classroom atmosphere to turn out stories during the course; but they stop writing the moment that stimulus is withdrawn. An astonishing number who really want ardently to write are unable even to do assigned themes, yet they turn up hopefully —

sometimes year after year. Obviously they are looking for help that is not being given them; and obviously they are in earnest—ready to spend what time, effort, and money they can to emerge from the class of novices and "yearners" and take their place among productive artists.

Two

❧

What Writers Are Like

If these are the difficulties, then we must try to cure them where they arise — in the life and attitudes and habits, in the very character itself. After you have begun to see what it is to be a writer, after you learn how the artist functions and also learn to act in the same way, after you have arranged your affairs and your relations so that they help you instead of hinder you on your way toward the goal you have chosen, those books on your shelves on the technique of fiction, or those others which set up models of prose style and story structure for emulation, will look quite different to you, and be infinitely more helpful. This volume is not intended to replace those books on craftsmanship. There are some handbooks so valuable that no writer should be without them. In the appended bibliography I give the titles of those I have found most helpful for myself and for my pupils; I have no doubt that the list could be doubled or trebled to advantage. This book is not even a companion volume to such works as those; it is a preliminary to them. If it is successful it will teach the beginner not how to write, but how to be a writer; and that is quite another thing.

Cultivating a Writer's Temperament

First of all, then, becoming a writer is mainly a matter of cultivating a writer's temperament. Now the very word "temperament" is justly suspect among well-balanced persons, so I hasten to say that it is no part of the program to inculcate a wild-eyed bohemianism, or to set up moods and caprices as necessary accompaniments of the author's life. On the contrary; the moods and tempers, when they actually exist, are the symptoms of the artist's personality gone wrong— running off into waste effort and emotional exhaustion.

I say "when they actually exist," for much of the bumptious idiocy which the average man believes is an inalienable part of the artist's makeup has no being except in the eye of the beholder. He has heard tales of artists all his life, and very frequently he really believes "poetic license" to mean that the artist claims the right to ignore every moral code which inconveniences him. What the non-writer thinks about the artist would be of little account if it did not influence those who would like to write; they are persuaded against their will and their better sense that there is something fearful and dangerous in an artist's life, and some of the very shyness which we have seen as a mischief-maker comes from their giving too much credence to such popular notions.

False and Real Artists

After all, very few of us are born into homes where we see true examples of the artistic temperament, and since artists do certainly conduct their lives—necessarily—on a different pattern from the average man of business, it is very easy to misunderstand what he does and why he does it when we see it from the outside. The picture of the artist as a monster made up of one part vain child, one part suffering martyr, and one part *boulevardier* is a legacy to us from the last century, and a remarkably embarrassing inheritance. There is an earlier and healthier idea of the artist than that, the idea of the genius as a man more versatile, more sympathetic, more studious than his fellows, more catholic in his tastes, less at the mercy of the ideas of the crowd.

The grain of truth in the fin de siècle notion, though, is this: the author of genius does keep till his last breath the spontaneity, the ready sensitiveness, of a child, the "innocence of eye" that means so much to the painter, the ability to respond freshly and quickly to new scenes, and to old scenes as though they were new; to see traits and characteristics as though each were new-minted from the hand of God instead of sorting them quickly into dusty categories and pigeon-holing them without wonder or surprise; to feel situations so immediately and keenly that the word "trite" has hardly any meaning for him; and always to see "the correspondences between things" of which Aristotle spoke two thousand years ago. This freshness of response is vital to the author's talent.

The Two Sides of a Writer

But there is another element to his character, fully as important to his success. It is adult, discriminating, temperate, and just. It is the side of the artisan, the workman and the critic rather than the artist. It must work continually with and through the emotional and childlike side, or we have no work of art. If either element of the artist's character gets too far out of hand the result will be bad work, or no work at all. The writer's first task is to get these two elements of his nature into balance, to combine their aspects into one integrated character. And the first step toward that happy result is to split them apart for consideration and training!

"Dissociation" Not Always Psychopathic

We have all read a great many Sunday "feature stories," magazine articles, and books of popularized psychology; so our first impulse is to shy violently away from the words "dissociation of personality." A dual personality, to the reader who has a number of half-digested notions about the constitution of the mind, is an unlucky fellow who should be in a psychopathic ward; or, at the happiest, a flighty, hysterical creature. Nevertheless, every author is a very fortunate sort of dual personality, and it is this very fact that makes him such a bewildering, tantalizing, irritating figure to the plain man of affairs who flatters himself that he, at least, is all of a piece. But there is no scandal and no danger in recognizing that you have more than one side to your character. The journals and letters of men of genius are full of admissions of their sense of being dual or multiple in their nature: there is always the workaday man who walks, and the genius who flies. The idea of the alter ego, the other self, or higher self, recurs wherever genius becomes conscious of its own processes, and we have testimony for it in age after age.

Everyday Examples of Dual Personality

Indeed, the dual character of the genius is almost a commonplace. As a matter of fact, it is a commonplace for all of us, to some extent. Everyone has had the experience of acting with a decision and neatness in an emergency which seem later to him to savor of the miraculous; this was the figure which Frederick W. H. Myers used to convey his idea of the activity of genius. Or there is the experience of the "second wind" that comes after long grinding effort, when suddenly fatigue seems to drop away and a new character to arise like a phoenix from the exhausted mind or body; and the work that went so haltingly begins to flow under the hand. There is the obscurer, but cognate, experience of having reached a decision, solved a problem, while we slept, and finding the decision good, the solution valid. All these everyday miracles bear a relation to genius. At such moments the conscious and the unconscious conspire together to bring about the maximum effect; they play into each other's hands, supporting, strengthening, and supplementing each other, so that the resulting action comes from the full, integral personality, bearing the authority of the undivided mind.

The man of genius is one who habitually (or very often, or very successfully) acts as his less gifted brothers only rarely do. He not only acts *in* an event, but he creates an event, leaving his record of the moment on paper, canvas, or in stone. As it were, he makes his own emergency and acts in it, and his willingness both to instigate and perform marks him off from his more inert, less courageous comrades.

Everyone who has seriously wanted to write has some hint of this. Often it is in the very moment of vision that the first difficulties arise. Embarkation on the career is easy enough; an inclination to reverie, a love of books, the early discovery that it is not too difficult to turn a phrase — to find any or all of these things in one's first adolescent consciousness is to believe that one has found the inevitable, and not too formidable, vocation.

The Slough of Despond

But then comes the dawning comprehension of all that a writer's life implies: not easy day-dreaming, but hard work at turning the dream into reality without sacrificing all its glamour; not the passive following of someone else's story, but the finding and finishing of a story of one's own; not writing a few pages which will be judged for style or correctness alone, but the prospect of turning out paragraph after paragraph and page after page which will be read for style, content, and effectiveness. Nor is this by any means all the beginning writer foresees. He worries to think of his immaturity, and wonders how he ever dared to think he had a word worth saying. He gets as stagestruck at the thought of his unseen readers as any sapling actor. He discovers that when he is able to plan a story step by step, the fluency he needs to write it has flown out the window; or that when he lets himself go on a loose rein, suddenly the story is out of hand. He fears that he has a tendency to make his stories all alike, or paralyzes himself with the notion that he will never, when this story is finished, find another that he likes as well. He will begin to follow current reputations and harry himself because he has not this writer's humor or that one's ingenuity. He will find a hundred reasons to doubt himself and not one for self-confidence. He will suspect that those who encouraged him are too lenient, or too far from the market to know the standards of successful fiction. Or he will read the work of a real genius in words, and the discrepancy between that gift and his own will seem a chasm to swallow his hopes. In such a state, lightened now and again by moments when he feels his own gift alive and surging, he may stay for months or years.

Every writer goes through this period of despair. Without doubt many promising writers, and most of those who were never meant to write, turn back at this point and find a lifework less exacting. Others are able to find the other bank of their slough of despond, sometimes by inspiration, sometimes by sheer doggedness. Still others turn to books or counselors. But often they are unable to tell the source of their baffled discomfort; they may even assign the reasons for their feeling of fright to the wrong causes, and think that they miss effectiveness because they "cannot write dialogue," or "are no good at plots," or "make all the characters too stiff." When they have worked as intensively as possible to overcome the weakness, only to find that their difficulties continue, there comes another unofficial weeding-out. Some drop away from this group; still others persist, even though they have reached the stage of dumb discomfort where they no longer feel that they can diagnose their own cases.

No ordeal by discouragement which editors, teachers, and older writers can devise is going to kill off the survivor of this type. What he needs to realize first is that he tried to do too much at once, and next, that although he started going about his self-education step by step, he took the wrong steps. Most of the methods of training the conscious side of the writer — the craftsman and the critic in him — are actually hostile to the good of the unconscious, the artist's side; and the converse of this proposition is likewise true. *But it is possible to train both sides of the character to work in harmony, and the first step in that education is to consider that you must teach yourself not as though you were one person, but two.*

Three

❦

The Advantages of
Duplicity

To see why training oneself to be a writer is a double task, let us go rapidly over the process of story formation.

The Process of Story Formation

Like any other art, creative writing is a function of the whole man. The unconscious must flow freely and richly, bringing at demand all the treasures of memory, all the emotions, incidents, scenes, intimations of character and relationship which it has stored away in its depths; the conscious mind must control, combine, and discriminate between these materials without hampering the unconscious flow. The unconscious will provide the writer with "types" of all kinds — typical characters, typical scenes, typical emotional responses; the conscious will have the task of deciding which of these are too personal, too purely idiosyncratic to be material for art, and which of them are universal enough to be useful. It may also be called upon to add intentionally those special traits which turn too universal a figure into an individual character, to undertake the humanizing of a type-form—a necessity if the fiction is to convey a sense of reality.

Each writer's unconscious will be found to have, if I may put it so, a type-story of its own: because of the individual's history, he will tend to see certain dilemmas as dramatic and overlook others entirely, as he will also have his own idea of the greatest possible happiness and personal good. Of course, it follows that each writer's stories will always bear a fundamental likeness to each other. This need not be seen as a threat of monotony, but the conscious mind must be enough aware of it to alter, recombine, introduce elements of surprise and freshness into each new story project.

Because of the tendency of the unconscious to see things in types, it is the unconscious, in the long run, which dictates the form of the story.

(But this will be taken up more fully later. All that needs pointing out here is that if this is so a great deal of instruction on plot making is a waste of time. Certain ingenuities can be suggested, the popular story of any given period can be isolated and studied, and formulas for its writing can be devised; but unless a given formula is already congenial to the student he will get little help by attempting to model his own work upon it.) At any rate, the story arises in the unconscious. It then appears, sometimes only vaguely prefigured, at other times astonishingly definite, in the consciousness. There it is scrutinized, pruned, altered, strengthened, made more spectacular or less melodramatic; and is returned into the unconscious for the final synthesis of its elements. After a period of intense activity—which, however, goes on at so deep a level that the author himself occasionally feels he has "forgotten" or "lost" his idea—it once again signals to the conscious that the work of synthesis has been done; and the actual writing of the story begins.

The "Born Writer"

In the genius, or the "born writer," we see this process taking place so smoothly and often so rapidly that even this overcompressed scheme seems to misrepresent the story's history. But the genius, you must remember, is the man who by some fortunate accident of temperament or education can put his unconscious completely at the service of his reasonable intention, whether or not he is aware that this is so. The proof of this statement will emerge later, for the process of making a writer is the process of teaching the novice to do by artifice what the born writer does spontaneously.

Unconscious and Conscious

The unconscious is shy, elusive, and unwieldy, but it is possible to learn to tap it at will, and even to direct it. The conscious mind is meddlesome, opinionated, and arrogant, but it can be made subservient to the inborn talent through training. By isolating as far as possible the functions of these two sides of the mind, even by considering them not merely as aspects of the same mind but as separate personalities, we can arrive at a kind of working metaphor, impossible to confuse with reality, but infinitely helpful in self-education.

The Two Persons of the Writer

So, for a period, while the conception is useful to you, think of yourself as two-persons-in-one. There will be a prosaic, everyday, practical person to bear the brunt of the day's encounters. It will have plenty of virtues to offset its stolidity; it must learn to be intelligently critical, detached, tolerant, while at the same time remembering that its first function is to provide suitable conditions for the artist-self. The other half of your dual nature may then be as sensitive, enthusiastic, and partisan as you like; only it will not drag those traits out into the workaday world. It distinctly will not be allowed, by the cherishing elderly side, to run the risk of being made miserable by trying to cope emotionally with situations which call only for reason, or of looking ludicrous to the unindulgent observer.

The Transparent Barrier

The first advantage that will be gained by your innocent duplicity is that you will have erected a transparent barrier between you and the world, behind which you can grow into your artistic maturity at your own pace. The average person writes just too much and not quite enough to have any great opinion of an author's life. It is unfortunate, but the unimaginative citizen finds something exquisitely funny about the idea that one aspires to make a name and a living by any such process as "stringing words together." He finds it presumptuous when an acquaintance announces that he has elected to give the world his opinion in writing, and punishes the presumption by merciless teasing. If you feel called upon to correct this unimaginative attitude you will have opportunities enough to keep you busy for a lifetime, but you will not—unless you have an extraordinary amount of energy—have much strength left for writing. The same plain man reacts as impulsively and naively to the successful writer. He is awestruck in his presence, but he is also very uncomfortable. Nothing but witchcraft, he seems to believe, could have made another human being so wise in the ways of his kind. He will turn self-conscious, and act either untypically or refuse to act at all; and if you alarm him you will find yourself barred from one source of your material. This is a low piece of advice to give, but I give it without apology: keep still about your intentions, or you will startle your quarry.

Keep Your Own Counsel

Then, too, the writer is at a disadvantage shared by no novice of the other arts. He does use the medium of ordinary conversation, of friendly letters and business letters, when he exercises his profession; and he has no impressive paraphernalia to impose respect on the layman. Now that everyone has his portable typewriter, not even that badge of his profession is left to the young writer. A musical instrument, canvas, clay, carry their own persuasiveness by seeming exotic to the uninitiated. Even a good singing voice does not issue from every throat. Until your name has been in print again and again you may get only teasing for your pains if you prematurely announce your allegiance to writing. At that, most young writers would benefit by taking a leaf from the practitioners of other arts; the violinist does not carry around his violin, the artist does not carry his palette and brushes, unless he is intending to use them, either privately or before a well-disposed audience. Give yourself the advantage of the same discretion, at least while you are finding your feet.

One excellent psychological reason for an author to keep his profession to himself is that if you confess so much you are likely to go further and talk of the things you mean to write. Now words are your medium, and effective use of them your profession; but your unconscious self (which is your wishful part) will not care whether the words you use are written down or talked to the world at large. If you are for the moment fortunate enough to have a responsive audience you often suffer for it later. You will have created your story and reaped your reward in approval or shocked disapproval; in either case you will have hit your mark. Afterward you will find yourself disinclined to go on with the laborious process of writing that story at full length; unconsciously you will consider it as already done, a twice-told tale. If you can conquer the disinclination to write you may still find that a slightly flat, uninterested note creeps in, in spite of you. So practice a wise taciturnity. When you have completed a fair first draft you can, if you like, offer it for criticism and advice; but to talk too early is a grave mistake.

There are other advantages in considering yourself a two-in-one character. It should not be your sensitive, temperamental self which bears the burden of your relations with the outside world of editors, teachers, or friends. Send your practical self out into the world to receive suggestions, criticisms, or rejections; by all means see to it that it is your prosaic self which reads rejection slips! Criticism and rejection are not personal insults, but your artistic component will not know that. It will quiver and wince and run to cover, and you will have trouble in luring it out again to observe and weave tales and find words for all the thousand shades of feeling that go to make up a story.

Your "Best Friend and Severest Critic"

For another thing, your writing self is an instinctive, emotional creature, and if you are not careful you will find yourself living the life that will give you the least annoyance and the greatest ease instead of a life that will continually feed and stimulate your talent. The "artistic temperament" is usually perfectly satisfied to exercise itself in reverie and amuse itself in solitude, and only once in a long while will the impulse to write rise spontaneously to the surface. If you leave it to the more sensitive side of your nature to set the conditions of work and living for you, you may find yourself at the end of your days with very little to show for the gift you were born with. A far better idea is to realize from the start that you are subject to certain caprices of action, and to study yourself objectively until you find which of your impulses are sound and which are likely to lead you into the bogs of inertia and silence. At first you will find it a great bore to be forever examining yourself for tendencies and habits; later you will find it second nature. Still later you will come to enjoy it rather too much, and the same critical attention will have to be given to the task of turning your scrutiny *away* from your own processes when your analysis has passed the stage where it bears beneficial fruits. In short, you will have to learn to be your own best friend and severest critic—mature, indulgent, stern and yielding by turns.

The Right Recreation

Observe, though, that you are to be your own best friend—not simply your stern and disciplinary elder. No one else will be in a position to discover for you what is best in the way of stimulation, amusement, and friends. Perhaps music (however little you know about music) may have the effect of starting up the obscure internal processes which send you to the typewriter. In that case it will be the task of your elder self to find and purvey music to you—and to see that you are not put on the defensive when you are questioned about your astonishing taste for symphony orchestras or Negro spirituals. You will find, too, that some friends are excellent for you as a writer who are worthless to you otherwise—and vice versa. Too stimulating a social life can be as hard on a budding talent as none at all. Only observation will show you the effect of any group or person *on you as a writer*. Seeing a dull soul whom you doggedly adore, or a brilliant friend who irritates you, may have to be treated as a very special form of indulgence, to be yielded to only rarely. If you feel, after an evening with the stolid friend, that the world is a dry and dusty place, or if you are exasperated to the point of speechlessness by your brilliant acquaintance, not the warmest emotion for them will justify your seeing much of them while you are trying to learn to write. You will have to find other acquaintances, persons who, for some mysterious reason, leave you full of energy, feed you with ideas, or, more obscurely still, have the effect of filling you with self-confidence and eagerness to write.

Friends and Books

If you are not fortunate enough to find them—well, you will discover fairish substitutes on library shelves, and occasionally in the strangest guises. I had a pupil who battened on medical case reports, and another who recorded that a few hours with a popular scientific monthly, which she could hardly understand in spite of its being insultingly elementary, induced in her such a feeling of being glutted with neat, hard little facts that she ran off to retrieve the balance by a debauch of imaginative writing. I know a popular author who abhors the works of John Galsworthy, but something in Galsworthy's rhythm starts up his own desire to write; he alleges that after a few pages of *The Forsyte Saga* he can hear an "internal hum" which soon turns into sentences and paragraphs; on the other hand,

Wodehouse, whom he considers a past master of modern humorous writing, plunges him into such depths of despond about his own performance that he takes care not to read the latest Wodehouse book until he has finished whatever he has in hand. Watch for a while, and see which authors are your meat and which your poison.

When the actual writing is to be done, your elder self must stand aside, only murmuring a suggestion now and again on such matters as your tendency to use repetitions, or to suggest that you are being too verbose, or that the dialogue is getting out of hand. Later you will call on it to consider the completed draft, or section, and with its help you will alter the manuscript to get the best possible effects. But at the time of writing, nothing is more confusing than to have the alert, critical, overscrupulous rational faculty at the forefront of your mind. The tormenting doubts of one's own ability, the self-conscious muteness that drops like a pall over the best story ideas, come from consulting the judge in oneself at the moment when it is the storyteller's turn to be in the ascendant. It is not easy at first to inhibit the running verdicts on every sentence, almost every word, that is written, but once the flow of the story has well set in, the critical faculty will be content to wait its turn.

The Arrogant Intellect

There is no arrogance like that of the intellect, and one of the dangers, as we have said, of studying the technique of story writing too solemnly is that the reason is confirmed in its delusion of being the more important member of the writing team. It is not. Its duties are indispensable but secondary; they come before and after the period of intensive writing. You will find that if you cannot rein in your intellect during this period it will be forever offering pseudo-solutions to you, tampering with motives, making the characters "literary" (which is often to make them stereotyped and unnatural), or protesting that the story which seemed so promising when it first dawned in your consciousness is really trite or implausible.

The Two Selves Not at War

But now I am in danger of making it seem that these two halves of the writing personality are at war with each other, when it is the exact contrary that is true. When each has found its place, when each is performing the functions which are proper to it, they play endlessly back and forth into each other's hands, strengthening, inciting, relieving each other in such a way that the resulting personality, the integral character, is made more balanced, mellow, energetic, and profound. It is precisely when they are at war that we get the unhappy artist—the artist who is working against the grain, or against his sober judgment, or, saddest of all, is unable to work. The most enviable writers are those who, quite often unanalytically and unconsciously, have realized that there are different facets to their nature and are able to live and work with now one, now another, in the ascendant.

The First Exercise

Now we come to the first exercise of a book which will be full of exercises. Its purpose is to show you how simple it is to see oneself objectively.

You are near a door. When you come to the end of this chapter put the book aside, get up, and go through that door. From the moment you stand on the threshold *turn yourself into your own object of attention.* What do you look like, standing there? How do you walk? What, if you knew nothing about yourself, could be gathered of you, your character, your background, your purpose just there at just that minute? If there are people in the room whom you must greet, how do you greet them? How do your attitudes to them vary? Do you give any overt sign that you are fonder of one, or more aware of one, than of the rest?

There is no deep, dark, esoteric purpose behind this exercise. It is a primer lesson in considering oneself objectively, and should be dismissed from your mind when you have learned what you can from it. Another time try sitting at ease and—using no gestures at all—tell yourself step by step how you comb your hair. (You will find it harder than you think.) Again, follow yourself at any small routine task. A little later take an episode of the day before; see yourself going up to it and coming away from it; and the episode itself as it might have looked to a stranger. At still another time think how you might have looked if you could follow yourself all day long from a little height. *Use the fiction maker's eye on yourself* to see how you would have appeared when you went in and out of houses, up streets and into stores, and back home at the end of the day.

Four

❧

Interlude: On Taking Advice

With the best of intentions, we usually go about the formation of a new habit or the eradication of an old one in the manner most calculated to defeat our purpose. Whenever you come across a piece of advice in these pages I exhort you not to straighten your spine, grit your teeth, clench your fists, and go at the experiments with the light of do-or-die on your countenance.

Save Your Energy

We customarily expend enough energy in carrying out any simple action to bring about a result three times greater than the one we have in view. This is true from the simplest matters to the most complex and of physical effort as well as mental. If we climb stairs, we climb them with every muscle and organ laboring as though our soul's salvation were to be found on the top step, and the result is that we grow resentful at the disproportionate returns we receive from our expended energy. Or, putting a great deal more energy out than we can use, we must take it up, somehow, in purposeless motion. Everyone has had the experience of pushing a door that looked closed with more vigor than was necessary and of falling into the next room as a consequence. Or we have picked up some light object which looked deceptively heavy. If you notice yourself on such an occasion, you will see that you *must* make a slight backward motion merely to retrieve your balance.

Imagination Versus Will in Changing Habits

In mental effort we are likely to go still more widely astray from some childish notion that it is laudable to exert that "slow, dead heave of the will" as often as possible. But in changing habits, you will find yourself getting your results far more quickly and with less "backwash" if you engage your imagination in the process instead of calling out the biggest gun of your character equipment first.

This is not a plea to abandon the will. There will be times and occasions when only the whole weight of the will brought to bear on the matter in hand will prove effective. But the imagination plays a far greater role in our lives than we customarily acknowledge, although any teacher can tell you how great an advocate the imagination is when a child is to be led into a changed course.

Displacing Old Habits

Old habits are strong and jealous. They will not be displaced easily if they get any warning that such plans are afoot; they will fight for their existence with subtlety and persuasiveness. If they are too radically attacked they will revenge themselves; you will find, after a day or two of extraordinarily virtuous effort, all sorts of reasons why the new method is not good for you, why you should alter it in line with this or that old habit, or actually abandon it entirely. In the end you will have had no good from the new advice; but you will almost certainly feel that you have given it a fair trial and that it has failed. Your mistake will have been that you tired yourself out and exhausted your good intentions before you had a chance to see whether or not the program was the right one for you.

This is a very simple but rather spectacular experiment which you can make that will teach you more about your own processes of putting an idea into operation than pages of exhortation and explanation. It is this:

A Demonstration

Draw a circle on a sheet of paper, using the bottom of a tumbler or something of that circumference as the guide; then make a cross through it. Tie a heavy ring or a key on a string about four inches long. Hold the end of the string with the ring hanging like the weight of a pendulum over the intersection of the cross, about an inch above the paper. Now *think* around the circle, following the circumference with your eyes and ignoring the ring and cord entirely.

After a few moments the little pendulum will begin to swing around in the direction you have chosen, at first making a very small circle, but steadily widening out as it goes on. Then reverse the direction *in thought only* and follow the circle with your eyes in the other direction. . . . Now

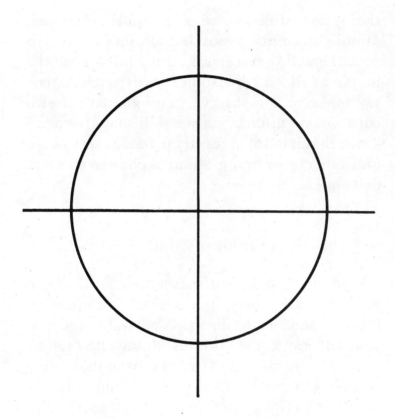

think up and down the perpendicular line; when that succeeds, shift to the horizontal. In each case the ring will stop for a moment and then begin to move in the direction of your thinking.

If you have not tried this experiment before you may feel that there is something uncanny about the result. There isn't. It is simply the neatest and easiest way of showing how important imagination can be in the sphere of action. Minute involuntary muscles take up the task for you. The will, you see, was hardly involved in the matter at all. And this, some French psychologists say, is the way to observe, in miniature, a "faith cure" in operation. At the least, it should demonstrate that it is not necessary to brace every nerve and muscle to bring about a change in your daily life.

The Right Frame of Mind

So, then, in doing the exercises in this book, turn yourself gently, in a relaxed and pleasant frame of mind, in the direction you want to go. See yourself, for a few minutes, doing the recommended experiment. After you have had a few successes by this method, you will find that it is capable of infinite extension. Consider that all the minor inconveniences and interruptions of habits are to the end of making a full and effective life for yourself. Forget or ignore for a while all the difficulties you have let yourself dwell upon too often; refuse to consider, in your period of training, the possibility of failure. You are not at this stage of your career in any position to estimate your chances justly. Things which look difficult or impossible to you now will be seen in truer perspective when you have gone a little further. Later you can take an inventory of yourself from time to time, see what is easy for you and what you do badly or imperfectly. You can consider then what steps to take to correct these definite faults, and by that time you will be able to work on yourself profitably, without discouragement or bravado.

Five

❦

Harnessing the Unconscious

To begin with, you must teach the unconscious to flow into the channel of writing. Psychologists will forgive us for speaking so airily about "teaching" the unconscious to do this or that. To all intents and purposes that is what happens; but less elegantly and more exactly we might say that the first step toward being a writer is to hitch your unconscious mind to your writing arm.

Wordless Daydreams

Most persons who are attracted by the idea of fiction at all are, or were in childhood, great dreamers. At almost any moment they can catch themselves, at some level, deep in reverie. Occasionally this reverie takes the form of recasting one's life, day by day or moment by moment, into a form somewhat nearer to the heart's desire: reconstructing conversations and arguments so that we come out with colors flying and epigrams falling around us like sparks, or imagining ourselves back in a simpler and happier period. Or adventure is coming toward us around the next corner, and we have already made up our minds as to the form it will take. All those naive and satisfying dreams of which we are the unashamed heroes or heroines are the very stuff of fiction, almost the *materia prima* of fiction. A little sophistication, a little experience, and we realize that we are not going to be allowed to carry off the honors in real life without a struggle; there are too many contenders for the role of leading lady or leading man. So, learning discretion and guile, we cast the matter a little differently; we objectify the ideal self that has caused us so much pleasure and write about him in the third person. And hundreds of our fellows, engaged secretly in just such daydreaming as our own, see themselves in our fictional characters and fall to reading when fatigue or disenchantment robs them of their ability to see themselves under any glamorous guise. (Not, thank heaven, that this is the only reason a book is ever read; but undoubtedly it is the commonest one.)

The little Brontës, with their kingdom of Gondaland, the infant Alcotts, young Robert Browning, and H. G. Wells all led an intensive dream-life which carried over into their maturity and took another form; and there are hundreds of authors who could tell the same stories of their youth. But there are probably thousands more who never grow up as writers. They are too self-conscious, too humble, or too solidly set in the habit of dreaming idly. After all, we begin our storytelling, usually, long before we are able to print simple words with infinite labor. It is little wonder that the glib unconscious should balk at the drudgery of committing its stories to writing.

Toward Effortless Writing

Writing calls on unused muscles and involves solitude and immobility. There is not much to be said for the recommendation, so often heard, to serve an apprenticeship to journalism if you intend to write fiction. But a journalist's career does teach two lessons which every writer needs to learn—that it is possible to write for long periods without fatigue, and that if one pushes on past the first weariness one finds a reservoir of

unsuspected energy—one reaches the famous
"second wind."

The typewriter has made the author's way
more rocky than it was in the old days of quill and
pen. However convenient the machine may be,
there is no doubt about the muscular strain involved in typewriting; let any author tell you of
rising stiff and aching from a long session.
Moreover, there is the distraction set up by the little clatter of keys, and there is the strain of seeing
the shafts continually dancing against the platen.
But it is possible to make either typing or writing
by hand second nature, so that muscular strain
will not slow you down or keep you from writing.

So if you are to have the full benefit of the
richness of the unconscious you must learn to
write easily and smoothly when the unconscious
is in the ascendant.

*The best way to do this is to rise half an hour, or
a full hour, earlier than you customarily rise. Just as
soon as you can—and without talking, without reading the morning's paper, without picking up the
book you laid aside the night before—begin to write.*
Write anything that comes into your head: last
night's dream, if you are able to remember it; the
activities of the day before; a conversation, real or
imaginary; an examination of conscience. Write
any sort of early morning reverie, rapidly and uncritically. The excellence or ultimate worth of
what you write is of no importance yet. As a mat-

ter of fact, you will find more value in this material than you expect, but your primary purpose now is not to bring forth deathless words, but to write any words at all which are not pure nonsense.

To reiterate, what you are actually doing is training yourself, in the twilight zone between sleep and the full waking state, simply *to write.* It makes no difference to the success of this practice if your paragraphs are amorphous, the thought vague or extravagant, the ideas hazy. Forget that you have any critical faculty at all; realize that no one need ever see what you are writing unless you choose to show it. You may, if you can, write in a notebook, sitting up in bed. If you can teach yourself to use the typewriter in this period, so much the better. Write as long as you have free time, or until you feel that you have utterly written yourself out.

The next morning begin without rereading what you have already done. Remember: you are to write *before* you have read at all. The purpose of this injunction will become clear later. Now all you need to concern yourself with is the mere performance of the exercise.

Double Your "Output"

After a day or two you will find that there is a certain number of words that you can write easily and without strain. When you have found that limit, begin to push it ahead by a few sentences, then by a paragraph or two. A little later try to double it before you stop the morning's work.

Within a very short time you will find that the exercise has begun to bear fruit. The actual labor of writing no longer seems arduous or dull. You will have begun to feel that you can get as much (far more really) from a written reverie as from one that goes on almost wordlessly in the back of your mind. When you can wake, reach out for your pencil, and begin to write almost on one impulse, you will be ready for the next step. Keep the material you have written—under lock and key if that is the only way to save yourself from self-consciousness. It will have uses you can hardly foresee.

As you take up the next exercise, you can return, in this morning task, to the limit that seems easy and natural. (But you should be able to write more words than when you began.) Watch yourself carefully; if at any time you find you have slipped back into inactive reverie, it is time to exert pressure on yourself. Throughout your writing life, whenever you are in danger of the spiritual drought that comes to the most facile writer from time to time, put the pencil and paper back on your bedside table, and wake to write in the morning.

Six

❧

Writing on Schedule

At once, when you have put the suggestion in the last chapter into operation, you will find that you are more truly a *writer* than you ever were before. You will discover that now you have a tendency to cast the day's experiences into words, to foresee the use that you will make of an anecdote or episode that has come your way, to transform the rough material of life into fictional shape, more consistently than you did when writing was a sporadic, capricious occupation which broke out from time to time unaccountably, or was undertaken only when you felt that you had a story firmly within your grasp.

The moment you reach that stage, you are

ready for the next step, which is to teach yourself to write at a given moment. The best way to do it is this:

Engaging to Write

After you have dressed, sit down for a moment by yourself and go over the day before you. Usually you can tell accurately enough what its demands and opportunities will be; roughly, at least, you can sketch out for yourself enough of your program to know when you will have a few moments to yourself. It need not be a very long time; fifteen minutes will do nicely, and there is almost no wage slave so driven that he cannot snatch a quarter of an hour from a busy day if he is in earnest about it. Decide for yourself when you will take that time for writing; for you are going to write in it. If your work falls off, let us say, after three-thirty in the afternoon, the fifteen minutes from four o'clock until quarter past four can safely be drafted as time of your own.

Well, then, at four o'clock you are going to write, come what may, and you are going to continue until the quarter-hour sounds. When you have made up your mind to that you are free to do whatever you like to do or must do.

A Debt of Honor

Now this is very important, and can hardly be emphasized too strongly: *you have decided to write at four o'clock, and at four o'clock write you must! No excuses can be given.* If at four o'clock you find yourself deep in conversation, you must excuse yourself and keep your engagement. Your agreement is a debt of honor, and must be scrupulously discharged; you have given yourself your word and there is no retracting it. If you must climb out over the heads of your friends at that hour, then be ruthless; another time you will find that you have taken some pains not to be caught in a dilemma of the sort. If to get the solitude that is necessary you must go into a washroom, go there, lean against the wall, and write. Write as you write in the morning—anything at all. Write sense or nonsense, limericks or blank verse; write what you think of your employer or your secretary or your teacher; write a story synopsis or a fragment of dialogue, or the description of someone you have recently noticed. However halting or perfunctory the writing is, *write.* If you must, you can write, "I am finding this exercise remarkably difficult," and say what you think are the reasons for the difficulty. Vary the complaint from day to day till it no longer represents the true state of affairs.

Extending the Exercise

For you are going to do this from day to day, but each time you are to choose a different hour. Try eleven o'clock, or a moment or two before or after lunch. Another time, promise yourself to write for fifteen minutes before you start for home in the evening; or fifteen minutes before you dine. The important thing is that *at* the moment, *on the dot of the moment,* you are to be writing, and that you teach yourself that no excuse of any nature can be offered when the moment comes.

While you are merely reading this recommendation you may be quite unable to see why it is put so emphatically. As you begin to put it into practice you will understand. There is a deep inner resistance to writing which is more likely to emerge at this point than in the earlier exercise. This will begin to "look like business" to the unconscious, and the unconscious does not like these rules and regulations until it is well broken in to them; it is incorrigibly lazy in its busy-ness and given to finding the easiest way of satisfying itself. It prefers to choose its own occasions and to emerge as it likes. You will find the most remarkable series of obstacles presented to you under the similitude of common sense: Surely it will be just as satisfactory to write from 4:05 to 4:20? If you break out of a circle you are likely to be cross-questioned, so why not wait till the circle breaks up by itself and then take your fifteen minutes? In the morning you could hardly foresee that you were going to work yourself into a headache that day; can work done under the handicap of a headache possibly be fit to do? And so on and on. But you must learn to disregard every loophole the wily unconscious points out to you. If you consistently, doggedly, refuse to be beguiled, you will have your reward. The unconscious will suddenly give in charmingly, and begin to write gracefully and well.

Succeed, or Stop Writing

Right here I should like to sound the solemnest word of warning that you will find in this book: *If you fail repeatedly at this exercise, give up writing. Your resistance is actually greater than your desire to write, and you may as well find some other outlet for your energy early as late.*

These two strange and arbitrary performances — early morning writing, and writing by prearrangement — should be kept up till you write fluently at will.

Seven

❦

The First Survey

When you have succeeded in establishing these two habits — early morning writing and writing by agreement with yourself — you have come a long way on the writer's path. You have gained, on the one hand, fluency, and on the other control, even though in an elementary way. You know a great deal more about yourself, in all likelihood, than you did when you embarked on the exercises. For one thing, you know whether it was easier to teach yourself to write on and on, or whether writing by prearrangement seemed more natural. Perhaps for the first time you see that if you want to write you can write, and that no life is actually so busy as to offer no opportunities if you are alert to find them. Then, too, you should begin to think it less than miraculous that writers can bring out book after book, having found in yourself the same inexhaustible resources that issue in the work of others. The physical mechanism of writing should have ceased to be tiring and begun to take its place as a simple activity. Your realization of the writer's life is probably more vivid, and nearer to the truth, than it was before—which is in itself a long stride to have taken.

Now it is time to consider yourself and your problems objectively again; and if you have followed the exercises well you should have plenty of material for an illuminating first survey.

Reading Your Work Critically

Up to this point it is best to resist the temptation to reread your productions. While you are training yourself into facility in writing and teaching yourself to start writing whenever and wherever opportunity offers, the less you turn a critical eye upon your own material the better—even for a cursory survey. The excellence or triteness of your writing was not the matter under consideration. But now, turning back to see what it may reveal under a dispassionate survey, you may find those outpourings very enlightening.

The Pitfalls of Imitation

You will remember that one of the conditions set was that you should not have read one word before beginning the morning's task, nor, if at all possible, so much as spoken until you have finished. This is the reason. We all live so surrounded by words that it is difficult for us to discover, without long experience, what our own rhythms are, and what subjects do really appeal to us. Those who are sensitive enough to want ardently to become writers are usually a little too suggestible for their own good. Consciously or not, they may have fallen into the temptation of imitating an established author. It may be a genuine master of writing; it may be (and too often is) the author whose work is having the greatest vogue at the moment. No one who has not taught fiction writing can believe how often a pupil will say some such thing as, "Oh, I've just thought of the most marvelous Faulkner story!" or, more ambitiously, "I think I can make a regular Virginia Woolf out of it." The teacher who crassly says she would rather see a good story of the pupil's own is damned for a prig, or outspokenly argued with; for the notion that playing the sedulous ape to the extent of copying not only the prose style but the very philosophies and narrative forms of current popular authors seems to have been so inculcated in our apprentice writers that they genuinely believe they will become original authors by the process of imitation. The men and women who have served as their models, since they are writing from a strong native talent and according to their own personal tastes, grow, alter, change their styles and their "formulas," and the poor sedulous apes are left imitating the work of an outmoded period.

Discovering Your Strength

The best way to escape the temptation to imitate is to discover as early as possible one's own tastes and excellences. Here, in the sheaf of pages you have written during this period of habit-making, is priceless laboratory material for you. What, on the whole, *do* you write, when you set down the first things that occur to you? Try to read, now, as though you had the work of a stranger in your hands, and to discover there what the tastes and talents of this alien writer may be. Put aside every preconception about your work. Try to forget any ambitions or hopes or fears you may have entertained, and see what you would decide was the best field for this stranger if he were to consult you. The repetitions, the recurrent ideas, the frequent prose forms in these pages will give you your clues. They will show you where your *native* gift lies, whether or not you eventually decide to specialize in it. There is no reason to believe that you can write only one type of work, that you may not be fully as successful in some other line; but this examination will show you where your richest and most easily tapped vein lies.

In my experience, the pupil who sets down the night's dream, or recasts the day before into ideal form, who takes the morning hour to write a complete anecdote or a passage of sharp dialogue, is likely to be the short story writer in embryo. Certain types of character sketching, when it is brief and concerned with rather general (or even obvious) traits, point the same way. A subtler analysis of characters, a consideration of motives, acute self-examination (as distinct from romanticizing one's actions), the contrasting of different characters faced by the same dilemma, most often indicate the novelist. A kind of musing introspection or of speculation only sketched in is found in the essay writer's notebook, although with a grain of drama added, and with the particularizing of an abstract speculation by assigning the various elements of the problem to characters who act out the idea, there is promise of the more meditative type of novelist.

When this stage of instruction is reached

there is often in my classes a burst of highly stimulating activity. Seeing the possibilities in the writing which they now feel came almost without effort, the pupils frequently branch into some type of work which they look on simply as recreation, and hammer away on their more difficult problems in their "working" time. These spontaneous manuscripts are usually very interesting, and often, with some shaping, can be turned into satisfactory finished work. They are a little rambling, a little discursive, but they have a fresh, unforced tone which is striking. About this time you will find that your work is already less patchy and uneven; you are striking your own stride and finding your own rhythm, as well as discovering which subjects have a perennial interest for you.

A Footnote for Teachers

Here I should like to add a footnote for other teachers, rather than for students of writing. I think that holding up the work of each pupil in class for the criticism of the others is a thoroughly pernicious practice, and it does not become harmless simply by allowing the manuscript to be read without assigning its authorship publicly.

The ordeal is too trying to be taken with equanimity, and a sensitive writer can be thrown out of his stride deplorably by it, whether or not the criticism is favorable. It is seldom that the criticism *is favorable*, when a beginner is judged by the jury of his peers. They seem to need to demonstrate that, although they are not yet writing quite perfectly themselves, they are able to see all the flaws in a story which is read to them, and they fall upon it tooth and fang. Until self-confidence arises naturally, and the pupil asks for group criticism, his work should be treated as utterly confidential by the teacher. Each will have his own rate of growth and it can only go on steadily if not endangered by the setbacks that come from embarrassment and self-consciousness. I recommend an almost inhuman taciturnity to my students, at least about work that is being done at the moment. There have been weeks when I have had nothing at all from the best workers in the class, only to have three or four full-length manuscripts from a single pupil at the end of the silent period. Beyond stipulating that each pupil must follow the exercises as they are given out, whether or not I see the material which is written from day to day, I assign no tasks.

Eight

❧

The Critic at Work on Himself

Now, we will suppose, you have a kind of rough preliminary idea of yourself as a writer. It will be a very rough idea, still distorted by humility in some directions and overconfidence in others, but at least it will bear enough resemblance to your ultimate professional self to be worth working on. Even in this unfinished state you will realize that there are definite things which you can do for yourself that will improve the quality of your writing, provide you with occasions for writing, or stimulate you so that writing will follow naturally. It is time now to call on your prosaic side

89

for the services it can render you. (As a matter of fact, it will already have been called on to read the material and find your self-revealed tastes, but that was only preliminary.) There are a hundred things it can do for you as soon as you have given it this much material to work on. If it is called in too soon, though, it hampers you more than it helps.

Here you are then, with all these pages and notebooks to be examined by your common sense, everyday character. By the cursory examination recommended in the last chapter you have already found the more obvious trends in your own work. Now it is time to be more specific, and to examine in detail what you have done. Your workaday self has been standing aside while you were about the business of teaching your unconscious to flow whenever you could find a moment for it; you will find now that it has been closely following the process, remarking your successes and failures, and getting ready with suggestions.

A Critical Dialogue

The next few paragraphs are much more naive and more outrageously dual than any dialogue you will ever have with yourself, but some such interchange as this between the sides of your nature should now take place:

"Do you know, I find that you write dialogue

very well; you evidently have a good ear. But your passages of description aren't well done. They're stilted."

Here the culprit will probably murmur something about liking to write dialogue, but feeling silly when describing anything without the protection of quotation marks.

"Of course you love to write dialogue," you must return, "just *because* you do it well. But don't you realize that if you can't do straight passages and transitions smoothly you're going to get a jerky story? You'd better make up your mind, I should say, whether you want to write fiction or to specialize in playwriting. Either way, you've got a lot of work to do."

"Which should *you* say? That's almost as much in your department as mine?"

"Well, fiction, on the whole. You don't show much interest yet in dramatic and spectacular effects, or in building up to a visually effective climax. You unfold a character slowly and by means of dialogue. If you had all the time and paper in the world you could undoubtedly get to your point by using dialogue alone, but, you see, you have space and effectiveness to consider. You'll have to do some of it in straight narrative form. No, all in all, I think we'd better work on your weak spots. You might read a lot of E. M. Forster in your spare time. He gets from point to point remarkably well. In the meanwhile, here's a passage for you to meditate upon. It's from Edith Wharton's *The Writing of Fiction:*

'The use of dialogue in fiction seems to be one of the few things about which a fairly definite rule may be laid down. It should be reserved for the culminating moments, and regarded as the spray into which the great wave of narrative breaks in curving toward the watcher on the shore. This lifting and scattering of the wave, the coruscation of the spray, even the mere material sight of the page broken into short, uneven paragraphs, all help to reenforce the contrast between such climaxes and the smooth effaced gliding of the narrative intervals; and the contrast enhances that sense of the passage of time for the producing of which the writer has to depend on his intervening narration. Thus the sparing use of dialogue not only serves to emphasize the crises of a tale, but to give it as a whole a greater effect of continuous development.' "

Or the exhortation may take the form of remarking a minor stylistic matter, and you will address yourself on it: "By the way, do you realize that you overwork the word 'colorful'? Every time you're in too much of a hurry to find the exact word you want you fall back on that; you're using it to death. Very sloppy habit. In the first place it's, usually, too vaguely inclusive to give the effect you want, and in the second, it is being used by all the advertising writers in the country just now. Stay away from it for a while."

Be Specific in Suggestions

Although you may not be quite so direct as this in your discourse, still you are advised to address yourself *directly* on these points, making the complaints specific, and, wherever possible, suggesting specific remedies. You will remember more easily, and you will have reenforced your own discontent with this or that element in your writing in such a way that you must take steps to correct the slipshod practice or confess that you are not working seriously at the profession you have chosen. Make a clean-cut issue for yourself wherever you are able to put your finger on a fault; if you suspect that there are weaknesses which you do not see for some reason, show your work to someone whose good taste and judgment you trust. You will often find that a reader who has no pretensions to literary knowledge can put a finger on your stylistic sins as directly as a writer, an editor, or a teacher; but turn to outside counsel only after you have done all you are able to do for yourself. In the long run, it is *your* taste and *your* judgment that must carry you over the pitfalls, and the sooner you educate yourself into being all things to your writing-character the better your prospects are.

Correction After Criticism

Press home all the points on which you have any doubts. Do you use too many short declarative sentences, or too many exclamation points? Is your vocabulary lush, or too severe? Are you so reticent that you slide over an emotional scene so rapidly that your reader may miss the very thing you are trying to convey? Do you indulge in blood-and-thunder past the point of credibility? Then try to find the antidote. The reticent writer can force himself to read Swinburne, or Carlyle, or any one of a number of contemporary authors who are more sensational than decorous. The over-sensational can reverse the recommendation. and read the eighteenth-century Englishmen, or such writers as William Dean Howells, Willa Cather, Agnes Repplier. If you have a dull and prosy note, a course in the novels and stories of G. K. Chesterton should be of advantage. There is almost no limit to the recommendations which could be made, but you must learn both to diagnose your own case and to find your own best medicine. When you have found your antidote, read with humility, determined to see the excellence in writers who are natively antipathetic to you; while you are performing your stylistic penance, give yourself no quarter. Leave the books which usually attract you severely alone.

The Conditions of Excellence

Next set yourself to discover if you can see any connection between a good morning's work and the conditions of the evening before. Can you tell whether or not the good writing came after you had spent an active day, or after a quiet one? Did you write more easily after going to bed early, or after a short sleep? Is there any observable connection between seeing certain friends and the vividness or dullness of the next morning's work? How did you write on the morning after you had been to a theater, or to an exhibition of pictures, or to a dance? Notice such things, and try to arrange for the type of activity which results in good work.

Dictating a Daily Regime

Then turn your attention to your daily regime. Most writers flourish greatly on a simple, healthy routine with occasional time off for gaiety. Here you will touch the very foundations of prosaic common sense, for you will have to decide on such matters as what diet suits you and what food you must leave alone. If you are going in for a lifetime of writing, it stands to reason that you must learn to work without the continual use of stimulants, so find what ones you can use in moderation and what must be dropped. Bursts of work are not what you are out to establish as your habit, but a good, steady, satisfying flow, rising occasionally to an extraordinary level of performance, but seldom falling below what you have discovered is your own normal output. A completely honest inventory, taken every two or three months, or twice a year at the least, will keep you up to the best and most abundant writing of which you are capable.

While you are having this honest showdown is the time to ask yourself whether you are allowing your temperamental side too much voice in the conduct of your daily life. Do you find yourself emotional and headstrong in situations where an unprejudiced observer would expect you to be dispassionate and judicial? Are you hampering yourself by being resentful or envious or easily depressed? These are all matters to be cleared up by quiet consideration. Envy, depression, resentment, will poison the very springs from which your work flows, and the sooner you eradicate the faintest traces of them the better your writing will be.

When you have these sessions, have them thoroughly. This close, analytical probing of yourself should be done rarely, but well. You must be not only strict with yourself but fair. A blanket condemnation will get you no further than uncritical self-approval. If there is a type of writing which you do well, by all means recognize it and encourage yourself by it. Hold your own good work up to yourself as a standard, and exact work of the same grade in other lines.

After each of these sessions you will see that you emerge with a clearer idea of yourself, your abilities, and your weaknesses. At first you are likely to emphasize some points over others, and later will be astonished at your own blindness to equally important items. But you will have learned how to keep a friendly, critical eye on your own progress, and what steps to take to bring yourself nearer your goal. Once more: don't follow yourself around, nagging and suggesting and complaining. When you feel that you would benefit by an inventory, set an hour for it, have it thoroughly, take the suggestions you have made; then come out and live without introspection till the next occasion for an overhauling arises.

Nine

❦

Reading as a Writer

To get the most benefit from the corrective reading you are going to do after these periodical inventories, you must take a little trouble to learn to read as a writer. Anyone who is at all interested in authorship has some sense of every book as a specimen, and not merely as a means of amusement. But to read effectively it is necessary to learn to consider a book in the light of what it can teach you about the improvement of your own work.

Most would-be writers are bookworms, and many of them are fanatical about books and libraries. But there is often a deep distaste at the idea of dissecting a book, or reading it solely for style, or for construction, or to see how its author has handled his problems. Some feeling that one will never again get the bewitched, fascinated interest from any volume that one got as an uncritical but appreciative reader makes many a student-writer protest at the idea of putting his favorite authors under a microscope. As a matter of fact, when you have learned to read critically you will find that your pleasure is far deeper than it was when you read as an amateur; even a bad book becomes tolerable when you are engaged in probing it for the reasons for its stiff, unnatural effects.

Read Twice

At first you will find that the only way to read as a writer is to go over everything twice. Read the story, article, or novel to be studied rapidly and uncritically, as you did in the days when you had no responsibility to a book but to enjoy it. When you have finished put it aside for a while, and take up a pencil and scratch pad.

Summary Judgment and Detailed Analysis

First make a short written synopsis of what you have just read. Now pass a kind of summary judgment on it: you liked it, or didn't like it. You believed it, or were left incredulous. You liked part of it, and disliked the rest. (You may, if you like later, pass a moral judgment on it, too, but now confine your decisions to what you believe were the author's intentions, as far as you are able to discern them.)

Go on to enlarge on these flat statements. If you liked it, why did you? Don't be discouraged if your answer to this is vague at first. You are going to read the book again, and will have another chance to see whether you can find the source of your response. If part of it seemed good to you and the rest weak, see whether you are able to tell when the author lost your assent. Were the characters drawn with uniform skill, badly drawn, or inconsistent only occasionally? Do you know why you felt this?

Do any of the scenes stand out in your mind? Because they were well done, or because an opportunity was so stupidly missed? Remember any passage which arrested your attention for any reason. Is the dialogue natural, or, if stylized, is the formality purposeful or a sign of the author's limitations?

By this time you know some of your own weaknesses. How does the author you have just read handle situations which would be difficult for you?

The Second Reading

If it is a good book your list of questions should be long and searching, your answers particularized as much as possible. If it is not especially good it will be enough, at first, to find the weak spots in it and lay it aside. When you have made your synopsis and answered your own questions as far as possible, make a check against those you were not able to answer fully, or that seem to promise more enlightenment if you pursue them. Now start at the first word again, reading slowly and thoroughly, noting down your answers as they become plain to you. If you find any passage particularly well done, and especially if the author has used adroitly material which would be hard for you to handle, mark them. Later you can return to them and use them as models after further analysis.

You know now how the story ends; be on the watch for the clues to that ending which come early in the book or story. Where was the character trait that brings about the major complication first mentioned? Was it brought in smoothly and subtly, or lugged in by the ears? Do you find, on second reading, that there are false clues—passages which do not make the book more real, or which distort the author's intention, but which have been allowed to pass although they introduce an unnecessary element or actually mislead the reader? Go over such passages carefully, to make sure that *you* are not missing the author's full meaning, and be sure that you are right before concluding that the author was at fault.

Points of Importance

There is no end to the amount of stimulation and help you can get from reading with critical attention. Read with every faculty alert. Notice the rhythm of the book, and whether it is accelerated or slowed when the author wishes to be emphatic. Look for mannerisms and favorite words, and decide for yourself whether they are worth trying for practice or whether they are too plainly the author's own to reward you for learning their structure. How does he get the characters from one scene to another, or mark the passing of time? Does he alter his vocabulary and emphasis when he centers his attention first on one character and then on another? Does he seem to be omniscient, is he telling only what would be apparent to one character and allowing the story to dawn on the reader by following that character's enlightenment? Or does he write first from the viewpoint of one and then another, and then a third? How does he get contrast? Is it, for instance, by placing character against setting incongruously—as Mark Twain put his Connecticut Yankee down into the world of King Arthur's day?

Each writer will ask his own questions and find his own suggestive points. After the first few books—which you *must* read twice if you are to make good use of the work of others—you will find that you can read for enjoyment and for criticism simultaneously, reserving a second reading only for those pages where the author has been at his best or worst.

Ten

🐦

On Imitation

Now as to imitation for practice. When you have learned to find in the writing of others the material which is suggestive for your own work, you are in a position to imitate in the only way in which imitation can be of any use to you. The philosophies, the ideas, the dramatic notions of other writers of fiction should not be directly adopted. If you find them congenial, go back to the sources from which those authors originally drew their ideas, if you are able to find them. There study the primary sources and take any items over into your own work only when they have your deep acquiescence — never because the author in whose work you find them is temporarily successful, or because another can use them effectively. They are yours to use only when you have made them your own by full acquaintance and acceptance.

Imitating Technical Excellences

But technical excellences can be imitated, and with great advantage. When you have found a passage, long or short, which seems to you far better than anything of the sort you are yet able to do, sit down to learn from it.

Study it even more closely than you have been studying your specimen book or specimen story as a whole. Tear it apart almost word by word. If possible, find a cognate passage in your own work to use for comparison. Let us assume, for instance, that you have trouble with that bugbear of most writers when they first begin to work seriously—conveying the passing of time. You either string out your story to no purpose, following your character through a number of unimportant or confusing activities to get him from one significant scene to another, or you drop him abruptly and take him up abruptly between two paragraphs. In the story you have been reading, which is about the length of the one you want to write, you find that the author has handled such transitions smoothly, writing just enough, but not a word too much, to convey the illusion of time's passing between two scenes. Well, then; how does he do it? He uses—how many words? Absurd as it may seem at first to think that anything can be learned by word-counting, you will soon realize that a good author has a just sense of proportion; he is artist enough to feel how much space should be given to take his character from the thick of action in one situation into the center of the next.

How to Spend Words

In a story of five thousand words, let us say, your author has given a hundred and fifty words to the passing of a night and a day, rather unimportant, in the life of his hero. And you? Three words, or a sentence perhaps: "The next day, Conrad, etc."* Something too skimpy about it altogether. Or, on the other hand, although there was nothing in Conrad's night and morning that was pertinent to the story in hand, and although you have already used up all the space you can af-

---

*I hasten to say that there are occasions on which the words, "The next day, Conrad, etc.," may be exactly the number of words and exactly the emphasis to be given to a transition. We are assuming for the moment that such a transition is, for the story you are engaged on, too abrupt.

ford in the sketching of your hero's character, by sheer inability to stop talking about him once you have started you may have given six hundred or a thousand words to the retailing of totally irrelevant matters about his day.

How does the author expend the words that you have counted? Does he drop for a few paragraphs into indirection, after having told the story up to this time straightforwardly? Does he choose words which convey action, in order to show that his hero, although not engaged during that time in anything that furthered the story, still has a full life while he is, as it were, offstage? What clues does he drop into the concluding sentence which allows him to revert to the true action? When you have found as much as you are able to find in that way, write a paragraph of your own, imitating your model *sentence by sentence*.

Counteracting Monotony

Again it may be that you feel that your writing is monotonous, that verb follows noun, and adverb follows verb, with a deadly sameness throughout your pages. You are struck by the variety, the pleasant diversity of sentence structures and rhythms in the author you are reading. Here is the real method of playing the sedulous ape: The first sentence has twelve words; you will write a twelve word sentence. It begins with two words of one syllable each, the third is a noun of two syllables, the fourth is an adjective of four syllables, the fifth an adjective of three, etc. Write one with words of the same number of syllables, noun for noun, adjective for adjective, verb for verb, being sure that the words carry their emphasis on the same syllables as those in the model. By choosing an author whose style is complementary to your own you can teach yourself a great deal about sentence formation and prose rhythm in this way. You will not wish, or need, to do it often, but to do it occasionally is remarkably helpful. You become aware of variation and tone in your reading, and learn as you read. Once having taken the trouble to analyze a sentence into its component parts and construct a similar one of your own, you will find that some part of your mind is thereafter awake to subtleties which you may have passed obliviously before.

Pick Up Fresh Words

Be on the alert to find appropriate words wherever you read, but before you use them be sure they are congruous when side by side with the words of your own vocabulary. Combing a thesaurus for what an old professor of mine used to call, contemptuously, "vivid verbs" will be far less useful than to find words in the midst of a living story; although a thesaurus is a good tool if it is used as it is meant to be.

Last of all, turn back to your own writing and read it with new eyes: read it as it will look if it makes its way into print. Are there changes you can make which will turn it into effective, diversified, vigorous prose?

Eleven

❦

Learning to See Again

The Blinders of Habit

The genius keeps all his days the vividness and intensity of interest that a sensitive child feels in his expanding world. Many of us keep this responsiveness well into adolescence; very few mature men and women are fortunate enough to preserve it in their routine lives. Most of us are only intermittently aware, even in youth, and the occasions on which adults see and feel and hear with every sense alert become rarer and rarer with the passage of years. Too many of us allow ourselves to go about wrapped in our personal problems, walking blindly through our days with our attention all given to some petty matter of no particular importance. The true neurotic may be engrossed in a problem so deeply buried in his being that he could not tell you what it is that he is contemplating, and the sign of his neurosis is his ineffectiveness in the real world. The most normal of us allow ourselves to become so insulated by habit that few things can break through our preoccupations except truly spectacular events — a catastrophe happening under our eyes, our indolent strolling blocked by a triumphal parade; it must be a matter which challenges us in spite of ourselves.

This dullness of apprehension to which we all submit spinelessly is a real danger to a writer. Since we are not laying up for ourselves daily observations, fresh sensations, new ideas, we tend to turn back for our material to the same period in our lives, and write and rewrite endlessly the sensations of our childhood or early years.

Causes of Repetitiousness

Everyone knows an author who seems to have, somehow, only one story to tell. The characters may be given different names from book to book, they may be put into ostensibly different situations; their story may end happily or on a tragic note. Nevertheless we feel each time we read a new book by that author that we have heard the same thing before. Whatever the heroine's name, we can be sure that snowflakes will fall and melt on her eyelashes, or that on a woodland walk her hair will be caught by a twig. A hero of D. H. Lawrence will drop into Lancashire dialect in moments of emotion, a heroine of Storm Jameson is likely to make a success at advertising writing and to have come from a shipbuilding family. Kathleen Norris will give you a blue mixing bowl in a sunny kitchen at least in every other book—and so on, ad infinitum. The temptation to rework material which has an emotional value for us is so great that it is almost never resisted; and there is no reason why it should be, if the reworking is well done. But often one is led to suspect that the episode is used through thoughtlessness and that with a little more trouble the author might have been able to turn up equivalent touches, just as valid, just as effective emotionally, and far less stale. The truth is that we all have a tendency to remember things which we saw under the clear, warm light of childhood, and to return to them whenever we wish to bring a scene to life. But if we continue to use the same episodes and items over and over we lose effectiveness.

Recapturing Innocence of Eye

It is perfectly possible to strip yourself of your preoccupations, to refuse to allow yourself to go about wrapped in a cloak of oblivion day and night, although it is more difficult than one might think to learn to turn one's attention outward again after years of immersion in one's own problems. Merely deciding that you will not be oblivious is hardly enough, although every writer should take the recommendation of Henry James, and register it like a vow: "Try to be one of the people on whom nothing is lost."* By way of getting to that desirable state, set yourself a short period each day when you will, by taking thought, recapture a childlike "innocence of eye." For half an hour each day transport yourself back to the state of wide-eyed interest that was yours at the age of five. Even though you feel a little self-conscious about doing something so deliberately that was once as unnoticed as breathing, you will still find that you are able to gather stores of new material in a short time. Don't plan to use the material at once, for you may get only the brittle, factual little items of the journalist if you do not wait for the unconscious mind to work its mira-

---

*In his essay "The Art of Fiction," in *Partial Portraits*. Macmillan.

cles of assimilation and accretion on them. But turn yourself into a stranger in your own streets.

A Stranger in the Streets

You know how vividly you see a strange town or a strange country when you first enter it. The huge red buses careening through London, on the wrong side of the road to every American that ever saw them — soon they are as easy to dodge and ignore as the green buses of New York, and as little wonderful as the drugstore window that you pass on your way to work each day. The drugstore window, though, the streetcar that carries you to work, the crowded subway, can look as strange as Xanadu if you refuse to take them for granted. As you get into your streetcar, or walk along a street, tell yourself that for fifteen minutes you will notice and tell yourself about every single thing that your eyes rest on. The streetcar: what color is it outside? (Not just green or red, here, but sage or olive green, scarlet or maroon.) Where is the entrance? Has it a conductor and motorman, or a motorman-conductor in one? What colors inside, the walls, the floor, the seats, the advertising posters? How do the seats face? Who is sitting opposite you? How are your neighbors dressed, how do they stand or sit, what are they reading, or are they sound asleep? What sounds are you hearing, what smells are reaching you, how does the strap feel under your hand, or the stuff of the coat that brushes past you? After a few moments you can drop your intense awareness, but plan to resume it again when the scene changes.

Another time speculate on the person opposite you. What did she come from, and where is she going? What can you guess about her from her face, her attitude, her clothes? What, do you imagine, is her home like?*

It will be worth your while to walk on strange streets, to visit exhibitions, to hunt up a movie in a strange part of town in order to give yourself the experience of fresh seeing once or twice a week. But any moment of your life can be used, and the room that you spend most of your waking hours in is as good, or better, to practice responsiveness on as a new street. Try to see your home, your family, your friends, your school or office, with the same eyes that you use away from your own daily route. There are voices you have heard so often that you forget they have a timbre of their own; unless you are morbidly hypersensitive, the chances are that you hardly realize that your best friend has a tendency to use some words so frequently that if you

---

*See the story entitled "An Unwritten Novel" in Virginia Woolf's *Monday or Tuesday.*

were to write a sentence involving those words anyone who knew him would realize whom you were imitating.

All such easy and minor exercises are excellent for you if you really want to write. No one cares to follow a dull and stodgy mind through innumerable pages, and a mind is so easily freshened. Remember that part of the advice is to put what you notice *into definite words* before you abandon it to the manipulation of the unconscious. Finding the exact words is not always necessary, but much usable stuff will slip through your fingers if you do not emphasize it in this way. If you think, "Oh, I'm sure to remember that," you will find that you are often merely begging off from a hard task. You aren't finding the words for the new sensation simply because the words do not come easily; persistently going after the right phrase will reward you with a striking, well-realized item sometime when you need it badly.

The Rewards of Virtue

Shortly after you begin looking about you like this you will see that your morning's pages are fuller and better than before. It is not only that you are bringing new material to them every day, but you are stirring the latent memories in your mind. Each fresh fact starts a train of associations reaching down into the depths of your nature, releasing for your use sensations and experiences, old delights, old sorrows, days that have been overlaid in your memory, episodes which you had quite forgotten.

This is one reason for the inexhaustible resources of the true genius. Everything that ever happened to him is his to use. No experience is so deeply buried that he cannot revive it; he can find a type-episode for every situation that his imagination can present. By the simple means of refusing to let yourself fall into indifference and boredom, you can reach and revive for your writing every aspect of your life.

Twelve

❦

The Source of Originality

It is a commonplace that every writer must turn to himself to find most of his material; it is such a commonplace that a chapter on the subject is likely to be greeted with groans. Nevertheless it must be written, for only a thorough understanding of the point will clear away the misapprehensions as to what constitutes "originality."

The Elusive Quality

Every book, every editor, every teacher will tell you that the great key to success in authorship is originality. Beyond that they seldom go. Some-

times they will point out to the persistent inquirer someone whose work shows the "originality" that they require, and those free examples are
often responsible for some of the direst mistakes
that young writers fall into. "Be original, like
William Faulkner," an editor will say, meaning
only to enforce his advice by an instance; or "Look
at Mrs. Buck; now if you could give me something
like that —!" And the earnest inquirer, quite missing the point of the exhortation, goes home and
tries with all his might to turn out what I have already complained of: "a marvelous Faulkner
story," or "a perfect Pearl Buck novel." Once in a
long while—a very long while, if my experience as
editor and teacher counts for anything—the im-
itative writer actually finds in his model some
quality so congenial that he is able to turn out an
acceptable story on the same pattern. But for one
who succeeds there are hundreds who fail. I could
find it in my heart to wish that everyone who cut
his coat by another man's pattern would find the
result a crass failure. For originality does not lie
down that road.

It is well to understand as early as possible in
one's writing life that there is just one contribution which every one of us can make: we can give
into the common pool of experience some comprehension of the world as it looks to each of us.

There is one sense in which everyone is unique. No one else was born of your parents, at just that time of just that country's history; no one underwent just your experiences, reached just your conclusions, or faces the world with the exact set of ideas that you must have. If you can come to such friendly terms with yourself that you are able and willing to say precisely what you think of any given situation or character, if you can tell a story as it can appear only to you of all the people on earth, you will inevitably have a piece of work which is original.

Now this, which seems so simple, is the very thing that the average writer cannot do. Partly because he has immersed himself in the writing of others since he was able to read at all, he is sadly apt to see the world through someone else's eyes. Occasionally, being imaginative and pliable, he does a very good job of it, and we have a story which is near enough to an original story to seem good, or not to show too plainly that it is derivative. But often those faults in comprehension, those sudden misunderstandings of one's own fictional characters, come from the fact that the author is not looking at the persons of his own creation with his own eyes; he is using the eyes of Mr. Faulkner, of Mr. Hemingway, of D. H. Lawrence or Mrs. Woolf.

Originality Not Imitation

The virtue of those writers is precisely that they have refused to do what their imitators do so humbly. Each of them has had a vision of the world and has set out to transcribe it, and their work has the forthrightness and vigor of all work that comes from the central core of the personality without deviation or distortion. There is always a faint flavor of humbug about a Dreiserian story written by some imitator of Mr. Dreiser, or one of those stark mystical Laurentian tales not directly fathered by D. H. Lawrence; but it is exceedingly hard to persuade the timid or hero-worshipping young writer that this must always be so.

The "Surprise Ending"

When the pitfall of imitation is safely skirted, one often finds that in the effort to be original an author has pulled and jerked and prodded his story into monstrous form. He will plant dynamite at its crisis, turn the conclusion inside out, betray a character by making him act uncharacteristically, all in the service of the God of Originals. His story may be all compact of horror, or, more rarely, good luck may conquer every obstacle hands down; and if the teacher or editor protests that the story has not been made credible, its author will murmur *"Dracula"* or "Kathleen Norris," and will be unconvinced if told that the minimum requirement for a good story has not been met: that he has not shown that he, the author, truly and consistently envisages a world in which such events could under any circumstances come to pass, as the authors whom he is imitating certainly do.

Honesty, the Source of Originality

So these stories fail from their own inconsistency, although the author has at his command, in the mere exercise of stringent honesty, the best source of consistency for his own work. If you can discover what you are like, if you can discover what you truly believe about most of the major matters of life, you will be able to write a story which is honest and original and unique. But those are very large "ifs," and it takes hard digging to get at the roots of one's own convictions.

Very often one finds a beginner who is unwilling to commit himself because he knows just enough about his own processes to be sure that his beliefs of today are not likely to be his beliefs of tomorrow. This operates to hold him under a sort of spell. He waits for final wisdom to arrive, and since it tarries he feels that he cannot commit himself in print. When this is a real difficulty, and not simply (as it sometimes is) a neurotic excuse to postpone writing indefinitely, you will find a writer who can turn out a sketch, a half-story with no commitments in it, but seldom more. Obviously what such a writer needs is to be made to realize that his case is not isolated; that we all continue to grow, and that in order to write at all we must write on the basis of our present beliefs. If you are unwilling to write from the honest, though perhaps far from final, point of view that represents your present state, you may come to your deathbed with your contribution to the world still unmade, and just as far from final conviction about the universe as you were at the age of twenty.

Trust Yourself

There are only so many dramatic situations in which man can find himself—three dozen, if one is to take seriously *The Thirty-six Dramatic Situations* of Georges Polti—and it is not the putting of your character in the central position of a drama which has never been dreamed of before that will make your story irresistible. Even if it were possible to find such a situation it would be an almost heartbreaking feat to communicate it to your readers, who must find some recognizable quality in the story they read or be hopelessly at sea. How *your* hero meets his dilemma, what *you* think of the impasse—those are the things which make your story truly your own; and it is your own individual character, unmistakably showing through your work, which will lead you to success or failure. I would almost be willing to go so far as to say that there is no situation which is trite in itself; there are only dull, unimaginative, or uncommunicative authors. No dilemma in which a man can find himself will leave his fellows unmoved if it can be fully presented. There is, for instance, a recognizable thematic likeness between *The Way of All Flesh*, *Clayhanger*, and *Of Human Bondage*. Which of them is trite?

"Your Anger and My Anger"

Agnes Mure MacKenzie, in *The Process of Litterature*, says, "Your loving and my loving, your anger and my anger, are sufficiently alike for us to be able to call them by the same names: but in our experience and in that of any two people in the world, they will never be quite completely identical"; if that were not literally true there would be neither basis nor opportunity for art. And again, in a recent issue of the *Atlantic Monthly,* Mrs. Wharton, writing *The Confessions of a Novelist,* declares: "As a matter of fact, there are only two essential rules: one, that the novelist should deal only with what is within his reach, literally or figuratively (in most cases the two are synonymous), and the other that the value of a subject depends almost wholly on what the author sees in it, and how deeply he is able to see into it."

By returning to those quotations from time to time you may at last persuade yourself that it is your insight which gives the final worth to your writing, and that there is no triteness where there is a good, clear, honest mind at work.

One Story, Many Versions

Very early in my classes I set out to prove this by direct demonstration. I ask for synopses of stories reduced to the very bones of an outline. Of those that are offered I choose the "tritest." In one class this was offered: "A spoiled girl marries and nearly ruins her husband by her attitude toward money." I confess that when I read this aloud to my pupils my heart misgave me. I could foresee, myself, only one elaboration of it, with one possible variation which would only occur to those who could perform the rather sophisticated feat of "dissociation" upon it—those, that is, who could discover what their immediate response to the idea was, and then deliberately alter their first association into its opposite. The class was asked to write for ten minutes, expanding the sentence into a paragraph or two, as if they were going to write a story on the theme. The result, in a class of twelve members, was twelve versions so different from each other that any editor could have read them all on the same day without realizing that the point of departure was the same in each.

We had, to begin with, a girl who was spoiled because she was a golf champion, and who, since she was an amateur, nearly ruined her husband by traveling around to tournaments. We had a story of a politician's daughter who had entertained her father's possible supporters and who entertained her husband's employer too lavishly, leading him to think that his young right-hand man was too sure of promotion. We had a story of a girl who had been warned that young wives were usually too extravagant, and who consequently pinched and pared and cut corners till she wore out her husband's patience. Before the second variation was half-read the class was laughing outright. Each member realized that she, too, had seen the situation in some purely personal light, and that what seemed so inevitable to her was fresh and unforeseen to the others. I wish I could conclude this anecdote by saying that I never again heard one of them complain that the only idea she could think of was too platitudinous to use, but this story really happened.

Nevertheless it is true that not even twins will see the same story idea from the same angle. There will always be differences of emphasis, a choice of different factors to bring about the dilemma and different actions to solve it. If you can once believe this thoroughly you can release for your immediate use any idea which has enough emotional value to engage your attention at all. If you find yourself groping for a theme you may take this as a fair piece of advice, simple as it sounds: "You can write about anything which has been vivid enough to cause you to comment upon it." If a situation has caught your attention to that extent, it has meaning for you, and if you can find what that meaning is you have the basis for a story.

Your Inalienable Uniqueness

Every piece of writing which is not simply the purveying of straightforward information—

as a recipe or a formula is, for example—is an essay in persuasion. You are persuading your reader, while you hold his attention, to see the world with your eyes, to agree with you that this is a stirring occasion, that that situation is essentially tragic, or that another is deeply humorous. All fiction is persuasive in this sense. The author's conviction underlies all imaginative representation of whatever grade.

Since this is so, it behooves you to know what you do believe of most of the major problems of life, and of those minor problems which you are going to use in your writing.

A Questionnaire

Here are a few questions for a self-examination which may suggest others to you. It is by no means an exhaustive questionnaire, but by following down the other inquiries which occur to you as you consider these, you can come by a very fair idea of your working philosophy:

Do you believe in a God? Under what aspect? (Hardy's "President of the Immortals," Wells' "emerging God"?)

Do you believe in free will or are you a determinist? (Although an artist-determinist is such a walking paradox that imagination staggers at the notion.)

Do you like men? Women? Children?

What do you think of marriage?

Do you consider romantic love a delusion and a snare?

Do you think the comment "It will all be the same in a hundred years" is profound, shallow, true or false?

What is the greatest happiness you can imagine? The greatest disaster?

And so on. If you find that you are balking at definite answers to the great questions, then you are not yet ready to write fiction which involves major issues. You must find subjects on which you are capable of making up your mind, to serve as the groundwork of your writing. The best books emerge from the strongest convictions — and for confirmation see any bookshelf.

Thirteen

❧

The Writer's Recreation

Authors are more given than any other tribe to the taking of busmen's holidays. In their off-hours they can usually be found reading in a corner, or, if thwarted in that, with other writers, talking shop. A certain amount of shoptalk is valuable; too much of it is a drain. And too much reading is very bad indeed.

Busmen's Holidays

All of us, whether we follow writing as a career or not, are so habituated to words that we cannot escape them. If we are left alone long enough and forbidden to read, we will very soon be talking to ourselves—"subvocally" as the behaviorists say. This is the easiest thing in the world to prove: starve yourself for a few hours in a wordless void. Stay alone, and resist the temptation to take up any book, paper, or scrap of printed matter that you can find; also flee the temptation to telephone someone when the strain begins to make itself felt—for you will almost surely scheme internally to be reading or talking within a few minutes. In a very short while you will find that you are using words at a tremendous rate: planning to tell an acquaintance just what you think of him, examining your conscience and giving yourself advice, trying to recapture the words of a song, turning over the plot of a story; in fact, words have rushed in to fill the wordless vacuum.

Prisoners who never wrote a word in the days of their freedom will write on any paper they can lay hands on. Innumerable books have been begun by patients lying on hospital beds, sentenced to silence and refused reading; the last one to be reported was, I think, Margaret Ayer Barnes' *Years of Grace*, and long ago I remember reading that William Allen White's *A Certain Rich Man* came to him when he was "tossing pebbles into the sea" on an enforced vacation. A two-year-old will tell himself stories, and a farmer will talk to a cow. Once we have learned to use words we must be forever using them.

Wordless Recreation

The conclusion should be plain. If you want to stimulate yourself into writing, amuse yourself in wordless ways. Instead of going to a theater, hear a symphony orchestra, or go by yourself to a museum; go alone for long walks, or ride by yourself on a bus-top. If you will conscientiously refuse to talk or read you will find yourself compensating for it to your great advantage.

One very well-known writer of my acquaintance sits for two hours a day on a park bench. He says that for years he used to lie on the grass of his back garden and stare at the sky, but some member of the family, seeing him so conveniently alone and aimless, always seized the occasion to come out and sit beside him for a nice talk. Sooner or later, he himself would begin to talk about the work he had in mind, and, to his astonishment, he discovered that the urgent desire to write the story disappeared as soon as he had got it thoroughly talked out. Now, with a purposeful air and in mysterious silence, he disappears daily, and can be found every afternoon (but fortunately seldom is) with his hands in his pockets staring at the pigeons in the park.

Another writer, almost tone-deaf, says that she can finish any story she starts if she can find a hall where a long symphony is being played. The lights, the music, her immobility, bring on a sort of artistic coma, and she emerges in a sleepwalking state which lasts till she reaches the typewriter.

Find Your Own Stimulus

Only experiment will show you what your own best recreation is; but books, the theater, and talking pictures should be very rarely indulged in when you have any piece of writing to finish. The better the book or the play is the more likely it is, not only to distract you, but actually to alter your mood, so that you return to your own writing with your attitude changed.

A Variety of Time-Fillers

Most established authors have some way of silent recreation. One found that horseback riding was the best relaxation for him; another, a woman, confessed that whenever she came to a difficult spot in a novel she was writing, she got up and played endless games of solitaire. (I believe it was Mrs. Norris, and I think she went so far as to say that she was not always certain to see an ace when she turned it up.) Another woman novelist found, during the war years, that she spun stories as fast as she knitted, and turned herself into a Penelope of the knitting needle, raveling a square of scarlet wool and starting on it again whenever she had a story "simmering." Fishing served a writer of detective stories, and another admits that he whittles aimlessly for hours. Still another said that she embroidered initials on everything she could lay her hands on.

Only an impassioned author could call some of these occupations by any name so glamorous as "recreation"; but it is to be noticed that successful writers, when talking about themselves *as writers*, say little about curling up in a corner with a good book. Much as they may love reading (and all authors would rather read than eat), they had all learned from long experience that it is the wordless occupation which sets their own minds busily at work.

Fourteen

❧

The Practice Story

A Recapitulation

When you have succeeded for some weeks in rising early and writing, and in the second step of going off by yourself at a given moment and beginning to write, you are ready to combine the two; and you are within measurable distance of being ready for the key procedure which every successful artist knows. Why it is kept such a secret, and why it should take a different form in almost every writer, is a mystery. Perhaps because each worked it out for himself and so hardly realizes that it is a part of his special knowledge. But that is matter for another chapter. Now it is time to bring together the work of the conscious and unconscious in an elementary manner.

You were warned not to reread your own work before starting on each morning's writing. You were to try to tap the unconscious directly, not simply to call up from it by way of association a certain limited set of ideas; and, further, if you were to find your own stride it was necessary to free you from the hampering effects of having any example before your eyes. A newspaper, a novel, the speech of someone else, or even your own writing so long as you are under the influence of others—all have a circumscribing effect. We are very easily drawn into a circle of ideas; we fall into the rhythm of any book or newspaper we read.

The Contagiousness of Style

If you seriously doubt this, it is very easy to demonstrate how one can be caught up into the current of another's style. Choose any writer whose work has a strong rhythm, a decided personal style: Dickens, Thackeray, Kipling, Hemingway, Aldous Huxley, Mrs. Wharton, Wodehouse—anyone you like. Read your author until you feel a little fatigue, the first momentary flagging of attention. Put the book aside and write a few pages on any subject. Then compare those pages with the writing you have done in the early morning. You will find a definite difference between the two. You have insensibly altered your own emphasis and inflection in the direction of the author's in whom you have been engrossed. Sometimes the similarity is so striking as to be almost ludicrous, although you intended no parody—may even have intended to write as independently as possible. We can leave it to the psychologists to discover that this is so, and to explain why it should be.

Find Your Own Style

The important matter is to find your own style, your own subjects, your own rhythm, so that every element in your nature can contribute to the work of making a writer of you. Study your own pages; among them you are to find some idea — preferably, this time, a fairly simple one — which offers you a good, obvious nucleus for a short story, an expanded anecdote (say, of *The New Yorker*'s style), or a brief essay. Story material will be best. Anything that is there in your early morning work has real value for you. You will have something to say on the subject which is more than superficial comment. Abstract your idea from its too discursive setting and get down to the matter of considering it seriously.

The Story in Embryo

What shall you make of it? Remember, you are to look for a simple idea—something that can be finished in one sitting. Then, in that case, what will it need? Emphasis? Characters to embody in concrete form the speculations you have made in your sleepy state? Does it need to have certain factors made very plain, so that the conflict, whatever it is, runs no danger of seeming unimportant or of being overlooked? When you have decided what can and should be made of it, consider the details with care.

The Preparatory Period

Mind you, you are not yet to write it. The work you are doing on it is preliminary. For a day or two you are going to immerse yourself in these details; you are going to think about them consciously, turning if necessary to books of reference to fill in your facts. Then you are going to dream about it. You are going to think of the characters separately, then in combination. You are going to do everything you can for that story by using alternately your conscious intelligence and unconscious reverie on it. There will seem no end to the stuff that you can find to work over. What does the heroine look like? Was she an only child, or the eldest of seven? How was she educated? Does she work? Now perform the same labor on the hero, and on any secondary characters you need to bring the story to life. Then turn your attention to the scene, and to those background scenes in each character's life which you may never need to write of, but a knowledge of which will make your finished story that much more convincing.*

When you have done everything you can in this way, say to yourself: "At ten o'clock on Wednesday I will begin to write it," and then dismiss it from your mind. Now and then it will rise to the surface. You need not reject it with violence, but

---

*In his latest book, *It Was the Nightingale*, Ford Madox Ford says, on just this point: "I may—and quite frequently do—plan out every scene, sometimes even every conversation, in a novel before I sit down to write it. But unless I know the history back to the remotest times of any place of which I am going to write I cannot begin the work. And I must know—from personal observation, not reading, the shapes of windows, the nature of doorknobs, the aspect of kitchens, the material of which dresses are made, the leather used in shoes, the method used in manuring fields, the nature of bus tickets. I shall never use any of these things in the book. But unless I know what sort of doorknob his fingers closed on how shall I—satisfactorily to myself—get my character out of doors?" This book will be found full of valuable sidelights on the process of literature.

reject it. You are not ready for it yet; let it subside again. Three days will do it no harm, will even help it. But when ten o'clock strikes on Wednesday you sit down to work.

Writing Confidently

Now; strike out at once. Just as you made yourself do the time exercises in the sixth chapter, take no excuses, refuse to feel any stage fright; simply start working. If a good first sentence does not come, leave a space for it and write it in later. Write as rapidly as possible, with as little attention to your own processes as you can give. Try to work lightly and quickly, beginning and ending each sentence with a good, clear stroke. Reread very little—only a sentence or two now and then to be sure you are on the true course.

In this way you can train yourself into good, workmanlike habits. The typewriter or the writing pad should not appear to you a good place to lose yourself in musing, or to work out matters you should have cleared up before. You may find it very helpful, before you begin to write, to settle on a first and last sentence for your story. Then you can use the first sentence as a springboard from which to dive into your work, and the last as a raft to swim toward.

A Finished Experiment

The exercise must end with a completed piece of work, no matter how long you labor at it. Later you will learn how to do writing which cannot be finished at a sitting; the best way is to make another engagement with yourself before you rise from the typewriter, and while the heat of work is still on you. You will find if you do this that you will come to meet yourself, as it were, in the same mood, and there will not be a noticeable alteration in the manner of your writing between one session and the next. But this story is to be finished on the day you begin it.

Whether or not you are going to like it when you read it later, whether or not you decide that you can do a better version of it if you try again, the exercise is not done properly unless you rise from the session with a complete practice story.

Time for Detachment

Put it away, and if your curiosity will let you, leave it alone for two or three days. At the very least let it stay unread overnight. Your judgment on it until you have slept is worth exactly nothing. One of two states of mind will interfere with any earlier appraisal. If you belong to one half the writing race, you will be worn and discouraged, and, reading your own story over with fatigue clouding every line, you will think it the dullest, most improbable, flattest tale ever told. Even if you reread it more favorably later when you are freshened by sleep and diversion, a memory of that first verdict is likely to cause you to wonder which of the judgments is right. And if the story is rejected by the first editor who sees it, you are likely to think that it is as bad as you feared, and you may refuse to give it another chance.

The other half of the brotherhood seems not to use up the last ounce of its energy in getting a story to its close. They, on reading their recent effort, will be still held by the impulse which set them writing in the first place. If they have fallen into errors of judgment, if they have been too verbose or compact, the same astigmatism that was responsible for the mistake in the first place will still operate to blind them to it.

You are simply not ready to read your story objectively when it is newly finished; and there *are* writers who cannot trust their objectivity toward their own work much under a month. So put it away and turn your attention to something else. Now is the time of times for the reading which you have been denying yourself. Your story is safely written, and will preserve the marks of your personality so tenaciously that not the deepest admiration for the work of another writer will be likely to endanger it. If even reading seems too great an effort, find some mild relaxation which takes your attention quite away from authorship. If you can make a definite break in your routine just here, so much the better. Some writers have an immediate impulse to begin work on another story; if you feel it, by all means give in to it. But if you feel that you never want to see paper and typewriter again, indulge yourself in that mood, too.

The Critical Reading

When you are refreshed, relaxed, and detached, take out your story and read it.

The chances are that you will find a great deal more in your manuscript than you are conscious of having put there. Something was at work for you while you wrote. Scenes which you thought absolutely vital to the proper telling of the story are not there at all; other scenes which you had not planned to write take their places. The characters have traits you had hardly realized. They have said things you had not thought of having them say. Here is a sentence cleverly emphasized which you had thought of as only a casual statement, but which needed that emphasis if the story was to be shapely. In short, you have written both less and more than you intended. Your conscious mind had less to do with it, your unconscious mind more, than you would have believed possible.

Fifteen

❧

The Great Discovery

The Five-Finger Exercises of Writing

Now those are the five-finger exercises of writing. To recapitulate before we go further, for you can hardly hear too often these primary truths about your art, the writer (like every artist) is a dual personality. In him the unconscious flows freely. He has trained himself so that the physical effort of writing does not tire him out of all proportion to the effect he achieves. His intellect directs, criticizes, and discriminates wherever two possible courses present themselves, in such a way as to leave the more sensitive element of his nature free to bring forth its best fruit. He learns to use his intellect both cursively, as he works, and later, as he considers what he has done during the period of the creative flow. He replaces by conscious intention, and day by day, the drains made on his funds of images, sensations, and ideas, by keeping awake to new observations. Ideally, the two sides of his nature are at peace with each other and work in harmony; at the least he must be able to suppress one or the other at discretion. Each side of his character must learn to be able to trust the other to do what is in its field and to carry the full responsibility for its own work. He restrains each side of his mind to its own functions, never allowing the conscious to usurp the privilege of the unconscious, and vice versa.

Now we go a little more deeply into the contribution of the unconscious, and the piece of writing you have just finished is your laboratory specimen. If you have worked according to instructions, foreseeing as many of the points of your story as you were able to, if you thought and daydreamed about the story without beginning to write prematurely; if then when you had promised yourself to write you got straight to work without hesitation or apology, it is very nearly certain that the resulting piece of writing will be both shapelier and fuller than you could have expected. The story will be balanced in a way which seems more adroit than you would have believed possible. The characters will be more fully, more expertly drawn, and at the same time drawn with more economy, than if you had labored at them with all your conscious mind in action. In short, a faculty has been at work which so far we have hardly considered. The higher imagination, you may call it; your own endowment of genius, great or small; the creative aspect of your mind, which is lodged almost entirely in the unconscious.

The Root of Genius

For the root of genius is in the unconscious, not the conscious, mind. It is not by weighing, balancing, trimming, expanding with conscious intention, that an excellent piece of art is born. It takes its shape and has its origin outside the region of the conscious intellect. There is much that the conscious can do, but it cannot provide you with genius, or with the talent that is genius' second cousin.

Unconscious, Not Subconscious

But we are badly handicapped when we come to talk or write of it, for the mind is not yet fully explored. And there is an even more serious difficulty to be encountered. When the Freudian psychology first reached us, we began to hear, unfortunately for us, about the *sub*conscious. Freud himself has corrected that error in terminology, and it is the *un*conscious that is now mentioned in the canonical works. But for most of us, that unlucky "sub" carried a derogatory connotation, and we have not entirely freed ourselves from the idea that the unconscious is, in some way, a less laudable part of our makeup than our conscious mind. F.W.H. Myers, in his excellent chapter on "Genius" in *Human Personality* (which should be read by every prospective author), fell subject to the same temptation and spoke continually of the "subliminal uprush." Now the unconscious is not, in its entirety, either below or less than the conscious mind. It includes in its scope everything which is not in the forefront of our consciousness, and has a reach as far above our average intellect as it has depths below.

The Higher Imagination

This spatial terminology is also unfortunate. The thing to realize is that the unconscious must be trusted to bring you aid from a higher level than that on which you ordinarily function. Any art must draw on this higher content of the unconscious as well as on the memories and emotions stored away there. A sound and gifted person is one who draws on and uses continually these resources, who lives in peace and amity with all the reaches of his being; not one who suppresses, at the cost of infinite energy and vitality, every echo from the far region.

Come to Terms with the Unconscious

The unconscious should not be thought of as a limbo where vague, cloudy, and amorphous notions swim hazily about. There is every reason to believe, on the contrary, that it is the great home of form; that it is quicker to see types, patterns, purposes, than our intellect can ever be. Always, it is true, you must be on the watch lest a too heady exuberance sweep you away from a straight course; always you must direct and control the excess of material which the unconscious will offer. But if you are to write well you must come to terms with the enormous and powerful part of your nature which lies behind the threshold of immediate knowledge.

If you can learn to do this, you have less tiring, difficult labor to perform than you believed you had when you first turned to writing. There is a great field of technical knowledge which the writer can study, many shortcuts to effectiveness which can be learned by taking thought. Yet on the whole it is the unconscious which will decide on both the form and the matter of the work which you are planning, and which will, if you can learn to rely on it, give you a far better and more convincing result if you are not continually meddling with its processes and imposing on it your own notions of the plausible, the desirable, the persuasive, according to some formula which you have painstakingly extracted from a work on the technique of fiction, or laboriously plotted out for yourself from long study of stories in print.

The Artistic Coma
and the Writer's Magic

The true genius may live his life long without ever realizing how he works. He will know only that there are times when he must, at all costs, have solitude; time to dream, to sit idle. Often he himself believes that his mind is empty. Sometimes we hear of gifted men who are on the verge of despair because they feel they are going through a "barren" period; but suddenly the time of silence is past, and they have reached the moment when they must write. That strange, aloof, detached period has been called "the artistic coma" by observers shrewd enough to see that the idleness is only a surface stillness. *Something* is at work, but so deeply and wordlessly that it hardly gives a sign of its activity till it is ready to externalize its vision. The necessity which the artist feels to indulge himself in solitude, in rambling leisure, in long speechless periods, is behind most of the charges of eccentricity and boorishness that are leveled at men of genius. If the period is recognized and allowed for, it need not have a disruptive effect. The artist will always be marked by occasional periods of detachment; the nameless faculty will always announce itself by an air of withdrawal and indifference, but it is possible to hasten the period somewhat, and to have it, to a limited extent, under one's control. To be able to induce at will the activity of that higher imagination, that intuition, that artistic level of the unconscious — that is where the artist's magic lies, and is his only true "secret."

Sixteen

❦

The Third Person, Genius

The Writer Not Dual But Triple

So, almost insensibly, one arrives at the understanding that the writer's nature is not dual but triple. The third member of the partnership is—feeble or strong, constantly or spasmodically showing—one's individual endowment of genius. The flashes of insight, the penetrating intuitions, the imagination which combines and transmutes ordinary experience into "the illusion of a higher reality" — all these necessities of art, or, on a humbler level, all these necessities of any interpretation of life, come from a region beyond those

155

we have been studying and learning to control. For most practical purposes it is enough to divide our minds roughly into conscious and unconscious; it is quite possible to live a lifetime (even the lifetime of an artist) without even so much comprehension of the mind's complexity. Yet by recognizing this third component of your nature, by understanding its importance to your writing, by learning to liberate it, to clear obstructions from its path so that it may flow unimpeded into your work, you perform the most vital service of which you are capable to yourself as a writer.

The Mysterious Faculty

Now you begin to see the basis of truth for that discouraging statement, "Genius cannot be taught." In a sense, of course, that is the literal truth; but the implications are almost entirely misleading. You cannot add one grain to this faculty by all your conscious efforts, but there is no reason why you should desire to. Its resources at the feeblest are fuller than you can ever exhaust. What we need is not to add to that natural endowment, but to learn to use it. The great men of every period and race—so great that we call them, for simplicity's sake, by the name of that one faculty alone, as though in them it existed with no admixture, the "geniuses"—are those who were able to free more of that faculty for use in their lives and in their works of art than the rest of mankind. No human being is so poor as to have no trace of genius; none so great that he comes within infinity of using his own inheritance to the full.

The average man fears, distrusts, ignores, or knows nothing of that element of his nature. In moments of deep emotion, in danger, in joy, occasionally when long sickness has quieted the body and the mind, sometimes in a remote, dim apprehension which we bring back with us from sleep, or from moments under an anesthetic, everyone has intimations of it. Traces of it may be seen at its most unmistakable and mysterious in the lives of the prodigies of music.* However mysterious and incomprehensible it is, it exists; and it is no more "an infinite capacity for taking pains"—as the old definition of genius would have it—than "inspiration is perspiration"; a pure American delusion if ever there was one. The process of *transmitting* one's intuitive knowledge, of conveying one's insight at all satisfactorily, may be infinitely laborious. Years may be spent finding the words to set forth the illumination of a

---

*Read any account of Mozart's life, for example.

moment. But to confuse the labor with the genius that instigated it is to be misled. When one learns to release this faculty even inexpertly, or when it is released fortuitously, one finds that so far from having to toil anxiously and painstakingly for his effects one experiences, on the contrary, the miracle of being carried along on the creative current.

Releasing Genius

Often the release does come accidentally. It is possible for an artist to count on the energy from this region to carry out a book, story, a picture, and yet never recognize it. He may even go so far as to deny that any such thing as "genius" is in question. He will assure you that, in his experience, it is all a matter of "getting into his stride"; but what getting into his stride implies he may never know, even though in that happy state he writes pages of clarity and beauty beyond anything of which he is capable in his pedestrian moments. Another may, in a burst of candor, tell you that after mulling an idea over till his head aches he comes to a kind of dead end: he can no longer think about his story or even understand why it once appealed to him. Much later, when he is least expecting it, the idea returns, mysteriously rounded and completed, ready for transcribing. And so on. Most successful writers arrive at their own method of releasing this faculty by a trial-and-error process, so obscure that they can seldom offer a beginner in search of the secret so much as a rule-of-thumb. Their reports of their writing habits are so at variance with each other that it is no wonder the young writer sometimes feels that his elders are all engaged in a conspiracy to delude and mislead him as to the actual process of literature.

Rhythm, Monotony, Silence

There is no conspiracy; there is, I should say, remarkably little jealousy or personal envy between writers. They will tell you what they can, but the more instinctively they are artists the less they are able to analyze their ways of working. What one finally gets, after long cross-questionings, after raking through reports, is no explanation, but usually simple statements of personal experience. They agree in reporting that the idea of a book or story is usually apprehended in a flash. At that moment many of the characters, many of the situations, the story's outcome, all may be—either dimly or vividly—prefigured. Then there is a period of intensive thinking and working over of the ideas. With some authors this is a period of great excitement; they seem intoxicated with the possibilities there before their minds. Later comes a quiescent period; and since almost every writer alive occupies himself in some quite idiosyncratic way in that interlude, it is seldom noticed that these occupations have a kind of common denominator. Horseback riding; knitting; shuffling and dealing cards; walking; whittling; you see they *have* a common denominator — of three figures, one might say. All these occupations are rhythmical, monotonous, and wordless. And that is our key.

In other words, every author, in some way which he has come on by luck or long search, puts himself into a very light state of hypnosis. The attention is held, but *just* held; there is no serious demand on it. Far behind the mind's surface, so deep that he is seldom aware (unless at last observation of himself has taught him) that any activity is going forward, his story is being fused and welded into an integrated work.

A Floor to Scrub

With no more clue than that you might be able to find some such occupation of your own; or you may recognize in some recurrent habit the promise of an occupation which would be useful to you. But the disadvantage of most of these accidentally discovered time-fillers is that they are only rude expedients. When they *have* been found they are seldom abandoned. Indeed, many writers reach a state of real superstition about the method which has worked for them. "I'd be all right if I had a floor to scrub," one of my pupils said to me, a professor's wife who had written in the intervals of bringing up a large family, and had found that her stories fell into line best when she was at work on the kitchen floor. A little success had brought her to the city to study; she convinced herself completely that she would be unable to write again till she got back to the rhythmical monotony of the scrubbing brush. This is an extreme case; but there are many famous authors with superstitions just as stubbornly and firmly, although less outspokenly, held as my middle-western housemother's. And indeed most of the methods which have been discovered accidentally are as arbitrary, wasteful, and haphazard as scrubbing floors.

There is a way to shorten that "incubating period" and produce a better piece of work. And that way is the writer's magic which you have been promised.

Seventeen

*

The Writer's Magic

X Is to Mind as Mind to Body

Let us pretend, for convenience, that this faculty, this genius which is present in all of us to a greater or less degree, has been isolated, analyzed, and studied; and found to stand in relation to the mind as the mind stands to the body. If the word "genius" is still too magniloquent a word for comfort, if you fear that under a wily guise you are being introduced to a spiritual quality which discomfits you, bear with the notions a little while, and call the faculty under consideration just ordinary X. Now X is to be thought of like a factor in an algebraic equation—

163

X : Mind :: Mind : Body. In order to think intensively you hold your body still; at the most you
engage it in some light, mechanical task which
you can carry on like an automaton. To get X into
action, then, you must quiet the mind.

This, you will observe, is exactly what those
rhythmical, monotonous, wordless activities had
as their obscure end: they were designed to hold
mind as well as body in a kind of suspension while
the higher, or deeper, faculty was at work. Insofar
as they were successful, they were adopted and
used over and over. But they are usually awkward,
unsatisfactory, and not always uniform in their
results. Moreover, they usually take far more time
than the unknown quality needs to fulfill its functions. So, if you are fortunate enough to be a
young writer who has not yet found a formula for
that gestation period of the story, you are in a
position to learn a quicker and better way to attain the same end.

Hold Your Mind Still

It is, in short, this: *learn to hold your mind as
still as your body.*

For some this advice is so easy to take that
they cannot believe anyone has difficulty in following it. If you belong to that happy group, do

not try any of the more intensive exercises that follow. You do not need them, and they will only confuse you. But as you come to this spot in the book, close the book over your finger and shut your eyes, holding your mind, for only a few seconds, as still as you can.

Were you successful—even if for only a fraction of a moment? If you have never tried it before, you may be surprised and confounded to find how busy, fluttering, and restless your mind seems. "The chattering monkey," an Indian will say of his mind, half in scorn, half in indulgence; much as St. Francis of Assisi called his body, "My Brother, the Ass." "It skitters around like a water bug!" one experimenter exclaimed, in surprise. But it will stop skittering for you, after a little practice; at least it will be still enough to suit your purposes.

Practice in Control

The best practice is to repeat this procedure once a day for several days. Simply close your eyes with the idea of holding your mind quite steady, but feeling no urgency or tension about it. Once a day; don't push it or attempt to force it. As you begin to get results, make the period a little longer, but never strain at it.

If you discover that you cannot learn to do it

so easily, try this way: Choose a simple object, like a child's gray rubber ball. (It is better not to select anything with a bright surface or a decided highlight.) Hold the ball in your hand and look at it, confining your attention to that one simple object, and calling your mind back to it quietly whenever it begins to wander. When you are able to think of the object and nothing else for some moments, take the next step. Close your eyes and *go on looking at the ball*, thinking of nothing else. Then see if you can let even that simple idea slip away.

The last method is to let your mind skitter all it pleases, watching it indulgently as it moves. Presently it will grow quieter. Don't hurry it. If it will not be entirely quiet, it will probably be still enough.

The Story Idea as the Object

When you have succeeded, even a little, try holding a story idea, or a character, in your mind, and letting your stillness center around that. Presently you will see the almost incredible results. Ideas which you held rather academically and unconvincingly will take on color and form; a character that was a puppet will move and breathe. Consciously or unconsciously every successful writer who ever lived calls on this faculty to put the breath of life into his creations.

Now you are ready to try the process in more extended form.

The Magic in Operation

Since this is practice work only (although more may come of the ideas you practice on than you expect) you may go at it rather mechanically. Choose any story idea at random. If you do not like to use one of your own cherished plots for this, here is a variation that will work as well: replace the character of a well-known book by someone you know in real life. If your sister had played the role of Becky Sharp, for example, what course would *Vanity Fair* have had to follow? Suppose Gulliver had been a woman? How vague, stiff, or incomplete the idea is, is of no importance. For our purposes, the less satisfactory it seems at the moment the more complete the demonstration of the method's effectiveness. Make a rough outline of the story. Decide on the main characters, then the secondary characters. See as plainly as possible what crucial situation you would like to put them into, and how you would like to leave them at the end. Don't worry about getting them either in or out of their dilemma; simply see them in it, and then see it resolved. Remember here the circle-and-ring experiment, and that envisaging the end was enough to set the means in motion.

Think over the whole story in a sort of pleasant, indulgent mood, correcting any obvious absurdities, reminding yourself of this or that item which you would like to include if it could be brought in naturally.

Now take that rough draft of a story out for a walk with you. You are going to walk till you are just mildly tired, and at that time you should be back at your starting place; gauge your distance by that. Get into a smooth and easy swing, not vigorous and athletic—a lazy, loafing walk is better at first, although it may become more rapid later. Now think about your story; let yourself be engrossed in it—but think of it *as a story*, not of how you are going to write it, or what means you will use to get this or that effect. Refuse to let yourself be diverted by anything outside. As you circle back to your starting place, think of the story's end, as though you were laying it aside after reading it.

Inducing the "Artistic Coma"

Now bathe, still thinking of it in a desultory way, and then go into a dim room. Lie down, flat on your back; the alternative position, to be chosen only if you find that the other makes you too drowsy, is to sit not quite fully relaxed in a low, large chair. When you have taken a comfortable position, do not move again: make your body quiet. Then quiet your mind. Lie there, not quite asleep, not quite awake.

After a while—it may be twenty minutes, it may be an hour, it may be two—you will feel a definite impulse to rise, a kind of surge of energy. Obey it at once; you will be in a slightly somnambulistic state indifferent to everything on earth except what you are about to write; dull to all the outer world but vividly alive to the world of your imagination. Get up and go to your paper or typewriter, and begin to write. The state you are in at that moment is the state an artist works in.

Valedictory

How good a piece of work emerges depends on you and your life: how sensitive, how discriminating you are, how closely your experience reflects the experience of your potential readers, how thoroughly you have taught yourself the elements of good prose writing, how good an ear you have for rhythm. But, limited or not, you will find, if you have followed the exercises, that you can bring forth a shapely, integrated piece of work by this method. It will have flaws, no doubt; but you will be able to see them objectively and work on eradicating them. By these exercises you have made yourself into a good instrument for the use of your own genius. You are flexible and sturdy, like a good tool. You know what it feels like to work as an artist.

Now read all the technical books on the writing of fiction that you can find. You are at last in a position to have them do you some good.

In Conclusion:
Some Prosaic Pointers

Typewriting

As soon as you can, learn to typewrite. Then, if possible, learn to compose on the typewriter. Unless you write very rapidly and plainly, a first draft written by hand is usually one long waste motion. But be sure that you are sacrificing nothing in making the shift from handwriting to writing on a machine. There are persons who are never able to get the same qualities in the machine-written work which they can catch by the more leisurely method. Write two rather similar ideas, one by each method; compare the two. If the typewritten draft is more abrupt, if you find

that ideas escape you there which are found in
your handwritten draft, composing at the typewriter is not your proper method.

Have Two Typewriters

The professional writer should have two
typewriters, a standard machine and a portable — preferably a noiseless portable. Choose
machines with the same typeface; they should
both be pica, or both be elite. This will enable you
to write at your own convenience, in any room, at
any free moment, or when traveling. And you can
also leave an incompleted piece of work in the
machine, as a mute reproach—if you find you
need that.

Stationery

Raid a stationery store. There are innumerable pencils on the market, of all grades of softness
and several colors. Try them all; you may find the
ideal pencil for your purposes. A medium-soft
lead is best for most writers: the pages do not
smudge, yet no particular pressure is necessary
when writing.

Try bond paper and "laid" paper—paper

with a sleek, smooth finish. Many amateurs use a bond paper because they have never had the good fortune to find the smoother finish, yet the grain in a bond paper may irritate them like the feeling of painted china.

Try writing on loose paper, on pads of various sizes, and in notebooks. Have a notebook full of fresh sheets ready to take on any short journey. On a long journey carry typewriter paper and a portable machine, and make the most of your time.

Don't buy the heaviest and most impressive grade of bond paper for your finished manuscripts. It makes too bulky and heavy a package, and the paper shows wear more quickly than the less expensive grades. "A good sixteen-pound paper," is the way to ask for what you need. If the clerk doesn't understand you, find a better stationery store.

At the Typewriter: WRITE!

Teach yourself as soon as possible to work the moment you sit down to a machine, or settle yourself with pad and pencil. If you find yourself dreaming there, or biting your pencil end, get up and go to the farthest corner of the room. Stay there while you are getting up steam. When you have your first sentence ready, go back to your tools. If you steadily refuse to lose yourself in reverie at your worktable, you will be rewarded by finding that merely taking your seat there will be enough to make your writing flow.

If you are unable to finish a piece of work at one sitting, make an engagement with yourself to resume work *before you rise from the table.* You will find that this acts like a posthypnotic suggestion, in more ways than one. You will get back to the work without delay, and you will pick up the same note with little difficulty, so that your story will not show as many different styles as a patchwork quilt when it is done.

For Coffee Addicts

If you have an ingrained habit of putting off everything until after you have had your morning coffee, buy a thermos bottle and fill it at night. This will thwart your wily unconscious in the neatest fashion. You will have no excuse to postpone work while you wait for your stimulant.

Coffee Versus Maté

If you tend to drink a great deal of coffee when in the throes of composition, try replacing half of it by maté, a South American drink much like tea, but stimulating and innocuous. It can be bought at any large grocer's, and is very easy to prepare.

Reading

If you are writing a manuscript so long that the prospect of not reading at all until you have finished is too intolerable, be sure to choose books which are as unlike your own work as possible: read technical books, history, or, best of all, books in other languages.

Book and Magazine Buying

Have periodical debauches of book-buying and magazine-buying, and try to formulate to yourself the editor's possible requirements from the type of periodical he issues. Buy a good handbook on fiction markets, and whenever you find an editor asking for manuscripts which sound like the type you are interested in writing, send for a copy of the magazine if you cannot buy it nearer home.

Bibliography

Edith Wharton, *The Writing of Fiction*, Scribner, 1925.

A. Quiller-Couch, *On the Art of Writing*, Putnam, 1916.

A. Quiller-Couch, *On the Art of Reading*, Putnam, 1920.

Percy Lubbock, *The Craft of Fiction*, Scribner, 1921.

E. M. Forster, *Aspects of the Novel*, Harcourt, Brace, 1927.

The Novels of Henry James, Definitive Edition, Scribner, 1917. In particular, see Preface to *The Ivory Tower*.

Graham Wallas, *The Art of Thought*, Harcourt, Brace, 1926.

Mary Austin, *Everyman's Genius*, Bobbs Merrill, 1925.

Thomas Uzzell, *Narrative Technique*, Harcourt, Brace, 1923.

F.W.H. Myers, *Human Personality and its Survival of Bodily Death*, Longmans, Green, 1920. In particular, see the chapter on Genius.

Edith Wharton, "The Confessions of a Novelist." *Atlantic Monthly*, April, 1933.

Percy Marks, *The Craft of Writing*, Harcourt, Brace, 1932.

S. T. Coleridge, *Biographia Literaria*. Various editions.

Conversations of Eckermann with Goethe, tr. by John Oxenford, Dutton, 1931.

Longinus, *On the Sublime*, tr. by W. Rhys Roberts, Macmillan, 1930.

Alexander Pope, *Essay on Criticism*. Various editions.

William Archer, *Play-Making*, Dodd, Mead, 1912.

George Saintsbury, *History of English Prose Rhythm*, Macmillan, 1922.

Charles Williams, *The English Poetic Mind*, Oxford, 1932.

Anonymous, *The Literary Spotlight*, Doran.

24 English Authors, *Mr. Fothergill's Plot*, Oxford, 1931.

Douglas Bement, *Weaving the Short Story*, Richard R. Smith, 1931.

Ford Madox Ford, *It Was the Nightingale*, Lippincott, 1933.

Arnold Bennett, *How to Live on 24 Hours a Day*, Doran, 1910.

T. S. Eliot, *Selected Essays*, Harcourt, Brace, 1932.

Virginia Woolf, *The Common Reader*, Harcourt, Brace, 1925.

Virginia Woolf, *Monday or Tuesday*, Harcourt, Brace, 1921.

The Journals of Katherine Mansfield, edited by J. Middleton Murry, Knopf, 1927.

Storm Jameson, *The Georgian Novel and Mr. Robinson*, Morrow, 1929.

Blanche Colton Williams, *Handbook on Story Writing*, Dodd, Mead, 1930.

Henry Seidel Canby, *Better Writing*, Harcourt, Brace, 1926.

Paul Elmer More, *The Shelburne Essays*, 11 vols., Houghton Mifflin.

Irving Babbitt, *The New Laokoon*, Houghton Mifflin, 1910.

Lafcadio Hearn, *Talks to Writers*, Dodd, Mead, 1920.

And, finally, those who read French will treble the number of these books by the works of Sainte-Beuve, Remy de Gourmont, Gustave Flaubert, the Journals of the brothers Goncourt, Jules Lemaître, Paul Valéry, André Gide (see particularly *Les Faux-Monnayeurs*, or the excellent English translation, published in this country under the title *The Counterfeiters*, Knopf, 1927).

Index

On Becoming a Novelist

by John Gardner

Foreword by Raymond Carver

For all my students

CONTENTS

ACKNOWLEDGMENTS

Some of the plot ideas examined in this book came out of writers' workshop discussions at SUNY–Binghamton.

FOREWORD

A long time ago—it was the summer of 1958—my wife and I and our two baby children moved from Yakima, Washington, to a little town outside of Chico, California. There we found an old house and paid twenty-five dollars a month rent. In order to finance this move, I'd had to borrow a hundred and twenty-five dollars from a druggist I'd delivered prescriptions for, a man named Bill Barton.

This is by way of saying that in those days my wife and I were stone broke. We had to eke out a living, but the plan was that I would take classes at what was then called Chico State College. But for as far back as I can remember, long before we moved to California in search of a different life and our slice of the American pie, I'd wanted to be a writer. I wanted to write, and I wanted to write anything—fiction, of course, but also poetry, plays, scripts, articles for *Sports Afield*, *True*, *Argosy*, and *Rogue* (some of the magazines I was then reading), pieces for the local newspaper—anything that involved putting words together to make something coherent and of interest to someone besides myself. But at the time of our move, I felt in my bones I had to get some education in order to go along with being a writer. I put a very high premium on education then—much higher in those days than now, I'm sure, but that's because I'm older and have an education. Understand that nobody in my family had ever gone to college or for that matter had got beyond the mandatory eighth grade in high school. I didn't *know anything,* but I knew I didn't know anything.

So along with this desire to get an education, I had this very strong desire to write; it was a desire so strong that, with the encouragement I was given in college, and the insight acquired, I kept on writing long after "good sense" and the "cold facts"—the "realities" of my life told me, time and again, that I ought to quit, stop the dreaming, quietly go ahead and do something else.

That fall at Chico State I enrolled in classes that most freshman students have to take, but I enrolled as well for something called Creative Writing 101. This course was going to be taught by a new faculty member named John Gardner, who was already surrounded by a bit of mystery and romance. It was said that he'd taught previously at Oberlin College but had left there for some reason that wasn't made clear. One student said Gardner had been fired—students, like everyone else, thrive on rumor and intrigue—and another student said Gardner had simply quit after some kind of flap. Someone else said his teaching load at Oberlin, four or five classes of freshman English each semester, had been too heavy and that he couldn't find time to write. For it was said that Gardner was a real, that is to say a practicing, writer—someone who had written novels and short stories. In any case, he was going to teach CW 101 at Chico State, and I signed up.

I was excited about taking a course from a real writer. I'd never laid eyes on a writer before, and I was in awe. But where were these novels and short stories, I wanted to know. Well, nothing had been published yet. It was said that he couldn't get his work published and that he carried it around with him in boxes. (After I became his student, I was to see those boxes of manuscript. Gardner had become aware of my difficulty in finding a place to work. He knew I had a young family and cramped quarters at home. He offered me the key to his office. I see that gift now as a turning point. It was a gift not made casually, and I took it, I think, as a kind of mandate—for that's what it was. I spent part of every Saturday and Sunday in his office, which is where he kept the boxes of manuscript. The boxes were stacked up on the floor beside the desk. *Nickel Mountain*, grease-pencilled on one of the boxes, is the only title I recall. But it was in his office, within sight of his unpublished books, that I undertook my first serious attempts at writing.)

When I met Gardner, he was behind a table at registration in the women's gym. I signed the class roster and was given a course card. He didn't look anywhere near what I imagined a writer should look like. The truth is, in those days he looked and dressed like a Presbyterian minister, or an FBI man. He always wore a black suit, a white shirt, and a tie. And he had a crewcut. (Most of the young men my age wore their hair in what was called a "DA" style—a "duck's ass"—the hair combed back along the sides of the head onto the nape and plastered down with hair oil or cream.) I'm saying that Gardner looked very square. And to complete the picture he drove a black four-door Chevrolet with black-wall tires, a car so lacking in any of the amenities it didn't even have a car radio. After I'd got to know him, had been given the key, and was regularly using his office as a place to work, I'd be at his desk in front of the window on a Sunday morning, pounding away on his typewriter. But I'd be watching for his car to pull up and park on the street out in front, as it always did every Sunday. Then Gardner and his first wife, Joan, would get out and, all dressed up in their dark, severe-looking clothes, walk down the sidewalk to the church where they would go inside and attend services. An hour and a half later I'd be watching for them as they came out, walked back down the sidewalk to their black car, got inside and drove away.

Gardner had a crewcut, dressed like a minister or an FBI man, and went to church on Sundays. But he was unconventional in other ways. He started breaking the *rules* on the first day of class; he was a chain smoker and he smoked continuously in the classroom, using a metal wastebasket for an ashtray. In those days, nobody smoked in a classroom. When another faculty member who used the same room reported on him, Gardner merely remarked to us on the man's pettiness and narrow-mindedness, opened windows, and went on smoking.

For short story writers in his class, the requirement was one story, ten to fifteen pages in length. For people who wanted to write a novel—I think there must have been one or two of these souls—a chapter of around twenty pages, along with an outline of the rest. The kicker was that this one short story, or the chapter of the novel, might have to be revised ten times in the course of the semester for Gardner to be satisfied with it. It was a basic tenet of his that a writer found what he wanted to say in the ongoing process of *seeing* what he'd said. And this seeing, or seeing more clearly, came about through revision. He *believed* in revision, endless revision; it was something very close to his heart and something he felt was vital for writers, at whatever stage of their development. And he never seemed to lose patience rereading a student story, even though he might have seen it in five previous incarnations.

I think his idea of a short story in 1958 was still pretty much his idea of a short story in 1982; it was something that had a recognizable beginning, middle, and an end to it. Once in a while he'd go to the blackboard and draw a diagram to illustrate a point he wanted to make about rising or falling emotion in a story—peaks, valleys, plateaus, resolution, *denouement*, things like that. Try as I might, I couldn't muster a great deal of interest or really understand this side of things, the stuff he put on the blackboard. But what I did understand was the way he would comment on a student story that was undergoing class discussion. Gardner might wonder aloud about the author's reasons for writing a story about a crippled person, say, and leaving out the fact of the character's crippledness until the very end of the story. "So you think it's a good idea not to let the reader know this man is crippled until the last sentence?" His tone of voice conveyed his disapproval, and it didn't take more than an instant for everyone in class, including the author of the story, to see that it wasn't a good strategy to use. Any strategy that kept important and necessary information away from the reader in the hope of overcoming him by surprise at the end of the story was cheating.

In class he was always referring to writers whose names I was not familiar with. Or if I knew their names, I'd never read the work. Conrad. Céline. Katherine Anne Porter. Isaac Babel. Walter van Tilburg Clark. Chekhov. Hortense Calisher. Curt Harnack. Robert Penn Warren. (We read a story of Warren's called "Blackberry Winter." For one reason or another, I didn't care for it, and I said so to Gardner. "You'd better read it again," he said, and he was not joking.) William Gass was another writer he mentioned. Gardner was just starting his magazine, *MSS,* and was about to publish "The Pedersen Kid" in the first issue. I began reading the story in manuscript, but I didn't understand it and again I complained to Gardner. This time he didn't tell me I should try it again, he simply took the story away from me. He talked about James Joyce and Flaubert and Isak Dinesen as if they lived just down the road, in Yuba City. He said, "I'm here to tell you who to read as well as teach you how to write." I'd leave class in a daze and make straight for the library to find books by these writers he was talking about.

Hemingway and Faulkner were the reigning authors in those days. But altogether I'd probably read at the most two or three books by these fellows. Anyway, they were so well-known and so much talked about, they couldn't be all that good, could they? I remember Gardner telling me, "Read all the Faulkner you can get your hands on, and then read all of Hemingway to clean the Faulkner out of your system."

He introduced us to the "little" or literary periodicals by bringing a box of these magazines to class one day and passing them around so that we could acquaint ourselves with their names, see what they looked like and what they felt like to hold in the hand. He told us that this was where most of the best fiction in the country and just about all of the poetry was appearing. Fiction, poetry, literary essays, book reviews of recent books, criticism of *living* authors *by* living authors. I felt wild with discovery in those days.

For the seven or eight of us who were in his class, he ordered heavy black binders and told us we should keep our written work in these. He kept his own work in such binders, he said, and of course that settled it for us. We carried our stories in those binders and felt we were special, exclusive, singled out from others. And so we were.

I don't know how Gardner might have been with other students when it came time to have conferences with them about their work. I suspect he gave everybody a good amount of attention. But it was and still is my impression that during that period he took my stories more seriously, read them closer and more carefully, than I had any right to expect. I was completely unprepared for the kind of criticism I received from him. Before our conference he would have marked up my story, crossing out unacceptable sentences, phrases, individual words, even some of the punctuation; and he gave me to understand that these deletions were not negotiable. In other cases he would bracket sentences, phrases, or individual words, and these were items we'd talk about, these cases were negotiable. And he wouldn't hesitate to add something to what I'd written —a word here and there, or else a few words, maybe a sentence that would make clear what I was trying to say. We'd discuss commas in my story as if nothing else in the world mattered more at that moment—and, indeed, it did not. He was always looking to find something to praise. When there was a sentence, a line of dialogue, or a narrative passage that he liked, something that he thought "worked" and moved the story along in some pleasant or unexpected way, he'd write "Nice" in the margin, or else "Good!" And seeing these comments, my heart would lift.

It was close, line-by-line criticism he was giving me, and the reasons behind the criticism, why something ought to be this way instead of that; and it was invaluable to me in my development as a writer. After this kind of detailed talk about the text, we'd talk about the larger concerns of the story, the "problem" it was trying to throw light on, the conflict it was trying to grapple with, and how the story might or might not fit into the grand scheme of story writing. It was his conviction that if the words in the story were blurred because of the author's insensitivity, carelessness, or sentimentality, then the story suffered from a tremendous handicap. But there was something even worse and something that must be avoided at all costs: if the words and the sentiments were dishonest, the author was faking it, writing about things he didn't care about or believe in, then nobody could ever care anything about it.

A writer's values and craft. This is what the man taught and what he stood for, and this is what I've kept by me in the years since that brief but all-important time.

This book of Gardner's seems to me to be a wise and honest assessment of what it is like and what is necessary to become a writer and stay a writer. It is informed by common sense, magnanimity, and a set of values that is not negotiable. Anyone reading it must be struck by the absolute and unyielding honesty of the author, as well as by his good humor and high-mindedness. Throughout the book, if you notice, the author keeps saying: "it has been my experience. . . ." It was his experience—and it has been mine, in my role as a teacher of creative writing—that certain aspects of writing can be taught and handed over to other, usually younger, writers. This idea shouldn't come as a surprise to any person seriously interested in education and the creative act. Most good or even great conductors, composers, microbiologists, ballerinas, mathematicians, visual artists, astronomers, or fighter pilots, learned their business from older and more accomplished practitioners. Taking classes in creative writing, like taking classes in pottery or medicine, won't in itself make anyone a great writer, potter, or doctor—it may not even make the person *good* at any of these things. But Gardner was convinced that it wouldn't hurt your chances, either.

One of the dangers in teaching or taking creative writing classes lies—and here I'm speaking from my experience again —in the overencouragement of young writers. But I learned from Gardner to take that risk rather than err on the other side. He gave and kept giving, even when the vital signs fluctuated wildly, as they do when someone is young and learning. A young writer certainly needs as much, I would even say more, encouragement than young people trying to enter other professions. And it ought to go without saying that the encouragement must always be honest encouragement and never hype. What makes this book particularly fine is the quality of its encouragement.

Failure and dashed hopes are common to us all. The suspicion that we're taking on water and that things are not working out in our life the way we'd planned hits most of us at some time or another. By the time you're nineteen you have a pretty good idea of some of the things you're *not* going to be; but more often, this sense of one's limitations, the really penetrating understanding, happens in late youth or early middle age. No teacher or any amount of education can make a writer out of someone who is constitutionally incapable of becoming a writer in the first place. But anyone embarking on a career, or pursuing a calling, risks setback and failure. There are failed policemen, politicians, generals, interior decorators, engineers, bus drivers, editors, literary agents, businessmen, basket weavers. There are also failed and disillusioned creative writing teachers and failed and disillusioned writers. John Gardner was neither of these, and the reasons why are to be found in this wonderful book.

My own debt is great and can only be touched on in this brief context. I miss him more than I can say. But I consider myself the luckiest of men to have had his criticism and his generous encouragement.

—RAYMOND CARVER

PREFACE

I assume that anyone looking at this preface to see whether or not it would perhaps be worthwhile to buy this book, or take it from the library, or steal it (don't), is doing so for one of two reasons. Either the reader is a beginning novelist who wants to know whether the book is likely to be helpful, or else the reader is a writing teacher hoping to figure out without too much wasted effort what kind of rip-off is being aimed this time at that favorite target of self-help fleecers. It's true that most books for beginning writers are not very good, even those written with the best of intentions, and no doubt this one, like others, will have its faults. Let me set down here how and why I've written it, and what I try to do.

After twenty-some years of giving readings and public lectures, along with making frequent visits to classes in creative writing, I have learned what questions to expect in the inevitable question-and-answer period—some questions at first glance merely polite ("Do you write with a pencil, a pen, or a typewriter?"); some professorial and freighted with vested interest ("Do you think it's important that the would-be novelist read widely in the classics?"); and some timid and serious, presented as if they were questions of life and death, which, for the person who asks them, they may well be, such as "How do I know if I'm really a writer?" This book puts together in one place my considered answers to the questions I take to be serious, including some questions I take to be more serious than they may sound to the casual ear. I answer each question directly but also discursively, trying to make sure I cover every aspect of the question, including those the questioner may have intended but didn't put in words. Some writers, I've found, make the general assumption that every question asked in an auditorium or a writing class is essentially frivolous, presented in order to draw attention to the asker, or to flatter the visitor and keep things rolling, or simply from mad whim. I try to err in the opposite direction. I assume, in classrooms and auditoriums, as elsewhere, that human beings are smarter and nobler than misanthropic souls imagine. I doubt that anyone whose interest in novel-writing is fake will bother to read this book, and I assume that anyone who cares deeply about writing will forgive me if I say, on any given subject, more than seems necessary, since he will sympathize with my purpose, which is to be useful and thorough.

Everything I say here is of course one writer's opinion—opinion grounded in years of writing, reading, teaching, editing, and arguing with my writer friends, but still only opinion, since art does not afford the testable certainties of geometry or physics. For that reason some of what I say will undoubtedly be, for some readers, off the mark or even offensive. On some subjects—for instance, writers' workshops—one is tempted to pull punches or rest satisfied with oversimplified answers; but I'm assuming, as the primary reader of this book, an intensely serious beginning novelist who wants the strict truth (as I perceive it) for his life's sake, so that he can plan his days and years in ways beneficial to his art; avoid false paths of technique, theory, and attitude; and become as quickly and efficiently as possible a master of his craft.

This book is elitist, in a sense. I do not mean that I write mainly for that very special novelist who desires only a small coterie of intensely sophisticated, well-educated, and subtle readers, though to that writer I would recommend this book, both as an aid and as an argument for humane moderation. The elitism I mean is more temperate and middle class. I write for those who desire, not publication at any cost, but publication one can be proud of—serious, honest fiction, the kind of novel that readers will find they enjoy reading more than once, the kind of fiction likely to survive. Fine workmanship—art that avoids cheap and easy effects, takes no shortcuts, struggles never to lie even about the most trifling matters (such as which object, precisely, an angry man might pick up to throw at his kitchen wall, or whether a given character would in fact say "you aren't" or the faintly more assertive "you're not")—workmanship, in short, that impresses us partly by its painstaking care, gives pleasure and a sense of life's worth and dignity not only to the reader but to the writer as well. This book is for the beginning novelist who has already figured out that it is far more satisfying to write well than simply to write well enough to get published.

This is not essentially a book on craft, though here and there I give what some may find valuable pointers. It's not that I disapprove of books on craft or believe no good book of the kind can be written—in fact, I've written such a book myself and use it with my students, changing and expanding it year by year, with the expectation that sooner or later it will seem to me worth making public. But the object of the present book is more grand and more humble: I try here to deal with, and if possible get rid of, the beginning novelist's worries.

Trying to help the beginning writer overcome his worries may at first seem a rather foolish project; my memory of my own apprentice years and my experience with other beginning writers suggest that it's not. The whole world seems to conspire against the young novelist. The young man or woman who announces an intention of becoming an M.D. or an electrical engineer or a forest ranger is not immediately bombarded with well-meant explanations of why the ambition is impractical, out of reach, a waste of time and intelligence. "Go ahead, try it," we say, secretly thinking: If he can't make the grade as an M.D., he can always become an osteopath. Writing teachers, on the other hand, and books about writing, not to mention friends, relatives, and professional writers, are quick to point out the terrible odds (thereby increasing them) against anyone's (ever, anywhere) becoming a successful writer. "Writing takes a rare and special gift," they say (not strictly true); "The market for writing gets worse every year" (largely false); or, "You'll starve!" (maybe so). And the discouragement offered by other human beings is the least of it. Writing a novel takes an immense amount of time, at least for most people, and can test the writer's psyche beyond endurance. The writer asks himself day after day, year after year, if he's fooling himself, asks why people write novels anyhow—long, careful studies of the hopes, joys, and disasters of creatures who, strictly speaking, do not exist. The writer may be undermined by creeping misanthropy, while the writer's wife, or husband, is growing sulky and embarrassed. The idiots who write for TV pull in money by the fistful, while this saint among mortals, the novelist, pumps gas, types memos, or sells life insurance to keep food in the mouths of his children. Or the writer may slide into alcoholism, the number one occupational hazard of the trade.

Almost no one mentions that for a certain kind of person nothing is more joyful or satisfying than the life of a novelist, if not for its financial rewards then for others; that one need not turn into a misanthrope or a drunk; that in fact one can be a more or less successful M.D., engineer, or forest ranger, even follow the unfashionable profession of housewife, and *also* be a novelist—at any rate, many novelists, both great and ordinary, have done it. This book tries to give honest reassurance by making plain what the life of a novelist is like; what the novelist needs to guard against, inside himself and outside; what he can reasonably expect and what, in general, he cannot. It is a book that celebrates novel-writing and encourages the reader to give it a try if he or she is seriously so inclined. The worst that can happen to the writer who tries and fails—unless he has inflated or mystical notions of what it is to be a novelist —is that he will discover that, for him, writing is not the best place to seek joy and satisfaction. More people fail at becoming successful businessmen than fail at becoming artists.

I.

THE WRITER'S
NATURE

Nearly every beginning writer sooner or later asks (or wishes he dared ask) his creative writing teacher, or someone else he thinks might know, whether or not he really has what it takes to be a writer. The honest answer is almost always, "God only knows." Occasionally the answer is, "Definitely yes, if you don't get sidetracked," and now and then the answer is, or should be, "I don't think so." No one who's taught writing for very long, or has known many beginning writers, is likely to offer an answer more definite than one of these, though the question becomes easier to answer if the would-be writer means not just "someone who can get published" but "a serious novelist," that is, a dedicated, uncompromising artist, and not just someone who can publish a story now and then—in other words, if the beginning writer is the kind of person this book is mainly written for.

The truth is that there are so many magazines in the United States—not to speak of all those elsewhere—that almost anyone, if he's stubborn enough, can sooner or later get a story published; and once the beginning writer has been published in one magazine (some obscure quarterly, let us say), so that he can say in his covering letter to other editors, "Previous fiction of mine has appeared in such and such a journal," the better his chances are of reaching publication in other magazines. Success breeds success. For one thing, publication in five or six obscure magazines virtually guarantees eventual success in some not so obscure magazine, because editors, when in doubt, tend to be swayed by a record of publication elsewhere. And for another thing, the more the beginning writer writes and publishes (especially when he publishes after an exchange of letters with an intelligent editor willing to give advice), the more confident and proficient the beginning writer becomes. As for getting a not very good novel published, the possibilities are richer than one might think—though the pay may not be good. There are always publishers looking for new talent and willing to take risks, including a good number of publishers actively seeking bad fiction (pornography, horror novels, and so forth). Some young writers, by a quirk of their nature, cannot feel they are really writers until they have published somewhere, *any*where. Such writers are probably wise to do it and get it over with, though they'd be wiser yet to improve their skills and publish somewhere better, for the future's sake. It's hard to live down one's shoddy publications, and it's hard to scrap cheap techniques once they've worked. It's like trying to stop cheating at marriage or golf.

To answer the serious young writer's question responsibly, the writing teacher, or whoever, needs to consider a variety of indicators, none of them sure but each of them offering a useful hint. Some of these have to do with visible or potential ability, some with character. The reason none of the indicators is foolproof is partly that they're relative, and partly that the writer can improve—changing old habits of technique or personality, getting better by stubborn determination—or simply grow at a later stage from a probable nonwriter to a probable success.

1

One might begin the list anywhere; for convenience, let me begin with verbal sensitivity.

Good grades in English may or may not go with verbal sensitivity, that is, with the writer's gift for, and interest in, understanding how language works. Good grades in English may have more to do with the relative competence, sensitivity, and sophistication of the teacher than with the student writer's ability. It is not quite true to say that every good writer has a keen feeling for sentence rhythms—the music of language— or for the connotations and diction levels (domains) of words. Some great writers are great in spite of occasional lapses— clunky sentences, feeble metaphors, even foolish word choices. Theodore Dreiser can write: "He found her extremely intellectually interesting"—language so cacophonous and dull most good writers would run from it; yet few readers would deny that Dreiser's *Sister Carrie* and *An American Tragedy* are works of art. The writer with a tin ear, if he's good enough at other things, may in the end write deeper, finer novels than the most eloquent verbal musician.

And it must be added that the true artist's verbal sensitivity may be something the ordinary English teacher, or even the most sophisticated user of language, may fail to recognize at first glance. Many people who care a good deal about language are horrified, for instance, to hear "hopefully" used in the sense "it is hoped," or to hear politicians say "forthcoming" when they mean "forthright," or businesspeople say "feedback" when they mean "reaction" or "response"; and given this distaste for linguistic change, or perhaps distaste for certain classes of humanity, the sophisticated stickler may dismiss without thought an ingenious and sensitive use of the suspect word or phrase. The true artist's verbal sensitivity may well be different, in other words, from that of the usual "writer of good English." Black street kids playing "The Dozens"—piling up ingenious metaphorical insults of one another's mothers, not all of the metaphors grammatical or unmixed—may in fact be showing more verbal sensitivity than the speechwriters who helped create the image of John Kennedy. Moreover, as the example of Dreiser perhaps suggests, not every kind of writer requires the same measure of verbal sensitivity. A poet, to practice his art with success, must have an ear for language so finely tuned and persnickety as to seem to the ordinary novelist almost diseased. The short story writer, since the emotional charge of his fiction must reveal itself quickly, has a similar need for lyrical compression, though a need less desperate than the poet's. In the novelist, a hypersensitive ear may occasionally prove a handicap.

But though some great writers may at times write awkwardly, it is nevertheless the case that one sign of the born writer is his gift for finding or (sometimes) inventing authentically interesting language. His sentence rhythms fit what he is saying, rushing along when the story rushes, turning somewhat ponderous to deal with a ponderous character, echoing the thunder of which the story tells, or capturing aurally the wobble of the drunk, the slow, dull pace of the tired old man, the touching silliness of the forty-year-old woman who flirts. The writer sensitive to language finds his own metaphors, not simply because he has been taught to avoid clichés but because he enjoys finding an exact and vivid metaphor, one never before thought of, so far as he knows. If he uses an odd word, it is never the fashionable odd word of his time and place—for instance (as of this writing), "ubiquitous," or "detritus," or "serendipitous"—he uses his *own* odd word, not solely because he wants to be noticed as original (though that is likely to be part of it) but also because he's fascinated by words. He's interested in discovering the secrets words carry, whether or not he ever puts them in his fiction—for instance, how "discover" means "to take the cover off." He's interested in playing with sentence formation, seeing how long he can make a sentence go, or how many short sentences he can use without the reader's noticing. In short, one sign of a writer's potential is his especially sharp ear—and eye—for language.

If once in a while the beginning writer does something interesting with language—shows that he's actually listening

to himself and looking closely at words, spying out their secrets—that is sign enough of the writer's promise. Only a
talent that doesn't exist at all can't be improved. Usually. On
the other hand, if as readers we begin to suspect that the writer
cares about nothing *but* language, we begin to worry that he
may be in for trouble. Normal people, people who haven't
been misled by a faulty college education, do not read novels
for words alone. They open a novel with the expectation of
finding a story, hopefully with interesting characters in it,
possibly an interesting landscape here and there, and, with any
luck at all, an idea or two—with real luck a large and interesting cargo of ideas. Though there are exceptions, as a rule the
good novelist does not worry primarily about linguistic brilliance—at least not brilliance of the showy, immediately obvious kind—but instead worries about telling his story in a moving way, making the reader laugh or cry or endure suspense,
whatever it is that this particular story, told at its best, will
incline the reader to do.

We read five words on the first page of a really good novel
and we begin to forget that we are reading printed words on
a page; we begin to see images—a dog hunting through garbage cans, a plane circling above Alaskan mountains, an old
lady furtively licking her napkin at a party. We slip into a
dream, forgetting the room we're sitting in, forgetting it's
lunchtime or time to go to work. We recreate, with minor and
for the most part unimportant changes, the vivid and continuous dream the writer worked out in his mind (revising and
revising until he got it right) and captured in language so that
other human beings, whenever they feel like it, may open his
book and dream that dream again. If the dream is to be *vivid*,
the writer's "language signals"—his words, rhythms, metaphors, and so on—must be sharp and sufficient: if they're
vague, careless, blurry, or if there aren't enough of them to let
us see clearly what is being presented, then the dream as we
dream it will be cloudy, confusing, ultimately annoying and

boring. And if the dream is to be *continuous*, we must not be roughly jerked from the dream back to the words on the page by language that's distracting. Thus, for example, if the writer makes some grammatical mistake, the reader stops thinking about the old lady at the party and looks, instead, at the words on the page, seeing if the sentence really is, as it seems, ungrammatical. If it is, the reader thinks about the writer, or possibly about the editor—"How come they let him get away with a thing like that?"—not about the old lady whose story has been interrupted.

The writer who cares more about words than about story (characters, action, setting, atmosphere) is unlikely to create a vivid and continuous dream; he gets in his own way too much; in his poetic drunkenness, he can't tell the cart—and its cargo —from the horse. So in judging the young writer's verbal sensitivity one does not ask only, "Has he got any?" but also, "Has he got too much?" If he has none, he's in for trouble, though as I've said, he may succeed anyway, either because he has something else that compensates for the weakness, or because, once the weakness has been pointed out, he's able to learn. If the writer has too much verbal sensitivity, his success —if he means to write novels, not poems—will depend (1) on his learning to care about other elements of fiction, so that, for their sake, he holds himself back a little, like a compulsive punster at a funeral, or (2) on his finding an editor and a body of readers who love, beyond all else, the same thing he loves, fine language. Such editors and readers do appear from time to time, refined spirits devoted to an exquisitely classy game we call fiction only by stretching the term to the breaking point.

The writer who cares chiefly or exclusively about language is poorly equipped for novel-writing in the usual sense because his character and personality are wrong for writing novels. By "character" I mean here what is sometimes called the individual's "inscribed" nature, his innate self; by "personality" I mean the sum of his typical and habitual ways of relating to those around him. I mean to distinguish, in other words, between the inner and outer selves. Those who inordinately love words as words are of a character type distinct enough, at least in broad outline, to be recognizable almost at a glance. Words seem inevitably to distance us from the brute existents (real trees, stones, yawling babies) that words symbolize and, in our thought processes, tend to replace. At any rate, so philosophers like Hobbes, Nietzsche, and Heidegger have maintained, and our experience with punsters seems to confirm the opinion. When a man makes a pun in a social situation, no one present can doubt—however we may admire the punster and the pun —that the punster has momentarily drawn back, disengaging himself, making connections he could not think of if he were fully involved in the social moment. For example, if we are admiring the art treasures of a family named Cheuse and the punster remarks, "Beggars can't be Cheuses!" we know at once that the punster is not peering deeply and admiringly into the Turner landscape at hand. The person profoundly in love with words may make an excellent poet, composer of crossword puzzles, or Scrabble player; he may write novel-like things which a select group admires; but he will probably not in the end prove a first-rate novelist.

For several reasons (first, because of his personality, which keeps the world of brute existence at arm's length), he is not likely to feel passionate attachment to the ordinary, mainstream novel. The novel's unashamed engagement with the world—the myriad details that make character come alive, the sustained fascination with the gossip surrounding the lives of imaginary beings, the naive emphasis on what happened next and what, precisely, the weather was that day—all these are likely to seem, to the word fanatic, silly and tedious; he feels himself buried in litter. And no one is much inclined to spend days, weeks, years, imitating an existence he does not really like in the first place. The word fanatic may love certain very special, highly intellectual novelists (Stendhal, Flaubert,

Robbe-Grillet, the Joyce of *Finnegans Wake*, possibly Nabokov), but he is likely to admire only for their secondary qualities novelists whose chief strength is the hurly-burly of vividly imitated reality (Dickens, Stevenson, Tolstoy, Melville, Bellow). I do not mean that the person primarily interested in linguistic artifice is blocked from all appreciation of good books whose main appeal comes from character and action; nor do I mean that, because by nature he distances himself from actuality, he is too icy of heart to love his wife and children. I mean only that his admiration of the mainstream novel is not likely to be sufficient to drive him to extend the tradition. If he's lucky enough to live in an aristocratic age, or if he can find the sanctuary of an aesthetic coterie—a walled enclave from which the great, fly-switching herd of humanity is excluded— the artificer may be able to work his quirky wonders. In a democratic age served largely by commercial publishers, only extraordinary ego and stubbornness can keep him going. We may all agree (and then again we may not) that the specialized fiction he writes is worthwhile; but to the extent that he suspects that his time and place are unworthy of his genius, to the extent that he feels detached from the concerns of the herd, or feels that his ideal is either meaningless or invisible to most of humanity, his will is undermined. Not caring much about the kind of novel most experienced and well-educated readers like to read, and not deeply in love with his special coterie—since ironic distance is part of his nature, perhaps even deep, misanthropic distrust like Flaubert's—he manages to bring out, in his lifetime, only one or two books. Or none.

By virtue of his personality—in the special sense in which I'm using that word—the brilliant artificer's novel is likely to suffer one of two harsh fates: either it never gets written at all (an excellent way of expressing one's scorn for one's audience and its interests) or it is spoiled by sentimentality, mannerism, or frigidity.

To publish a work of novel length, one must find, as I've

said, a coterie or else find some means of satisfying the ordinary reader's first requirement for any piece of writing longer than fifteen pages, namely profluence—the sense that things are moving, getting somewhere, flowing forward. The common reader demands some reason to keep turning the pages. Two things can keep the common reader going, argument or story. (Both are always involved, however subtly, in good fiction.) If an argument just keeps saying the same thing, never progressing from *a* to *b*, or if a story seems to be moving nowhere, the reader loses interest. To put it another way, if the reader finds nothing to feel suspense about (Where is this argument leading? or, What will happen if the rationalistic philosopher begins to believe in the warnings of his psychic student?), he eventually puts down the book. Every writer knows, in his bones if not elsewhere, that the vast majority of readers expects some kind of progress in a book (even if, according to some theory the writer holds, they are wrong to expect it), and the writer who sets out to do what he knows most of his readers don't want him to do—the writer who refuses to tell a story or advance an argument—is likely to find, sooner or later, that he simply cannot go on. Spending a lifetime writing novels is hard enough to justify in any case, but spending a lifetime writing novels nobody wants is much harder. If ten or twelve critics praise one's work and the rest of the world ignores it, it is hard to keep up one's conviction that the friendly critics are not crackpots. This is not to say that the serious writer should try to write for everyone—try to win the audience both of Saul Bellow and of Stephen King. But if one tries to write for nobody, only for some pure and unearthly ideal of aesthetic perfection, one is apt to lose heart.

Needless to say, most writers who care immoderately about language don't go to the extreme of refusing to tell a story at all. More commonly such writers do present characters, actions, and the rest, but becloud them in a mist of beautiful noise, forever getting in the way of *what* they are saying by the splendor of their way of saying it. Eventually one begins to suspect that the writer cares more about his gift than about his characters. Granted, the suspicion may be wrong. I think no fair-minded reader can doubt that in the fiction of Dylan Thomas the fundamental impulse is to capture real life, the special quality of country-Welsh craziness. Yet it's the metaphors, the slam-cram poetry we remember, not so much the people. Or think of John Updike. The brilliant language with which he describes a minor character cannot help but suggest that the words he chooses are more important to him than the token secretary behind the desk.

It is true that one of the pleasures afforded by good books is the writer's fine handling of language. But the dazzling poetry of Mercutio's Queen Mab speech is not the same poetry Hamlet speaks, while Hamlet's murderer-stepfather Claudius favors dull pentameters. Shakespeare fits language to its speaker and occasion, as the best writers always do. Both Hamlet and Mercutio are in some sense unbalanced, but the difference between the two kinds of imbalance is marked. Mercutio's madness is fantastic and phantasmic; Hamlet's is the madness of diseased irony and constraint. Mercutio flails and howls, piling metaphor on metaphor; Hamlet is so subtle in his neurotic meanness that his enemies often don't know they've been insulted. For instance, when his stepfather has asked him to adjust, be reasonable, stop wearing mourning clothes and harping on his father's death, be a dutiful citizen, Hamlet answers, "I'll serve you in my best." In the old medieval sense, "in my best" means "in black," in other words, in mourning clothes. He is saying, in the sly way of the hostile neurotic, both "I will do as you say" and "I defy you." In the work of Shakespeare, brilliant language always serves character and action. However splendid it may be, Shakespeare's language is finally subservient to character and plot.

If a writer cares more for his language than for other elements of fiction, if he continually calls our attention away from the story to himself, we call him "mannered" and eventually we tire of him. (Smart editors tire of him quickly and reject him.) If the writer seems to have less feeling for his characters than we feel they deserve, insofar as they reflect actual humanity, we call the writer "frigid." If he fakes feeling, or appears to do so—especially if he tries to achieve sentiment by cheap, dishonest means (for instance, by substituting language, "rhetoric," for authentically moving events)—we call him "sentimental."

So one of the things one considers when asked if the young writer has what it takes to become a good novelist is his feeling for language. If he's capable of writing expressively, at least sometimes, and if his love for language is not so exclusive or obsessive as to rule out all other interests, one feels the young writer has a chance. The better the writer's feel for language and its limits, the better his odds become. They are very good indeed for the writer who has a fine ear for language and *also* a fascination with the materials—character, action, setting—that make up fictional realities. He may develop into the virtuoso stylist (Proust, the later Henry James, or Faulkner) who has the best of both worlds.

The writer with the worst odds—the person to whom one at once says, "I don't think so"—is the writer whose feel for language seems incorrigibly perverted. The most obvious example is the writer who cannot move without the help of such phrases as "with a merry twinkle in her eye," or "the adorable twins," or "his hearty, booming laugh"—dead expressions, the cranked-up zombie emotion of a writer who feels nothing in his daily life or nothing he trusts enough to find his own words for, so that he turns instead to "she stifled a sob," "friendly lopsided smile," "cocking an eyebrow in that quizzical way he had," "his broad shoulders," "his encircling arm," "a faint smile curving her lips," "his voice was husky," "her face framed by auburn curls."

The trouble with such language is not only that it is cliché (worn out, overused); but also that it is symptomatic of a crippling psychological set. We all develop linguistic masks (arrays of verbal habits) with which to deal with the world; different masks for different occasions. And one of the most successful masks known, at least for dealing with troublesome situations, is the Christian Pollyanna mask embodied and atrophied in phrases like those I've mentioned. Why the mask turns up more often in writing than in normal speaking—why, that is, the art of writing becomes a way of prettifying and tranquilizing reality—I cannot say, unless it has to do with how writing is taught, in our early years, as a form of good manners, and also perhaps with the emphasis our first teachers give to the goody-goody (or taming) emotions fashionable in school readers. In any event, the Pollyanna mask, if it cannot be torn off, will spell ruin for the novelist. People who regularly seek to feel the bland optimism the Pollyanna mask supports cannot help developing a vested interest in seeing, speaking, and feeling as they do—with two results: they lose the power to see accurately, and they lose the power to communicate with any but those who see and feel in the same benevolently distorted way. Once one has made a strong psychological investment in a certain kind of language, one has trouble understanding that it distorts reality, and also trouble understanding how others—in this case those who take a more cautious or warily ironic view—can be so blind. No one with a distorted view of reality can write good novels, because as we read we measure fictional worlds against the real world. Fiction elaborated out of attitudes we find childish or tiresome in life very soon becomes tiresome.

The Pollyanna mask is only one among many common evasions of reality. Consider a few lines by a well-known science fiction writer:

> It's not often people will tell you how they *really* feel about gut-level things. Like god or how they're afraid they'll go insane

like their grandfather or sex or how obnoxious you are when you pick your nose and wipe it on your pants. They play cozy with you, because nobody likes to be hated, and large doses of truth from any one mouth tend to make the wearer of the mouth *persona non grata*. Particularly if he's caught you picking your nose and wiping it on your pants. Even worse if he catches you eating it.*

This is not the Pollyanna style favored by hack writers of the twenties and thirties but the hack-writer style that superseded it, disPollyanna. Sunny optimism, with its fondness for italics, gives way to an ill-founded cynicism, also supported by italics ("It's not often people will tell you how they *really* feel"), and "broad shoulders" give way to "gut-level things," or worse. Sentence fragments become common (a standard means of falsely heightening the emotion of what one says), and commas disappear ("grandfather or sex or how obnoxious you are") in rhetorical imitation of William Faulkner, who was also on thin ice. (Dropping commas is all right except if one's purpose is to increase the rush of the sentence and thus suggest emotion not justified by what is being said.) Instead of giving "friendly lopsided smiles" people "play cozy with you," which means that they're false, unreal, not even the owners (just the wearers) of their mouths. (The same stock depersonalization of human beings gives cheap detective fiction one of its favorite rhetorical devices, the transformation of "the man in the gray suit" to "Gray Suit," and the man in the sharkskin to "Sharkskin," as in "Gray Suit looks over at Sharkskin. 'Piss off,' he says." This tends to happen even in fairly good detective fiction. It's hard to rise above your class.) Crude jokes and images, slang phrases borrowed from foreign languages, are all stock in disPollyanna fiction—in an attempt to shock prudes. No one is shocked, of course, though a few may misread their annoyance as shock. One is annoyed because the whole thing is phony, an imitation of things too often imitated before. The problem with such

*Harlan Ellison, *Over the Edge* (New York: Belmont Books, 1970), p. 18.

writers, it ought to be mentioned, is not that they are worse people than those who wrote in Pollyanna. They are almost exactly the same people: idealists, people who simple-mindedly long for goodness, justice, and sanity; the difference is one of style. This same science fiction writer's character Jack the Ripper reacts in howling moral outrage when he learns how the Utopians have made him their plaything:

> A psychopath, a butcher, a lecher, a hypocrite, a clown.
> "You did this to me! Why did you do this?"
> Frenzy cloaked his words. . . .*

A young writer firmly hooked on bad science fiction, or the worst of the hard-boiled detective school, or tell-it-like-it-is so-called serious fiction, fashionably interpreting all experience as crap, may get published, if he works hard, but the odds are that he'll never be an artist. That may not bother him much. Hack writers are sometimes quite successful, even admired. But so far as I can see, they are of slight value to humanity.

Both Pollyanna and disPollyanna limit the writer in the same ways, leading him to miss and simplify experience, and cutting him off from all but fellow believers. Marxist language can have the same effects, or the argot of the ashram, or computer talk ("input"), or the weary metaphors of the business-and-law world ("where the cheese starts to bind"). When one runs across a student whose whole way of seeing and whose emotional security seem dependent on adherence to a given style of language, one has reason to worry.

Yet even linguistic rigidity of the kind I've been discussing is no sure sign of doom. Though some would-be writers may be incurably addicted to a particular way of oversimplifying language, others who seem no better off prove curable, once they've understood the problem and worked on it. What the writer must do to cure himself is rise above his own acquired bad taste, figure out how his language habits are like and unlike

*Over the Edge, p. 96.

the language habits of other people, and learn to recognize the relative virtues (and limitations) of language styles surrounding his own. This may mean working closely with a teacher who is sensitive to language, not only "good English" in the sense of "standard English," but vivid, expressive English, "standard" or not. Or it may mean thinking hard about words, phrases, sentence structure, rhythm, and the like; reading books about language; and above all, reading the work of universally acclaimed literary artists.

Every word and phrase, from holy to clinical to obscene, has its proper domain, where it works effectively and comfortably, offending no one. For instance, the phrase "We are gathered this day" is hardly noticeable floating from a pulpit, sounds ironic coming from a professor in a classroom, and in a business letter may sound insane. A phrase like "the blond youth" may be all but invisible in the foliage of an old-time novel but stands out in a modern one written in colloquial style. A comic vision of culture may help: the recognition that all human beings and literary styles have their amusing imperfections—the tendency of people and their language to slip into puffed-up pride, fake humility, dumb cunning, pretentious or fake-unpretentious intelligence. If all human styles are prone to reflect our human clownishness, we need not view any style with superstitious awe nor dismiss any style out of hand. We need only to figure out exactly what it is that we're trying to say—partly by saying it and then by looking it over to see if it says what we really mean—and to keep fiddling with the language until whatever objections we may consider raising seem to fall away.

To put all this more philosophically, language inevitably carries values with it, and unexamined language carries values one might, if one knew they were there, be ashamed of accidentally promoting. People sensitive to the disadvantage placed on women in our culture are likely to be annoyed each time common English usage makes us say "man" or "men" or "mankind" when we really mean "people"—or "he," as I mostly do (not that I like it) when I am speaking of the writer, whoever he or she may be. All of us are to some extent tricked by our language, thinking of the brain in terms of telephone circuits, or of the sun as "rising," or of "discovery" as (in faintly Platonic fashion) the uncovering of something that was always there ("He discovered a new way of eliminating fumes"). But the writer excessively tricked by language, "stuck" in the norms and prejudices of some narrow community, or unable to shake the influence and vision of some literary model—Faulkner or Joyce or the common locutions of bad science fiction—will never be a writer of the first rank because he will never be able to see clearly for himself.

The writer who knows himself to be insufficiently sensitive to language might try some of the following:

Get a first-rate freshman composition book (the best, in my opinion, is W. W. Watt's *An American Rhetoric*) and work hard, with or without a teacher, on everything you're unsure of, especially those sections dealing with style, diction, and sentence structure.

Create and work hard on exercises of your own. For example:

> —*Write an authentic sentence four pages long (do not cheat by using colons and semicolons that are really periods).*
> —*Write a two- or three-page passage of successful prose (that is, prose that's not annoying or distracting) entirely in short sentences.*
> —*Write a brief incident in five completely different styles —such an incident as: A man gets off a bus, stumbles, looks over and sees a woman, smiling.*

Improve your vocabulary, not in the *Reader's Digest* way (which encourages the use of fashionable big words) but by systematically copying from your dictionary all the relatively short, relatively common words that you would not ordinarily think to use, with definitions if necessary, and then making an effort to use them as if they'd come to you naturally—use them, in other words, as naturally and casually as you'd use words at a party.

Read books and magazines, paying careful attention to the language. If what you're reading is bad (you can generally count on women's magazine fiction), underline or highlight the words and phrases that annoy you by their triteness, cuteness, sentimentality, or whatever—in other words, anything that would distract an intelligent, sensitive reader from the vivid and continuous dream. If what you are reading is good (you can usually count on *The New Yorker*, at least for diction), account for why the language succeeds. Perhaps even type out a masterpiece such as James Joyce's "The Dead."

If the promising writer keeps on writing—writes day after day, month after month—and if he reads very carefully, he will begin to "catch on." Catching on is important in the arts, as in athletics. Practical sciences, including the verbal engineering of commercial fiction, can be taught and learned. The arts too can be taught, up to a point; but except for certain matters of technique, one does not learn the arts, one simply catches on.

If my own experience is representative, what one mainly catches on to is the value of painstaking—almost ridiculously painstaking—work. I'd been writing happily since the age of eight, the age at which I first discovered the joys of doggerel; I'd written poems, stories, novels, and plays in high school; in college and graduate school I'd taken good courses in understanding fiction and good creative writing courses, some with well-known writers and editors, and I'd worked with real devotion through the other sorts of courses one takes to get a PhD; but somehow, for all that, I wasn't very good. I worked more hours at my fiction than anyone else I knew, and I was lavishly praised by friends and teachers, even published a little;

but I was dissatisfied, and I knew my dissatisfaction was not just churlishness. The study where I buried myself alive, the first year or two after graduate school (a toolshed so small I could touch the outer walls from the center, and so poorly ventilated that the smoke of my pipe made my typewriter vanish in fog), came to be so crammed with my manuscripts and drafts that I couldn't move my chair—yet still nothing I wrote seemed worth the trouble.

I had by this time already faced the painful truth every committed young writer must eventually face, that he's on his own. Teachers and editors may give bits of good advice, but they usually do not care as much as does the writer himself about his future, and they are far from infallible; in fact, I am convinced, after years of teaching and editing, and watching others do the same, that a large sample of comments by teachers and editors, myself included, would show these comments to be more often wrong, for the particular writer, than right. I, at any rate, had worked with teachers generally considered outstanding, had done my best at the young writers' hothouse, the Iowa Workshop, and had weaseled whatever help I could get out of other writers I admired. But now nothing was clearer than that I must figure out on my own what was wrong with my fiction.

Then I fell into an odd piece of luck. In conversation with a slightly older colleague at the California State University, Chico, where I was teaching at the time, I suggested that the two of us do an anthology of fiction including (as anthologies did not then do and most anthologies do not do now) not only short stories but also other forms—fables, tales, yarns, sketches, etc. The result was *The Forms of Fiction,* a book (now long out of print and almost impossible to get hold of) that provided a close analysis of the narratives we included. A more important result, for me, was that I learned about taking pains. Lennis Dunlap, my collaborator, was and remains one of the most infuriatingly stubborn perfectionists I have ever known. Night after night for two full years we would work for five, six, seven hours on what sometimes added up to three or four sentences. He drove me crazy, and he wasn't so kind to himself, either: often we had to stop because the stress of working with a young man as impatient as I was would give Lennis a histamine headache. Gradually I came to feel as unwilling as he was to let a sentence stand if the meaning was not as unambiguously visible as a grizzly bear in a brightly lit kitchen. I discovered what every good writer knows, that getting down one's exact meaning helps one to discover what one means. Looking back now at our writing in *The Forms of Fiction*, I find the style overly cautious, a bit too tight. (Sometimes saying a thing twice is a good idea.) But that painful two years—the midnight fights and sometimes the shock of joy we would both experience when the right choice of words made us grasp the idea that had until that instant teased and eluded us—showed me what was wrong with my fiction.

Needless to say, since I was writing fiction throughout this period, and since Lennis Dunlap has a mind worth consulting, from time to time I showed him my own fiction. He went over it with the same eye for detail he gave to our work on other people's writing, and though I cannot say he wasn't helpful, I soon learned the limits of even the best advice. Coming from Tennessee, he did not speak the same English I speak, or know the same kinds of people, or interpret life experience in quite the same ways I do. When he suggested changes and I accepted his suggestions, the story almost invariably went wrong. What I learned from him, in short, is that a writer must take infinite pains—if he writes only one great story in his life, that is better than writing a hundred bad ones—and that finally the pains the writer takes must be his own.

2

Another indicator of the young writer's talent is the relative accuracy and originality of his "eye." The good writer sees things sharply, vividly, accurately, and selectively (that is, he chooses what's important), not necessarily because his power of observation is by nature more acute than that of other people (though by practice it becomes so), but because he cares about seeing things clearly and getting them down effectively. Partly he cares because he knows that careless seeing can undermine his project. Imagining the fictional scene imprecisely—failing to notice, for instance, the gesture that would in real life accompany some assertion by a character (the dismissive wave that takes back part of what has been said, or the clenched fist that reveals stronger emotion than the character has expressed) —the writer may be tricked into developing his situation in some way that is unconvincing. This is perhaps the chief offense in bad fiction: we sense that characters are being manipulated, forced to do things they would not really do. The bad writer may not intend to manipulate; he simply does not know what his characters would do because he has not been watching them closely enough in his mind's eye—has not been catching the subtle emotional signals that, for the more careful writer, show where the action must go next. Both because the cogency of his story depends on it and because he has learned to take pride in getting his scenes exactly right, the good writer scrutinizes the imagined or remembered scene with full concentration. Though his plot seems to be rolling along beautifully and his characters seem to be behaving with authentic and surprising independence, as characters in good fiction always do, the writer is willing to stop writing for a minute or two, or even stop for a long while, to figure out precisely what some object or gesture looks like and hunt down exactly the right words to describe it.

One of the best eyes in recent fiction belongs to the novelist David Rhodes. Look closely at the following:

> The old people remember Della and Wilson Montgomery as clearly as if just last Sunday after the church pot-luck dinner they had climbed into their gray Chevrolet and driven back out to

their country home, Della waving from the window and Wilson leaning over the wheel, steering with both hands. They can remember as if just yesterday they had driven by the Montgomerys' brownstone house and seen them sitting on their porch swing, Wilson rocking it slowly and conscientiously back and forth, Della smiling, her small feet only touching the floor on the back swing, both of them looking like careful, quiet children.

Della's hands were so small they could be put into smallmouth jars. For many years she was their only schoolteacher, and, except for the younger ones, they all had her, and wanted desperately to do well with spelling and numbers to please her. Without fail, screaming children would hush and hum in her arms. It was thought, among the women, that it was not necessary to seek help or comfort in times of need, because Della would sense it in the air and come. The old people don't talk of her now but what a shadow is cast over their faces and they seem to be talking about parts of themselves—not just that Della belonged to the old days, but that when she and Wilson were gone it was unnatural that anything else from back then should go on without them.*

The first visual detail in this passage, the abstractly introduced pot-luck dinner, is not especially remarkable: anyone dealing with this culture might have thought of it, and Rhodes doesn't dwell on it, though it's worth including as a quick way of characterizing Della and Wilson Montgomery. The "gray Chevrolet" is a little more specific, with its useful connotations of drabness, humble normality; but it's with the next image that Rhodes begins to bear down: Della waving, Wilson "leaning over the wheel, steering with both hands." The image of Wilson, though not extraordinary, is specific and vivid; we recognize that we're dealing with a careful author, one worth our trust. We see more than that Wilson leans over the wheel and steers with both hands: we see, for some reason, the expression on his face, something about his age; we know, without asking ourselves how we know, that he's wearing a hat. (Hints of his

*David Rhodes, *Rock Island Line* (New York: Harper & Row, 1975), p. 1.

nearsightedness, nervousness, age, and culture lead us to un-conscious generalization.) In other words, by selecting the right detail, the writer subtly suggests others; the telling detail tells us more than it says.

Now the images become much sharper: on the porch swing, Wilson rocks slowly and *conscientiously*—a startling word that makes the scene spring to life (adverbs are either the dullest tools or the sharpest in the novelist's toolbox)—and then, better yet: "Della smiling, her small feet only touching the floor on the back swing, both of them looking like careful, quiet children." Only the keenest novelistic eye would notice where it is that the feet touch; only a fine novelistic mind would understand how much that detail tells us of how Della sits, how she feels; and yet Rhodes treats it as a passing detail, moving on to his climactic image, "like careful, quiet children."

The first line of the second paragraph, "Della's hands were so small they could be put into small-mouth jars," presents a new level of technique, as when a magician who's been doing rather ordinary tricks suddenly reveals how good he really is. It matters, of course, that the jars are a part of Della's country culture, but that's the least of it. No general statement, such as "Della had small hands," could touch the vividness of this image. We do not doubt, as we read, that any grown woman's hands could be so small (though it's questionable); we accept the metaphor and all it carries in its train—Della's childlike character and delicacy, her dutifulness and devotion (canning food), her saintly abstractedness, a quality hard to account for in terms of anything Rhodes has said, yet somehow present. After this, we are willing to accept quite odd assertions—that her pupils strain to please her, that children stop crying in her arms (they even "hush and hum"), and that intelligent, grown women somehow think they have no need to call her when they need her. And now, just when things are turning a touch mystical, Rhodes introduces another sharply observed detail:

when those who remember her talk of Della, "a shadow is cast over their faces and they seem to be talking about parts of themselves." The old people, in other words, think of Della Montgomery as they think of their own failing kidneys, slight chest pains, or arthritic fingers. What Rhodes' eye has caught is the queer similarity of people's expressions when they talk of their own lost youth and approaching death, on one hand, and, on the other, their feelings about the long-absent Della. Who wouldn't raptly turn the page and read on?

Rhodes' eye, like any fine novelist's, is accurate both about literal details (where one's feet touch on a porch swing) and about metaphorical equivalencies. Sitting in his study twenty years later, he summons in his mind's eye exactly how things looked and finds precise expression for what he sees, sometimes literal expression (Wilson bending over the steering wheel, Della's feet as she swings), sometimes metaphorical expression (the point that the two are like quiet, careful children, the point that the old people, talking about Della, wear the same look they wear when talking about parts of their own lives). The visual power of metaphor, it should be noticed, is as available to novelists as to poets. Often an important gesture or complex of gestures (the man who walks through a hostile crowd like a tired plowhorse, the man who jerks up and looks at his alarm clock like a startled chicken) cannot be captured so efficiently by any other means. Rhodes, like many good writers, depends at least as heavily on metaphor as on the naming of significant details. The main point to be noticed here, however, is that nothing in Rhodes' vision is secondhand: what he offers he has taken from life experience, not from Faulkner or, say, *Kojak*.

The unpromising writer sees derivatively. I once visited a class taught by a graduate-student creative writing teacher, one of whose methods was the use of psychodrama. While three students performed the psychodrama assigned, the rest of the class was to write a description of what each of them saw. The performers were asked to play the parts of a psychologist, a troubled mother, and a tuned-out, pot-smoking, troublesome son. The mother and son arrive, the mother explains her problem to the psychologist, and the son puts his feet on the psychologist's desk, defending his behavior at home only insofar as he's forced to do so. One of the most interesting things that happened in this psychodrama was that the woman playing psychologist, in trying to get the son to explain himself, repeatedly held out her hands to him, then looped them back like a seaman drawing in rope, saying in gesture, "Come on, come on! What have you to say?"—to which the son responded with sullen silence. When the drama was over and the descriptions by the class were read, not one student writer had caught the odd rope-pulling gesture. They caught the son's hostile feet on the desk, the mother's fumbling with her cigarettes, the son's repeated swipes of one hand through his already tousled hair —they caught everything they'd seen many times on TV, but not the rope gesture.

Much of the dialogue one encounters in student fiction, as well as plot, gesture, even setting, comes not from life but from life filtered through TV. Many student writers seem unable to tell their own most important stories—the death of a father, the first disillusionment in love—except in the molds and formulas of TV. One can spot the difference at once because TV is of necessity—given its commercial pressures—false to life. Films and series installments on TV are tremendously expensive, though less expensive than commercials. Costs change, always for the worse, but when I was last involved with TV work, a few years ago, a hundred thousand dollars a minute was not unusual. If you're putting together a thirteen-installment series for TV, you look for ways to beat the numbers. You set up your lights, cameras, and so on, at a particular location—Hollywood and Vine, or Lexington and Fifty-third—and you show the actors their tapes (the places where their feet must go), and you hand each of them a pink slip of paper with words on it, such as, "Walter? I haven't seen him. I swear it!" or, "Oh, Michael! Not again!" (Sometimes the lines have directions: *angrily*, or *wearily*, or *obviously lying*.) You shoot the scene, send the actors to the wardrobe truck for a change of clothes, then hand the actors a different set of slips (it may be a slightly different set of actors), and you shoot a second scene, which will be edited into a wholly different episode in the series. The point is that it pays to make the most of any given location and setup. In this kind of production nobody but the director— sometimes not even the director—knows what the story is. For this reason a serious, thoughtful speech is impossible in the ordinary television series. Any good actor can say, "Walter? I haven't seen him," with conviction; but if you hand him a difficult, thoughtful set of lines, the actor is likely to ask, "What's the context?" TV production costs often prohibit serious concern about context.

I am not denying that TV has value—as an opiate, if nothing else. My point is only that TV is not life, and the young novelist who has watched TV and failed to notice the difference is in trouble, except perhaps if his ultimate goal is to write for TV. (TV movies are sometimes more artistic. Interesting speeches are allowable, up to a point, since TV movie production allows more rehearsal and shooting time than does the usual TV series; but commercial pressures are never entirely absent. The beginning TV writer is given precise instructions on how to time his dramatic crescendos so that they lead to the breaks for "messages.")

What is wrong with the young writer who imitates TV instead of life is essentially no different from what's wrong with the young writer who imitates some earlier writer. It may feel more classy to imitate James Joyce or Walker Percy than *All in the Family*; but every literary imitation lacks something we expect of good writing: the writer seeing with his own eyes.

This is not to say that imitation cannot be a useful tool of the writer's apprenticeship. Some writing teachers favor literary imitation as a means of learning, and in the eighteenth century imitation was the chief way of learning to write. As I said earlier, one can learn a good deal by typing out, word for word, a great writer's story: the activity helps the beginning writer pay close attention. And one can learn by studying a writer one admires and transforming all he says to one's own way of seeing. But as a rule, the more closely one looks at the writer one admires, the more clearly one sees that his way can never be one's own. Open a novel of Faulkner's and copy a few paragraphs, but change the particulars to fit the world you know yourself. Take, for instance, the opening of Faulkner's *The Hamlet:*

> Frenchman's Bend was a section of rich river-bottom country lying twenty-miles southeast of Jefferson. Hill-cradled and remote, definite yet without boundaries, it had been the original grant site of . . .

If I were to translate this to something I know, I might begin:

> Putnam Settlement was a section of drab high ground in low, drab country, six miles south of Batavia. . . .

Already I find myself in trouble. People in western New York don't think in terms of "sections"; I must substitute some more appropriate word, and except for some vague evasion like "stretch," I can think of no word the people with whom I'm familiar would really use. Moreover, Putnam Settlement would not think of itself in relation to Batavia or anywhere else, partly because Putnam Settlement, like Batavia, isn't really a "place," not even a "definite yet without boundaries" sort of place. Faulkner has treated in his opening sentence something of grave importance to those who proudly proclaim themselves Southerners, namely, place and all that implies— history, kin connections, identity. Perhaps because they were never humiliated by the loss of a civil war, perhaps because their culture is more open to strangers, perhaps for other reasons, western New Yorkers don't feel the same fierce concern about place that traditional Southerners feel. Where I come from, one place runs into another without much noticing. Place names are less matters of pride than points of orientation. Not far from Putnam Settlement there's a village called Brookville where there hasn't been a house or barn in years. People still speak of it as if they knew what they meant, which they do, but no one knows who lived there in 1800 or would dream of describing it to a stranger as a place. One mentions Brookville when directing someone to Charley Walsh's farm.

Faulkner's second sentence, "Hill-cradled and remote . . . ," raises further problems. First there's the sonorous Southern grandeur of the opening phrase, with its rhetorical suspension of meaning. Anyone with Putnam Settlement in mind would be embarrassed to be caught framing sentences in the style of a congressman or the *National Geographic*. The place, insofar as it is one, won't support it. (That's why people frequently don't talk, in western New York; they just point.) Nor would anyone who lives in the proximity of Putnam Settlement think about mentioning the lay of the land. If you live in rich bottom country with hills surrounding, like the people of Faulkner's Frenchman's Bend, it makes sense to think in terms of large, enclosed landscapes. In Putnam Settlement you think of the weeds along the road (Queen Anne's lace), the large, dead cherry and apple trees, the sagging, long-since-abandoned barns. The main value of trying to use Faulknerian devices for western New York turns out to be that the attempt shows dramatically how subject matter influences style.

A good novelist creates powerfully vivid images in the reader's mind, and nothing is more natural than that the beginning novelist should try to imitate the effects of some master, because he loves that writer's vivid world. But finally imitation is a bad idea. What writers of the past saw and said, even the recent past, is history. It is obvious that no one any longer talks or thinks like the characters of Jane Austen or Charles Dickens. It is perhaps less obvious that hardly anyone under thirty talks like the characters of Saul Bellow or his imitators. The beginning novelist can learn from his betters their tricks of accurate observation, but what he sees must be his own time and place or else, as in the very best historical fiction, the past as we, with our special sensibility (not better but new), would see it if we went back. The beginning writer need not worry too much if his work is in trivial respects derivative—in fact, nothing is more tiresome than writing that strains after what the poet Anthony Hecht once called "a fraudulent and adventitious novelty." Aping another writer's style is foolish, but the noblest originality is not stylistic but visionary and intellectual; the writer's accurate presentation of what he, himself, has seen, heard, thought, and felt.

The writer's accuracy of eye has partly to do with his character. For some novelists, as for most poets and many short story writers, the main accuracy required by their art has to do with self-understanding. Novelists of this kind—Beckett, Proust, many writers who favor first-person narration—specialize in private vision. What they need to see clearly and document well is their own feelings, experience, prejudice. Such a novelist may hate nearly all of humanity, as Céline does, or large groups of people, as does Nabokov. What counts in this case is not that we believe the private vision to be right but that we are so convinced by and interested in the person who does the seeing that we are willing to follow him around. Sometimes, as in the case of a writer like Waugh, we laugh at a misanthropic cynicism we would not consider adopting for ourselves—much as we might laugh at an amusing crank at a party. All that is required to keep us following such a writer is that he fully understand that he is, in the ordinary view, a crackpot, and that he present himself as such, creating a distinct and interesting persona. He must work up his act with the skill of a master clown—however grim his ultimate purpose—understanding how normal people are likely to react to him and manipulating that reaction to his advantage. In other words, he must understand, with a full measure of ironic detachment, his tics and oddities, so that he can present them to us by conscious art, and not by slips that cause us embarrassment for him and lead us to avoid him. Think of the superbly controlled sadist-snob image Alfred Hitchcock created for himself. Think of Nabokov as he presented himself both in his writing and in television interviews; using a snob accent as artfully fabricated as the language of Donald Duck, he reveled in such goofiness as, breaking in on himself, "Careful now! Here comes a metaphor!" The persona need not be comic, as these examples would seem to suggest. Another writer might play Wolfman; yet another might put on, as William S. Burroughs has done, the zombie style.

If we ask ourselves what usefulness or value such writers have, we at once recognize that they're so various as to make no single answer possible. Some, like Evelyn Waugh, allow us the pleasure of a moral holiday: we relax our fair-mindedness and civility and for a brief period take nasty delight in hearing the worst said of people and institutions we, too, in our more childish moments, love to scorn. Some, like Nabokov, present serious and moral visions of the world but do it in such a way (by irony and nastiness) that no underlying softness or piety undermines the effect. Some, like Donald Barthelme, simply present themselves as fascinating oddities of nature—or of literature gone awry. The list of possibilities might be extended. What all such writers have in common is their bold idiosyncrasy, their happy pursuit of their own unique paths in the labyrinthine pluralistic woods. Sometimes such writers explicitly deny, as William Gass does, that fiction is capable of presenting anything broader than a quirky individual vision. Whatever their claims, they present, in effect, portraits or comic cartoons of the artist, and we judge them exactly as we judge stand-up comedians like Bill Cosby or comic actors like

W. C. Fields, by the consistency and accuracy of observation with which they present to us their staged selves, their friends, enemies, memories, peculiar hopes and crank opinions.

For another kind of novelist the accuracy required is, I think, of a higher order, infinitely more difficult to achieve. This is the novelist who moves like a daemon from one body —one character—to another. Rather than master the tics and oddities of his own being and learn how to present them in an appealing way—and rather than capture other people in the manner of a cunning epigrammist or malicious gossip—he must learn to step outside himself, see and feel things from every human—and inhuman—point of view. He must be able to report, with convincing precision, how the world looks to a child, a young woman, an elderly murderer, or the governor of Utah. He must learn, by staring intently into the dream he dreams over his typewriter, to distinguish the subtlest differences between the speech and feeling of his various characters, himself as impartial and detached as God, giving all human beings their due and acknowledging their frailties. Insofar as he pretends not to private vision but to omniscience, he cannot as a rule, love some of his characters and despise others.

What chiefly astonishes us in the work of this highest class of novelists—Tolstoy, Dostoevsky, Mann, Faulkner—is the writer's gift for rendering the precise observations and feelings of a wide variety of characters, even entering the minds (in Tolstoy's case) of animals. The beginning novelist who has the gift for inhabiting other lives has perhaps the best chance for success.

The writer who does not have this gift can usually develop it to some extent, once he has decided he needs it. True, if his irrational hatreds or loves run deep he may be permanently stymied. (No one readily admits that his hatreds are irrational. The stubborn conviction that one is right to spurn most kinds of people can itself be a stymieing force. Character defects fed by self-congratulation are the hardest to shed.) Once one has recognized that the novelist ought to be able to play advocate for all kinds of human beings, see through their eyes, feel with their nerves, accept their stupidest settled opinions as self-evident facts (for them), one simply begins to do it; and doing it again and again—carefully rereading, reconsidering, revising—one gets good at it.

By certain tricks and certain exercises one can sharpen one's gift for seeing the world as others see it. Every writer finds his own. Some may pore over fat astrology books, not for comfort or a head start on disaster but for hints to the complex oddities of human character (the total character of a Pisces vs. the total character of a Leo, whether or not one believes these respective traits have to do with people's birth dates). Some read psychological case studies or "ladies' magazines" or, alas, "men's"; some play with phrenology, palmistry, or the Tarot. What one has to get, one way or another, is insight—not just knowledge—into personalities not visibly like one's own. What one needs is not the facts but the "feel" of the person not oneself.

For some people, of course, no tricks or exercises can help. For one reason or another these people seem never able to guess what others are thinking and feeling. They walk through a lifelong mystery, wondering why people are smiling at them or frowning at them, puzzling over exactly what so-and-so might have meant by that kiss on the cheek or that peculiar sneer in the supermarket. What works for most human beings doesn't work for them. We see a given expression on someone's face, and by mentally or even physically imitating that expression we understand what *we* would have meant by it, and by a leap of faith we assume that the other person meant the same. Or someone speaks crossly to us for no apparent reason, and on the basis of the theory that other people are essentially like ourselves we are able to figure out the real or imagined slight, or the stomach pain, or whatever, that caused the person's anger. Why some people cannot do this (assuming that we who think we can are not fooling ourselves) is probably a question for psychologists. It seems obvious that at least in some cases the problem lies in a neurosis. We have all encountered people who displace their anger at parents or themselves into anger at some social group: the Klansman who hates liberals and imputes evil motives to the liberal's most casual remarks, or the liberal who confidently imputes racial bigotry to anyone who expresses doubt about the value of welfare programs. But whatever the cause, it seems likely that some people can never learn to empathize with their neighbors, at least not with the confidence and clarity it takes to be a novelist of Tolstoy's kind. Such people have no choice, if they wish to be novelists, but to be the spokesmen of private, idiosyncratic vision. They are committed by character to one kind of novel and not the other.

To be psychologically suited for membership in what I have called the highest class of novelists, the writer must be not only capable of understanding people different from himself but fascinated by such people. He must have sufficient self-esteem that he is not threatened by difference, and sufficient warmth and sympathy, and a sufficient concern with fairness, that he wants to value people different from himself, and finally he must have, I think, sufficient faith in the goodness of life that he can not only tolerate but celebrate a world of differences, conflicts, oppositions.

Both the novelist of idiosyncratic vision and the novelist who seeks a more dispassionate understanding can improve the vividness of his fiction by learning to see characters in the light of their metaphoric equivalencies, though in one case the character who emerges will be someone seen from outside, colored by the writer's bias, and in the other case the character may seem someone as real and complex as we are ourselves. Perhaps the best exercise for heightening one's gift for discovering such equivalencies is the game called "Smoke." The player who is

It thinks of some personage living or dead and gives his fellow players a starting clue—"living American," "dead Asian," or whatever—then each player in turn asks a question in the form: "What kind of —— are you?" (What kind of smoke, what kind of vegetable, what kind of weather, building, part of the body, and so forth.) As the answers pile up, everyone playing the game finds he has a clearer and clearer sense of the personage whose name he is seeking, and when someone finally guesses the right answer, the effect is likely to have something like the power of a mystical revelation. No one who has played the game with even moderately competent players—people capable of suspending intellect for the deeper knowledge of the poetic mind—can doubt the value of metaphor for the creation of vivid character.

The writer with a truly accurate eye (and ear, nose, sense of touch, etc.) has an advantage over the writer who does not in that, among other things, he can tell his story in concrete terms, not just feeble abstractions. Instead of writing, "She felt terrible," he can show—by the precise gesture or look or by capturing the character's exact turn of phrase—subtle nuances of the character's feeling. The more abstract a piece of writing is, the less vivid the dream it sets off in the reader's mind. One can feel sad or happy or bored or cross in a thousand ways: the abstract adjective says almost nothing. The precise gesture nails down the one feeling right for the moment. This is what is meant when writing teachers say that one should "show," not "tell." And this, it should be added, is *all* that the writing teacher means. Good writers may "tell" about almost anything in fiction except the characters' feelings. One may tell the reader that the character went to a private school (one need not show a scene at the private school if the scene has no importance for the rest of the narrative), or one may tell the reader that the character hates spaghetti; but with rare exceptions the characters' feelings must be demonstrated: fear, love, excitement, doubt, embarrassment, despair become real only when they take the form of events—action (or gesture), dialogue, or physical reaction to setting. Detail is the lifeblood of fiction.

3

Another indicator of the novelist's talent is intelligence—a certain kind of intelligence, not the mathematician's or the philosopher's but the storyteller's—an intelligence no less subtle than the mathematician's or the philosopher's but not so easily recognized.

Like other kinds of intelligence, the storyteller's is partly natural, partly trained. It is composed of several qualities, most of which, in normal people, are signs of either immaturity or incivility: wit (a tendency to make irreverent connections); obstinacy and a tendency toward churlishness (a refusal to believe what all sensible people know is true); childishness (an apparent lack of mental focus and serious life purpose, a fondness for daydreaming and telling pointless lies, a lack of proper respect, mischievousness, an unseemly propensity for crying over nothing); a marked tendency toward oral or anal fixation or both (the oral manifested by excessive eating, drinking, smoking, and chattering; the anal by nervous cleanliness and neatness coupled with a weird fascination with dirty jokes); remarkable powers of eidetic recall, or visual memory (a usual feature of early adolescence and mental retardation); a strange admixture of shameless playfulness and embarrassing earnestness, the latter often heightened by irrationally intense feelings for or against religion; patience like a cat's; a criminal streak of cunning; psychological instability; recklessness, impulsiveness, and improvidence; and finally, an inexplicable and incurable addiction to stories, written or oral, bad or good. Not all writers have exactly these same virtues, of course. Occasionally one finds one who is not abnormally improvident.

I have described here, you may think, a curious and dangerous beast. (In fact, good writers are almost never dangerous—a point I will need to develop, but not just yet.) Though the tone is half-joking, my description of the writer is meant to be accurate. Writers would clearly be madmen if they weren't so psychologically complicated ("too complex," a famous psychiatrist once wrote, "to settle on any given madness")—and some go mad anyway. The easiest way to talk about this special sort of intelligence is perhaps to describe what it does, what the young novelist must sooner or later be equipped to do.

I have said that writers are addicted to stories, written or oral, bad or good. I do not mean, of course, that they can't tell the difference between bad and good stories, and I must now add that some bad stories make them furious. (Some writers get more angry, some less; some, in the presence of the kind of fiction that makes other good writers howl and throw things, do not show their anger, but turn their fury inward, sinking into suicidal gloom.) The kind of fiction that makes good writers cross is not *really* bad fiction. Most writers will occasionally glance through a comic book or a western, even a nurse novel if they find it at the doctor's office, and finish the thing with no hard feelings. Some happily read bad and good detective fiction, sci-fi's, sodbusters (fat novels about families in the South or West), even—perhaps especially—children's books. What makes them angry is bad "good" fiction, whether it's for children or for grownups.

It would be a mistake to blame the anger on professional jealousy. No one is more generous with his praise than a novelist who has just read a good novel by someone else, even if the author has been his lifelong enemy. One may be nearer the mark in blaming the anger on the novelist's insecurity, though that is not quite right, either. If one works very hard at doing a thing one considers important (telling a story extremely well), one is annoyed to see someone else do it badly or, worse, fraudulently, while claiming to belong in the same high league. One's honor is sullied—the honor of the whole profession is sullied—and one's purpose in life is undermined, especially if readers and reviewers seem unable to tell the difference between the real thing and the fake, as often they can't. One begins to doubt that one's standards have any value, even any roots in reality. One becomes crabby, petulant, eager to fight. Since excellence in the arts is a matter of taste—since one cannot really prove one work better than another, at least not in the same clear way mathematicians can prove one another right or wrong—the widespread celebration of a stupid book offends the true writer. Like a child who knows he's right but cannot make his parents see, and has neither the power nor the authority to beat them, the writer offended by an alleged masterpiece that he knows to be phony may throw the tantrums of the helpless, or sulk, or turn sly (may turn to, as Joyce put it, silence, exile, cunning).

Nothing is harder on the true writer's sense of security than an age of bad criticism, and in one way or another, sad to say, almost every age qualifies. No depressed and angry writer at the present moment can fail to notice, if he raises his heavy head and looks around, that fools, maniacs, and jabberers are everywhere—mindless, tasteless, ignorant schools of criticism publishing fat journals and meeting in solemn conclave, completely misreading great writers, or celebrating tawdry imitation writers to whom not even a common farm duck would give his ear; other schools maintaining, with much talk of Heidegger, that nothing a writer writes means anything, the very existence of his page is an amusing accident, all the words are a lunatic blithering (for all the writer's care), since language is by nature false and misleading, best read from the bottom of the page to the top. (Even Dante's *Divine Comedy*, critics like Harold Bloom and Stanley Fish maintain in their dissimilar ways, is mere raw material for "the art of criticism.") In a literary culture where the very notion of a "masterpiece" is commonly thought barbaric, where good writing is called reactionary or otherwise self-limiting, and where the worst writers are regularly admired (so it seems to the novelist in his gloomy funk, and a twenty-year list of best-sellers and Book-of-the-Month Club selections would prove him right), who's to say that all the carefully achieved standards of the bravest, most disciplined writer are not quackery and lob law? (Even in his funk the writer clings to his rhetoric and his OED.)

But it is not finally insecurity (his sense that his honor and purpose cannot survive the blind stampede of Nietzsche's "herd") that makes the true novelist hate fake art, though insecurity is involved. The practice of reading and writing fiction, like the practice of law or medicine, gives benefits only the man engaged in the practice can really know, know immediately and fully, in the quality of his life and vision. An analogy from the experience of painters may help. A man who regularly does oil paintings—landscapes, let us say—develops an acute eye for color and light, shapes, volumes, details of form. The novelist develops an acute eye, sometimes bordering on the psychic, for human feelings and behavior, tastes and habitats, pleasures, sufferings. The fake novelist not only fails to develop that gift but by his fakery impedes it, not only in himself but in his readers as well, at least insofar as they're tricked.

I said earlier that the writer who works closely with detail —studying his characters' most trivial gestures in the imagined scene to discover exactly where the scene must go next—is the writer most likely to persuade and awe us. That close scrutiny is one among many elements that make up the practice of fiction; let it serve as a clue to the value of authentic practice —and to the waste and harm in fictional malpractice. The true writer's scrutiny of imagined scenes both feeds on and feeds his real-life experience: almost without knowing he's doing it, the writer becomes an alert observer. He may even become such a watcher of people that he seems an oddity to his friends. It is said (I think—sometimes by accident I make these things up) that Anthony Trollope, when he went to a party, would sit for ten minutes or more, intently staring at one guest after another, hardly answering when people addressed him, much to the embarrassment of the company. Whether or not that story is true, it is a fact that a party with good writers can be, for the uninitiated, unnerving. Joyce Carol Oates's gazelle eyes dominate the room, especially when she chooses not to talk, trying to be (one suspects) inconspicuous. Stanley Elkin's style is to keep the floor at any cost, telling funny stories; but behind the thick glasses, the enlarged, keenly focused myopia makes the listener wonder if perhaps *he* will be the next funny story. (In fact, Elkin's stories are always generous. If anyone must play the fool in one, he takes the part for himself.) Bernard Malamud has an alarming way of listening when people speak. He focuses intently on gestures, turns of phrase; he may abruptly ask why the person speaking with him wears dark glasses. One could say the same kinds of things about other writers, though of course not about all other writers; many are highly socialized and never let it show that they are watching. The point is, whether or not they show it at dinner parties, writers learn, by a necessity of their trade, to be the sharpest of observers. That is one of the joys, as well as one of the curses, of the writer's occupation. Psychologists perhaps get some of this same pleasure, but psychologists, whatever their claims and intentions, are essentially interested in the aberrant mind. Writers care about all possibilities of human nature.

I might mention another embarrassment involved in the writer's habit of close attention. Once when I was driving through Colorado with a friend, traveling down a narrow mountain pass, we came upon an accident. A pickup truck and a car had collided, and from fifty feet away we could see the blood. We pulled over and ran to help. All the time I was running, all the time I was trying, with my friend's help, to pry open the door of the car in which a nine-months-pregnant woman had been impaled through the abdomen, I was thinking: I must remember this! I must remember my feelings! How would I describe this? I do not think I behaved less efficiently than my nonliterary friend, who was probably not thinking such thoughts; in fact, I may possibly have behaved more swiftly and efficiently, trying in my mind to create a noble scene. Nonetheless, what I felt above all was disgust at my mind's detachment, its inhumane fascination with the precise way the blood pumped, the way flesh around a wound becomes instantly proud, that is, puffed up, and so on. I would have been glad at that moment to be a literary innocent.

For better or worse, the practice of fiction changes a person. The true novelist knows things another man with his own specialization does not know and might not wish to. The false practitioner, on the other hand, knows less than nothing. Not only can it be said that reality is obscure to him; his bad techniques—his learned misapprehensions (think of the dis-Pollyanna science fiction writer)—distort his vision, so that he sees falsely. The true novelist despises the false one both because the false practitioner fools himself, manipulating characters instead of trying to understand them, and because he teaches his readers (at best) nothing.

What the novelist does besides despise false novels is try to write true ones. His complex intelligence, in other words, gathers its various and disparate powers to make up a satisfying story. The best way I can think of to make this point concrete is to speak of what good fiction requires.

Good fiction sets off, as I said earlier, a vivid and continuous dream in the reader's mind. It is "generous" in the sense that it is complete and self-contained: it answers, either explicitly or by implication, every reasonable question the reader can ask. It does not leave us hanging, unless the narrative itself justifies its inconclusiveness. It does not play pointlessly subtle games in which storytelling is confused with puzzle-making. It does not "test" the reader by demanding that he bring with him some special knowledge without which the events make no sense. In short, it seeks, without pandering, to satisfy and please. It is intellectually and emotionally significant. It is elegant and efficient; that is, it does not use more scenes, characters, physical details, and technical devices than it needs to do its job. It has design. It gives that special pleasure we get from watching, with appreciative and impressed eyes, a *performance*. In other words, noticing what it is that the writer has brought off, we feel well served: "How easy he makes it look!" we say, conscious of difficulties splendidly overcome. And finally, an aesthetically successful story will contain a sense of life's strangeness, however humdrum its makings.

If a young novelist fully appreciates all these qualities of successful fiction and regularly pursues them in his own work, one does not need to make guesses about his potential: he's already there. Most young novelists are aware of, and interested in, only some few of these qualities and might even deny that others are important. Partly this is an effect of lost innocence, the innocence the writer must now regain. Every child knows intuitively (insofar as he likes stories at all; some children don't) what the requirements are for good fiction, but by the time he's reached high-school age, he's grown a trifle confused, bullied by his teachers into reading what is in fact trash, scorned if he reads a good comic book, and warned, if he picks up *Crime and Punishment*, "Harold, you're not ready for that." By the time he's a sophomore or junior in college, he's likely to be quite profoundly confused, imagining, for instance, that "theme" is the most important value in fiction.

Nothing, let me pause to argue, could be farther from the truth than the notion that theme is all. Theme is what, at its deepest level, the story is about; it is the philosophical and emotional principle by which the writer selects and organizes his materials. Real literary artists are always conscious of their theme; but this does not assure good writing. Both theme and message (that is, subject and specific preachment) are likely to be more visible in a cheap western than in Proust's *Remem-*

brance of Things Past. And on the other hand, in some of our most beloved fictions the theme is difficult to isolate. What, exactly, is the theme of "Jack and the Beanstalk"? Any given reader may think he knows, but he should be given pause by the fact that for Bruno Bettelheim, whom most people would consider a competent psychologist (or at least not stupid), the story is about penis envy—surely a minority opinion. Some might say that the story is about the victory of childish innocence; some might say other things. The point is that what makes us take pleasure in "Jack and the Beanstalk" is not necessarily our sense, as we read or listen, that some basic philosophical question is being dramatized and illuminated, though in other fictions theme may indeed be what chiefly moves us. In *Pilgrim's Progress* the allegory may be the central appeal, though some might argue more or less persuasively that what we like most about that book is its style. Certainly, in Melville's *Bartleby the Scrivener* or Mann's *Death in Venice*, philosophical content is part of what holds us rapt. If theme is not what we chiefly love about a given story, not chiefly what makes us reread it and recommend it to our friends, then theme is not universally the most important quality of good fiction. Theme is like the floors and structural supports in a fine old mansion, indispensable but not, as a general rule, what takes the reader's breath away. More often than not, theme, or meaning, is the statement the architecture and decor make about the inhabitants. When we think about it, it seems to me, the all but universal fascination with theme in high-school and college English courses has to do with the teacher's need to say something intellectual and surprising. A flawlessly told story by Boccaccio, Balzac, or Borges is hard to talk about simply as a story, and since all stories "mean" things—sometimes quite odd and surprising things—the temptation to talk about the meaning rather than the story may be nearly irresistible.

For this reason the college-age student is easily persuaded to the view that great writers are primarily philosophers and teachers; they write to "show" us things. This is the message teachers and professional critics suggest in such misleading locutions as "Jean Rhys is *showing* us" or "Flaubert is *demonstrating* . . ." Teaching creative writing, one constantly hears students say of their work, "I am trying to show . . ." The error in this is obvious once it's pointed out. Does the twenty- or twenty-five-year-old writer really have brilliant insights that the intelligent reading public (doctors, lawyers, professors, skilled machinists, businessmen) has never before heard or thought of? If the young novelist's answer is an emphatic *yes*, he would do the world a favor by entering the ministry or the Communist party. If I belabor the point, I do so only because the effect of English literature courses is so often, for a certain kind of student, insidious.

Though it may not be universal, and though in any case it's a matter of degree, it often seems that people in their late teens or twenties cannot help but feel that their parents and most other so-called adults are fools, sell-outs, or at the very least, disappointing. Their disdain has partly to do with the developing psyche's struggle, the imperative Joyce treated, that the young animal assert his power and replace the elder. No doubt it is often a class trait: the child of the lower or lower middle class is urged in both overt and subtle ways to surpass his background, his well-meaning parents and friends never anticipating that if their dream of upward mobility is realized, the child may adopt the prejudices of the class to which he's lifted and, with a touch of neurotic distress, may permanently scorn his former life and also, to a certain extent, himself, since the class he's invaded is unlikely to accept him fully. And no doubt the arrogance of the young has also to do with the age-old idealism of teachers, who forever harp, not without some justice, on how the former generation failed and the world's salvation is up to the new generation. Whatever the cause, the young person—the young novelist—is encouraged to feel that *he* is life's hope, *he* is the Messiah.

There's nothing wrong with that feeling. It's natural—part of nature—and no artist ever became great by violating his deepest feelings, however youthful, neurotic, or wrongheaded. Nonetheless, adolescent emotion cannot create real art, usually, and if the young novelist can understand his inclination he can avoid an undue misuse of his energies. One of the great temptations of young writers is to believe that all the people in the subdivision in which he grew up were fools and hypocrites in need of blasting or instruction. As he matures, the writer will come to realize, with luck, that the people he scorned had important virtues, that they had better heads and hearts than he knew. The desire to show people proper beliefs and attitudes is inimical to the noblest impulses of fiction.

In the final analysis, what counts is not the philosophy of the writer (that will reveal itself in any case) but the fortunes of the characters, how their principles of generosity or stubborn honesty or stinginess or cowardice help them or hurt them in specific situations. What counts is the characters' story.

Just as it is easy for the student of literature to believe he, his teacher, and his classmates are better people than those unfamiliar with Ezra Pound, it is easy for him to be persuaded by his coursework that "entertainment" is a low if not despicable value in literature. Properly indoctrinated, the student may come to be convinced that certain classics he instinctively dismissed, at first, as insipid (good candidates, some would say, are Langland's *Piers Plowman* and Richardson's *Clarissa*) are in fact immensely interesting books, though not entertaining in the common sense, like the *Canterbury Tales*, or *Tom Jones*, or the sci-fi of Walter M. Miller, Jr. (*A Canticle for Leibowitz*). If he takes enough English literature courses, the young would-be writer can learn to block every true instinct he has. He learns to dismiss from mind the persistent mean streak in J. D. Salinger, the tough-guy whining sentimentality in Hemingway, Faulkner's bad habit of breaking the vivid and continuous dream by pouring on the rhetoric, Joyce's mannerisms, Nabokov's frigidity. He can learn that writers he at first thought quite good, usually women (Margaret Mitchell, Pearl Buck, Edith Wharton, Jean Rhys), are "really" second class. With the right teacher he can learn that Homer's *Iliad* is a poem against war, that the *Canterbury Tales* is a disguised sermon, or—if he studies with Professor Stanley Fish and his cohorts—that we have no objective grounds for saying that Shakespeare's work is "better" than that of Mickey Spillane. If he also takes courses in creative writing, he may learn that one should always write about what one knows, that the most important thing in fiction is point of view, perhaps even that plot and character are the marks of antiquated fiction. To a wise and secure innocent all this would seem very odd, but students in a college classroom are defenseless, and the rewards offered for giving in are many, the chief one being the seductive sweetness of literary elitism.

It is the power of miseducation's blandishments that makes stubbornness, even churlishness, a valuable quality in young writers. The good young writer, the potentially successful one, knows what he knows and will not budge—chiefly knows that the first quality of good storytelling is storytelling. A profound theme is of trifling importance if the characters knocked around by it are uninteresting, and brilliant technique is a nuisance if it pointlessly prevents us from seeing the characters and what they do.

The stubbornness that saves a writer in college will continue to serve him all his life, guarding and preserving his ego if the world refuses to notice how good he is and saving him, if necessary, from the potential suckerdom of fame. (The famous author tends to be less meticulously edited than the unknown one, tends to be asked for his opinion on subjects he knows nothing about, tends to be sought out for reviews or jacket blurbs of bad books by his friends.) And stubbornness will prove useful, in later life as in college, in protecting the writer from those who try to give him bad advice. As inept college writing teachers try to get the beginning writer to write fiction more like that of Jane Austen, or Grace Paley, or Raymond Carver, so well-meaning nincompoops later (editors, reviewers, academicians) are sure to put pressure on the writer to make him more nearly what they would be if they could write fiction. Not, of course, that the writer's stubbornness should be absolute. Some advice turns out to be good, however distasteful at first.

If the writer understands that stories are first and foremost stories, and that the best stories set off a vivid and continuous dream, he can hardly help becoming interested in technique, since it is mainly bad technique that breaks the continuousness and checks the growth of the fictional dream. He quickly discovers that when he unfairly manipulates his fiction—pushing the characters around by making them do things they wouldn't do if they were free of him; or laying on the symbolism (so that the strength of the fiction is diminished, too much of its energy going into mere intellect); or breaking in on the action to preach (however important the truth he's out to preach); or pumping up his style so that it becomes more visible than even the most interesting of his characters—the writer, by these clumsy moves, impairs his fiction. To notice such faults is to begin to correct them. One reads other writers to see how they do it (how they avoid overt manipulation), or one reads books about writing—even the worst are likely to be of some use—and above all, one writes and writes and writes. Let me add, before I leave this subject, that when he reads the work of other writers, the young novelist should read not in the manner of an English major but in the manner of a novelist. The good English major studies a work to understand and appreciate its meaning, to perceive its relationship to other works of the period, and so on. The young writer should read to see how effects are achieved, how things are done, sometimes reflecting on what he would have done in the same situation and on whether his way would have been better or worse, and why. He reads the way a young architect looks at a building, or a medical student watches an operation, both devotedly, hoping to learn from a master, and critically, alert for any possible mistake.

The development of fully competent technique calls for further psychological armor. If a writer learns his craft slowly and carefully, laboriously strengthening his style, not publishing too fast, people may begin to look at the writer aslant and ask suspiciously, "And what do *you* do?" meaning: "How come you sit around all the time? How come your dog's so thin?" Here the virtue of childishness is helpful—the writer's refusal to be serious about life, his mischievousness, and his tendency to cry, especially when drunk, a trick that makes persecutors quit. If the pressure grows intense, the oral and anal fixations swing into action: one relieves pressure by chewing things, chattering mindlessly, or straightening and re-straightening one's clothes.

The point is a serious one, and I do not mean to trivialize it. In my own experience, nothing is harder for the developing writer than overcoming his anxiety that he is fooling himself and cheating or embarrassing his family and friends. To most people, even those who don't read much, there is something special and vaguely magical about writing, and it is not easy for them to believe that someone they know—someone quite ordinary in many respects—can really do it. They tend to feel for the young writer a mixture of fond admiration and pity, a sense that the poor fellow is somehow maladjusted or misinformed. No human activity I know of takes more time than writing: it's highly unusual for anyone to become a successful writer if he cannot put in several hours every day at his typewriter. (Even for a successful professional, it can take a while to get into the mood, takes hours to get a few good pages of rough draft, and many many hours to revise them until they will bear repeated readings.) Of necessity the writer is unlike those of his friends who quit work at five; if he has a wife and children, the writer cannot pay as much attention to them as his neighbors do to theirs, and if the writer is worthy of his profession, he feels some guilt over this. Because his art is such a difficult one, the writer is not likely to advance in the world as visibly as do his neighbors: while his best friends from high school or college are becoming junior partners in prestigious law firms, or opening their own mortuaries, the writer may be still sweating out his first novel. Even if he has published a story or two in respectable periodicals, the writer doubts himself. In my teaching years, I have again and again seen young writers with obvious talent berate themselves almost to the point of paralysis because they feel they're not fulfilling their family and social obligations, feel—even when several stories have been accepted—that they're deluding themselves. Each rejection letter is shattering, and a parent's gentle prod— "Don't you think it's time you had children, Martha?"—can be an occasion of spiritual crisis. Only strong character, reinforced by the encouragement of a few people who believe in the writer, can get one through this period. The writer must somehow convince himself that he *is* in fact serious about life, so serious that he is willing to take great risks. He must find ways—mischievous humor, or whatever—of deflecting malicious or benevolent blows to his ego.

Only the writer who has come to understand how difficult it is simply to tell a first-rate story—with no cheap manipulations, no breaks in the dream, no preening or self-consciousness—is able to appreciate fully the quality of "generosity" in fiction. In the best fiction, plot is not a series of surprises but an increasingly moving series of recognitions, or moments of understanding. One of the most common mistakes among young writers (those who understand that fiction is storytelling) is the idea that a story gets its power from withheld information—that is, from the writer's setting the reader up and then bushwhacking him. Ungenerous fiction is first and foremost fiction in which the writer is unwilling to take the reader as an equal partner.

Say, for example, that the writer has decided to tell the story of a man who has moved into the house next door to the house of his teen-age daughter, a girl who does not know that the man is her father. The man—call him Frank—does not tell the girl—she may as well be Wanda—that she is his daughter. They become friends and, despite the difference in age, she begins to feel a sexual attraction.

What the foolish or inexperienced writer does with this idea is hide the father-daughter relationship from the reader as well as from the daughter until the last minute, at which point he jumps out and yells: "Surprise!" If the writer tells the story from the father's point of view and withholds the important information, the writer is false to the traditional reader-writer contract—that is, he has played a trick on the reader. (The so-called unreliable narrator favored in much contemporary fiction is not a violation of the contract. It is not the storyteller but a fictitious narrator, a character, that we must watch and learn to distrust. If the storyteller *himself* is unreliable, we avoid him as we would a mad sea captain or axe murderer.)

If, on the other hand, the story is told from the daughter's point of view, the device is legitimate, since the reader can only know what the daughter knows; but the writer has mishandled his idea. The daughter is simply a victim in this story, since she doesn't know the facts by means of which she could make significant choices—namely, struggle with her feelings and come to some decision, accepting her role as daughter or else, conceivably, choosing to violate the incest taboo. When the central character is a victim, not someone who *does* but someone who's *done to*, there can be no real suspense. Admittedly it is not always easy to see, in great fiction, the central character's agency. The governess in James's *The Turn of the Screw* would hotly deny that she herself is acting in complicity with the forces of evil, but gradually, to our horror, we realize that she is; and some stories—for instance those of Kafka—adapt to the purposes of "serious" fiction the central device of a certain kind of comic fiction, the clown-hero knocked around by the universe, a character we laugh at because his misapplied strategies and beliefs parody our own. (It is not that Kafka's heroes —or Beckett's—do not try to do things; it is only that the things they try don't work.) In the final analysis, real suspense comes with moral dilemma and the courage to make and act upon choices. False suspense comes from the accidental and meaningless occurrence of one damned thing after another.

The wiser or more experienced writer gives the reader the information he needs to understand the story moment by moment, with the result that instead of asking, as he reads, "What's going to happen to the characters next?" the reader asks, "What will Frank do next? What would Wanda say if Frank were to . . ." and so on. Involving himself in the story in this way, the reader feels true suspense, which is to say, true concern for the characters. He takes an active part, however secondary, in the story's growth and development: he speculates, anticipates; and because he has been provided with relevant information, he is in a position to catch the mistake if the writer draws false or unconvincing conclusions, forcing the action in a direction it would not naturally go, or making the characters feel things no human being would really feel in the situation.

If Frank is clearly drawn and interesting, a lifelike human being, the reader worries about him, understands him, cares about the choices he makes. Thus if Frank at some point, out of cowardice or indecisiveness, makes a choice any decent human being would recognize as wrong, the reader will feel vicarious embarrassment and shame, as he would feel if some loved one, or the reader himself, were to make such a choice. If Frank sooner or later acts bravely, or at least honestly, selflessly, the reader will feel a thrill of pride as if he himself or some loved one had behaved well—a pride that, ultimately, expresses pleasure in what is best not just in the made-up character but in all humankind. If Frank finally behaves well, and Wanda shows unexpected (but not arbitrary or writer-manipulated) nobility, the reader will feel even better. This is the morality of fiction. The morality of the story of Frank and Wanda does not reside in their choosing not to commit incest or in their deciding they *will* commit incest. Good fiction does not deal in codes of conduct—at least not directly; it affirms responsible humanness.

The young writer who understands why it is wisest to tell the Frank and Wanda story as one of dilemma, suffering, and choice is in a position to understand good fiction's generosity in the broadest sense of the word. The wise writer counts on the characters and plot for his story's power, not on tricks of withheld information, including withheld information at the end—will they commit incest or won't they, now that they know? In other words, the writer lays himself wide open, dancing on a high wire without a net. The writer is generous, too, in that, for all his mastery of technique, he introduces only those techniques useful to the story: he is the story's servant, not a donzel for whom the story serves as an excuse to show off pyrotechnics. This is not to say that he's indifferent to the value of performance. Those techniques he uses because the story needs them he uses brilliantly. He works entirely in service of the story, but he works with class. On this, more later.

It is the importance of this quality of generosity in fiction that requires a measure of childishness in the writer. People who have strong mental focus and a sense of purpose in their lives, people who have respect for all that grownups generally respect (earning a good living, the flag, the school system, those who are richer than oneself, those who are beloved and famous, such as movie stars), are unlikely ever to make it through the many revisions it takes to tell a story beautifully, without visible tricks, nor would they be able to tolerate the fame and fortune of those who tell stories stupidly, with hundreds of tricks, all of them old and boring to the discriminating mind. First, with his stubborn churlishness the good writer scoffs at what the grownups are praising, then, with his childish forgetfulness and indifference to what sensible people think, he goes back to his foolish pastime, the making of real art.

The remaining qualities in good fiction, and the personality traits in the writer that are likely to help him achieve them, need not delay us long. Good fiction, I have said, is intellectually and emotionally significant. All this means is that a story with a stupid central idea, no matter how brilliantly the story is told, will be a stupid story. Take an easy example. A young newspaperman discovers that his father, who is the mayor of the city and has always been a hero to him, is the secret owner of brothels, sex shops, and a vicious loan-shark operation. Shall the newspaperman spill the beans on his father? Whatever his secret life, our newspaperman's father taught our newspaperman all the values he knows, including integrity, courage, and concern for the community. What is the newspaperman to do?

Who cares? The whole story is a moronic setup, good enough for writers of pop fiction but useless as a vehicle for art. The first thing wrong with it is that the clash of ideas implied is a clash of boring ideas, namely, which is more important, personal integrity (telling it like it is) or personal loyalty? Only very odd people don't realize that truth-telling is always a relative value. If you're living in Germany during World War II and a Jew is hiding in your basement, you do nothing wrong in the sight of God by telling the Nazi at the door you're the only one home. Personal integrity (not telling lies) is so obviously bendable in the name of a higher integrity that the question's not worth talking about. And in the case of this hypothetical story, the father's nastiness is so deep and broad (at least as we've set it up) that only a fool would agonize over the claim of personal loyalty. Almost no one doubts that personal loyalty is a good thing, up to a point: the worth of the value is transparent and needs no defense. It will be objected that the fictional situation I've just set up is almost exactly the situation in Robert Penn Warren's *All the King's Men*. I am tempted to answer, yes, that's so, and notice the streak of sentimentality that impairs that novel, from its tour-de-force opening blast of rhetoric through all its gothic delays to its end; but in fairness to the success of that book, despite its sentimentality, I must say, anticipating the next point I mean to turn to, it is Penn Warren's characters that save what might have been, in another writer's hands, a bad idea for a novel. If the essential plot idea is melodramatic, the complexity of the characters enriches and complicates the idea and partly saves it.

What is most deeply wrong with our newspaperman story idea is that it starts in the wrong place, not with character but with situation. Character is the very life of fiction. Setting exists so that the character has someplace to stand, something that can help define him, something he can pick up and throw, if necessary, or eat, or give to his girlfriend. Plot exists so the character can discover for himself (and in the process reveal to the reader) what he, the character, is really like: plot forces the character to choice and action, transforms him from a static construct to a lifelike human being making choices and paying for them or reaping the rewards. And theme exists only to make the character stand up and *be* somebody: theme is elevated critical language for what the character's main problem is.

Consider again our story of Frank and his daughter Wanda. One might write that story very well without ever bothering to figure out what the theme is: it would be enough for the writer to understand clearly that Frank has an interesting problem (some details of which the writer will have to pause and figure out). For some reason (any persuasive reason will do), Frank has moved next door to his daughter; he knows her, she doesn't know him (any explanation of this odd fact will suffice, as long as it's so convincing that no reader would think of doubting it); and he decides not to tell her (by reason of something in his character and situation; again, any reason will do, so long as it's convincing and fits with everything else in the story). Our character's interesting situation, then, is that *(a)* perhaps somewhat to his surprise, he begins to feel a father's love for, and maybe pride in, the daughter he never knew, and *(b)* he likes seeing her, the oftener the better, but *(c)* she's beginning to feel an undaughterly love for him, so that he must either tell her how things are or not tell her, and in either case the ultimate question is, What are they going to do?

Every detail that enters the story will have an influence on the degree to which the characters suffer and eventually on what they choose. Say the daughter lives with her stepfather and her mother is dead. If the stepfather is indifferent to her, or a drunkard, or crazy, or always away on trips to Cleveland, her admiration of Frank and her opportunity for seeing him will increase. Say Frank lost his daughter and now-dead wife because he spent seventeen years in prison, a fact of which he is bitterly ashamed. In this case both his longing for his daughter and his fear of telling her the truth may be intense. Obviously it doesn't matter which particulars the writer selects—if he's smart he'll simply select those details he'd most enjoy finding in a story by someone else—but whichever details he chooses, he commits himself to exploring those details for all significant implications.

The Frank-Wanda story, as we've begun to flesh it out, may at first glance seem as much a situation story as the newspaperman-and-his-father story, but on closer inspection we see it's not. The initial situation in the Frank-Wanda story exists because of a conflict within Frank's character: he simultaneously wants to reveal his identity to his daughter and also hide that identity, or to put the problem in broader philosophical terms, he wants to be both independent and involved—an impossibility. The internal conflict inevitably leads to an external conflict, easily dramatized: Wanda, falling in love with the man she doesn't know to be her father, must necessarily send out signals of her sexual interest and must necessarily receive confusing signals in return. We can predict the line of action: from joys to trouble and distress to spats and tears to revelation and decision. (There is nothing wrong with fiction in which the plot is relatively predictable. What matters is how things happen, and what it means that they happen, to the people directly involved and to the larger humanity for whom the characters serve as representatives. Needless to say, it is always best if the predictable comes in some surprising way.)

In nearly all good fiction, the basic—all but inescapable—plot form is: *A central character wants something, goes after it despite opposition (perhaps including his own doubts), and so arrives at a win, lose, or draw.* In a novel the pros and cons of the character's project get complicated (each force, pro or con, dramatized by minor characters, subplots, and so on), but the form, however disguised, remains. The "victim story," as I described it earlier, can never work because the victim cannot know and, out of that knowledge, act. (If the victim's desire is not to be a victim, and if he or she acts on it, the victim's story is not a "victim story.") I have said "nearly all good fiction," since we do find exceptions. I have already mentioned Kafka's use, and Beckett's, of the always unsuccessful clown-hero, and I should register in passing the special case of the "epiphany" story as Joyce developed it in *Dubliners*—a story form in which, for all practical purposes, the reader takes the place of the conventional central character: it is the reader who actively pursues, the reader who, at the climax of the story, achieves his "win"—a sudden shift of vision, a new understanding, an "epiphany." Not all of the stories in *Dubliners* work this way, of course; for example, "The Dead" does not. In any case, no one denies the effectiveness of epiphany fiction; but if my analysis of how it works is correct, it is closer to convention than it appears at first blush.

Before we leave our newspaperman story we should admit, reminded by Kafka's practice, that it does have one chance of success. All aesthetic rules give way for comedy. Let us say our newspaperman is a true dolt—but an interesting one. He believes fervently everything his father has ever said; his father's words are the law of his life. He also fervently loves his father. Obviously we are involved not in drama but in clown drama, the drama of lovable moron heroes like the Marx Brothers or Laurel and Hardy. The newspaperman (Laurel), his father (Hardy), and everybody else who blunders into the story must be, in effect, clowns whose comment on the human condition is not that of realistic fiction or even of, say, the gothic tale, with its systematically altered realism, but something quite different, a special kind of loving satire. The story can now work, at least theoretically, because, though the clash of ideas is not in itself interesting, the characters involved may be interesting and appealing, in a cartoonish way, and they're stupid enough to be interested in what we see through at once. Though the characters are patently inferior to us, their agonies, perplexities, and triumphs clowningly parallel our own. No one will claim that the story has been made intellectually significant, but it is at least no longer an expression of authorial weak-mindedness. As for the emotional significance of the piece, the only way we can judge such things, in the case of comedy, is by giving the story to readers and seeing if they laugh.

If the young writer is to achieve intellectual and emotional significance in his fiction, he must have the common sense to tell foolish ideas from interesting ones and important emotions from trivial ones. These abilities can be guided a little, for instance by the teacher's pointing out, as I've done above, that stories beginning in character and conflict are bound to be more interesting than stories that do not—a principle applicable even to thrillers, sodbusters, and horror stories. And the writer's sense of what questions are really interesting and what ones aren't worth bothering with may be heightened a little by wide reading, by conversation with intelligent people, and by the conscious attempt to, as James said, "be someone on whom nothing is lost."

On the whole, the capacity for recognizing the significant is a gift. It helps not to be a dupe, to be, instead, a person of independent mind, not carried away by fads; and it may help to be a slow, deep thinker rather than a brilliant, facile one. If the young writer is by nature a foolish person, his chances are bad, though perhaps, to tell the truth, not all *that* bad. Every teacher of middle age or more can count up instances of highly successful former students who, as freshmen or sophomores, even juniors or seniors, seemed silly beyond all hope of reclamation. People change, sometimes because of outside forces—sickness, a failed marriage, a shattering family death, sometimes love or success—sometimes from a gradual process of maturing and reconsideration.

As for the quality of strangeness, it is hard to know what can be said. There can be no great art, according to the poet Coleridge, without a certain strangeness. Most readers will recognize at once that he's right. There come moments in every great novel when we are startled by some development that is at once perfectly fitting and completely unexpected—for instance, the late, surprising entrance of Svidrigailov in *Crime and Punishment*, Mr. Rochester's disguise in *Jane Eyre*, the rooftop scene in *Nicholas Nickleby*, Tommy's stumbling upon the funeral in *Seize the Day*, the recognition moment in *Emma*, or those moments we experience in many novels when the ordinary and the extraordinary briefly interpenetrate, or things common suddenly show, if only for an instant, a different face. One has to be just a little crazy to write a great novel. One must be capable of allowing the darkest, most ancient and shrewd parts of one's being to take over the work from time to time. Or be capable of cracking the door now and then to the deep craziness of life itself—as when in *Anna Karenina* Levin proposes to Kitty in the same weird way Tolstoy himself proposed to his wife. Strangeness is the one quality in fiction that cannot be faked.

If I could explain exactly what I mean here, I could probably do what I think no one has ever done successfully: reveal the very roots of the creative process. The mystery is that even when one has experienced these moments, one finds, as mystics so often do, that after one has come out of them, one cannot say, or even clearly remember, what happened. In some apparently inexplicable way the mind opens up; one steps out of the world. One knows one was away because of the words one finds on the page when one comes back, a scene or a few lines more vivid and curious than anything one is capable of writing —though there they stand. (That experience, I suspect, is the motivating impulse behind the many stories of unearthly experiences confirmed in the final paragraph by some ring or coin or pink ribbon left behind by the otherworldly intruder.) All writing requires at least some measure of trancelike state: the writer must summon out of nonexistence some character, some scene, and he must focus that imaginary scene in his mind until he sees it as vividly as, in another state, he would see the typewriter and cluttered desk in front of him, or the last year's calendar on his wall. But at times—for most of us, all too occasionally—something happens, a demon takes over, or nightmare swings in, and the imaginary *becomes the real*.

I remember that once, writing the last chapter of *Grendel*, this altered sense of things came over me with great force. It was not at the time a new or surprising experience; the one respect in which it was odd was that after I came out of it I seemed to remember vividly what had happened. Grendel has just had his arm torn off and recognizes that he will die. He has stubbornly insisted throughout the novel that we have no free will, that all life is brute mechanics, all poetic vision a cynical falsehood, and he clings even now to those opinions, partly for fear that optimism is cowardice, partly from stubborn self-love: even though Beowulf has banged Grendel's head against a wall, bullying him into making up a poem about walls, Grendel is hanging on for dear life to his convictions, in terror of being swallowed by the universe and convinced that his opinions and his identity are one and the same. The "inspired" passage (I am of course not talking about its aesthetic value) begins approximately here:

> No one follows me now. I stumble again and with my one weak arm I cling to the huge twisted roots of an oak. I look down past stars to a terrifying darkness. I seem to recognize the place, but it's impossible. "Accident," I whisper. I will fall. I seem to desire the fall, and though I fight it with all my will I know in advance that I can't win. Standing baffled, quaking with fear, three feet from the edge of a nightmare cliff, I find myself, incredibly, moving toward it. I look down, down, into bottomless blackness, feeling the dark power moving in me like an ocean current, some monster inside me, deep sea wonder, dread night monarch astir in his cave, moving me slowly to my voluntary tumble into death.

Throughout the novel I'd made occasional allusions to the poetry and prose of William Blake, a major influence on my ideas about the imagination (its power to transform and redeem). Here, when I was simply following Grendel in my imagination, trying to feel in myself what it might be like to flee through deep woods, bleeding to death, I suddenly fell, without having planned it, into what I can only describe as a powerful dream of a Blakean landscape: the huge twisted roots of the oak, then a dizzying reversal of up and down (I had the sense of Grendel as fallen onto his back, looking up past the tree but imagining he was looking down, an image that recalls my childhood fear that if the planet is indeed round, I might one day fall off). Though the oak tree is from Blake, it was

tinged in my mind with other associations. In Chaucer's poetry, with which I was then deeply involved, the oak is associated with Christ's cross and with sorrow in general; by
another line it is associated with druids and human sacrifice,
notions darkened for me by my childhood reaction to songs
like "The Old Rugged Cross" (stained with blood so divine),
grizzly and sickening reminders of beheaded chickens, butch-
ered cows, child thoughts of death with undertones of guilt
and the ultimate moral ugliness of God.

I did not, in my writing trance, separate these ideas out. I
saw Blake's tree, exactly the same tree I saw when I read
Chaucer's *The Book of the Duchess,* and its force was that of the
cross I imagined in childhood, messy with blood and gobbets
of flesh (an unorthodox image, I realize). I think, though I'm
not sure, that it was this sense of the tree as tied to my childhood vision that made me react to it with a sense of déjà vu.
Imitating (in fact feeling) Grendel's terror, I react in Grendel's
way, clinging to my (his) opinion: "Accident!"—that is, Beowulf's victory has no moral meaning; all life is chance. But the
fear that it may not all be accident strikes back instantly, prodded a little by childhood notions of the cross—blood, guilt,
one's desperate wish to be a good boy, be loved both by one's
parents and by that terrifying superfather whose otherness
cannot be more frighteningly expressed than by the fact that
he lives beyond the stars. So for all his conscious belief that it's
all accident, Grendel *chooses* death, morally aligning himself
with God (hence trying to save himself); that is, against his will
he notices that he seems to "desire the fall." Abruptly the
nightmare landscape shifts, from looking "down" past the tree
into the abyss of night to another source of vertigo, looking
down from the edge of a cliff. I did not consciously make this
shift because of the nightmare I'd had in my sleep the night
before I wrote this page; rather, I noticed as I made the shift
that in fact what I was writing was a nightmare that I'd had
and until that instant had forgotten.

A day or two before, my family and I had been watching Olympic ski jumpers practice—a terrifying business, to me at least, frightened as I am by heights. In a dream, the night before the writing of this passage, I'd found myself moving very slowly—but inexorably—toward the edge of the ski jump, the snow below me unspeakably far away. I'd felt in my nightmare, for whatever reason, exactly this same sense that I was willing the fall, in spite of myself. (I think there is some strange pun in the word "fall"; at any rate, it's a word I've often used elsewhere in its Edenic sense: so that the fear I felt as I was writing this passage—or enduring this entrancement— may have to do with moral paradox of the kind the unconscious takes wicked delight in: willing his death, Grendel is unconsciously trying to please God so that God will not slaughter him; willing "the Fall," he is defying the God he hates and fears.) Grendel feels the movement in himself to be in some way the movement of the universe. He is like "an ocean current," such a current as brought Beowulf to kill him; he feels that something inside him (his heart, his *id*) is at one with that current; and since earlier in the novel it was Grendel himself who lived "inside" (a cave), he is, since he houses the *id* monster, the mountain whose steeps he fears; he is some fabled mystery ("deep sea wonder"); and if the whole night sky is conceived as God's cave, then Grendel, "dread night monarch astir in his cave," is God. At the time I wrote the passage, I made all these connections (ocean current, monster, sea wonder, etc.) without consciously thinking: the mystical oneness, the calmly accepted paradox, were inherent in the entrancement.

The only point I mean to make out of this long and possibly self-indulgent analysis is this: All I myself know for sure, when I come out of one of these trance moments, is that I seem to have been taken over by some muse. Insofar as I'm able to remember what happened, it seems to me that it was this: for a moment the real process of our dreams has been harnessed. The magic key goes in, all the tumblers fall at once and the door swings open. Or: mental processes that are usually discrete for some reason act together. I was of course conscious, throughout my writing of *Grendel,* that what I was trying to talk about (or dramatize, or seek to get clear) was an annoying, sometimes painful disharmony in my own mental experience, a conflict between a wish for certainty, a sort of timid and legalistic rationality, on the one hand, and, on the other, an inclination toward childish optimism, what I might now describe as an occasional, flickering affirmation of all that was best in my early experience of Christianity. Surrounded by university people who had, as we say, "outgrown religion," and feeling uneasy about joining their party because to do so might be a cowardly surrender and a betrayal of my background, though refusing to do so might also be cowardice, and a betrayal of myself, I had gloomed through writers like Jean-Paul Sartre who seemed confident that they knew what they were talking about (I was not convinced); I'd joined churches and, finding them distasteful, had left; and I'd become, more or less by accident, a specialist in medieval Christian poetry, including of course *Beowulf,* source of, among other things, the quasi-mystical macrocosm/microcosm equations at the end of the passage I've been discussing. All the elements to be fused in the trance moment were in place, like the assembled components of the Frankenstein monster's body before the lightning strikes. What I can't really explain is the lightning. It may have to do with entering as fully as possible into the imaginary experience of the character, getting "outside" oneself (a paradox, since the character to be entered is a projection of the writer's self). It may have to do with the sense of mental strain one experiences at such moments: the whole mind seems tightened like a muscle, fierce with concentration. Anyway, if one is lucky the lightning strikes, and the madness at the core of the fictional idea for a moment glows on the page.

4

After verbal sensitivity, accuracy of eye, and a measure of the special intelligence of the storyteller, what the writer probably needs most is an almost daemonic compulsiveness. No novelist is hurt (at least as an artist) by a natural inclination to go to extremes, driving himself too hard, dissatisfied with himself and the world around him and driven to improve on both if he can.

A psychological wound is helpful, if it can be kept in partial control, to keep the novelist driven. Some fatal childhood accident for which one feels responsible and can never fully forgive oneself; a sense that one never quite earned one's parents' love; shame about one's origins—belligerent defensive guilt about one's race or country upbringing or the physical handicaps of one's parents—or embarrassment about one's own physical appearance: all these are promising signs. It may or may not be true that happy, well-adjusted children can become great novelists, but insofar as guilt or shame bend the soul inward they are likely, under the right conditions (neither too little discomfort nor too much), to serve the writer's project. By the nature of his work it is important that one way or another the novelist learn to depend primarily on himself, not others, that he love without too much need and dependency, and look inward (or toward some private standard) for approval and support. Often one finds novelists are people who learned in childhood to turn, in times of distress, to their own fantasies or to fiction, the voice of some comforting writer, not to human beings near at hand. This is not to deny that it also helps if a novelist finds himself with one or more loved ones who believe in his gift and work.

The novelist is in a fundamentally different situation from the writer of short stories or the poet. Generally speaking, if he wins, he wins more handsomely than they do: a commercially successful artistic novel—especially a third or fourth one —may bring in upwards of a hundred thousand dollars (no real win by businesspeople's standards; it may have taken him ten years to write) and in addition may bring stature, honor, maybe love letters from photogenic strangers. None of that is —or ought to be—the reason the novelist chose the genre he works in. He is the particular kind of writer he is, what William Gass has called a "big-breath writer," and in effect he does what is most natural for him. He has, unlike the poet or short story writer, the endurance and pace of a marathon runner. As Fitzgerald put it, there is a peasant in every good novelist. And he has, besides, the kind of ambition peculiar to novelists—a taste for the monumental. He may begin as a short story writer; most novelists do. But he quickly comes to find himself too narrowly caged: he needs more space, more characters, more world. So he writes his large book and, as I began by saying, if he wins, he wins handsomely. The trouble is (and this is the point, I've been struggling toward), the novelist does not win nearly as often as do poets and writers of short stories. That is why he needs to be a driven man, or at any rate directed by inner forces, not daily or monthly bursts of applause. A good poem takes a couple of days, maybe a week, to write. A good short story takes about the same. A novel may take years. All writers thrive on praise and publication; the novelist is the writer who makes the huge, long-term investment, one that may or may not pay off.

A writer's successes bring him more than praise, publication, or money: they also help him toward confidence. With each success, writers, like stunt riders and ballet dancers, learn to dare more: they take on riskier projects and become more exacting in their standards. They get better. Here the novelist is at a disadvantage in comparison to writers of shorter forms. Especially in his apprentice years, when it matters most, success comes rarely.

Let us look more closely at the process a novelist must

depend upon. First of all, the serious novelist can seldom punch straight through, write from beginning to end, knock off a quick revision, and sell his book. The idea he's developing is too large for that, contains too many unmanageable elements —too many characters, each of whom the writer must not just create but figure out (as we figure out peculiar people in real life) and then must present convincingly; and the story contains too many scenes, too many moments, each of which the writer must imagine and render with all the intensity and care of his being. He may work for weeks, even months, without losing his focus and falling into confusion, but sooner or later —at least in my experience—the writer comes to the realization that he's lost. His overfamiliarity with the characters, after endless hours of writing and rewriting, may lead to his suddenly feeling bored with them, irritated by everything they say or do; or he may become so close to them that, for lack of objectivity, he's baffled by them. Just as we can often predict how casual acquaintances will behave in a given situation, though we cannot make out what we ourselves or those close to us would do, so writers often have a clearer fix on their characters when the novel is still a fresh idea than they do months later, when the writing is well along and the characters are like family. I myself am stopped cold when I cannot make out how a character would deal with the situation presented to him. If the situation presented is trivial, one's perplexity can be maddening. Once during the writing of *Mickelsson's Ghosts* I found the novel's heroine being offered an hors d'oeuvre, and I couldn't tell whether she would accept it or not. I forced the issue, made her refuse it; but then I found myself stuck. It didn't matter a particle which choice she made, but damned if I could move to the next sentence. "This is ridiculous," I told myself, and tried a little gin—to no avail. It seemed to me now that I knew nothing about this woman; I wasn't even sure she'd have come to the party in the first place. *I* wouldn't have. Stupidest party in all literature. I quit writing, put the manuscript away, and took out my frustration on woodworking tools, making furniture. A week or so later, in the middle of a band-saw cut, I saw, as if in a vision, the woman taking the hors d'oeuvre. I still didn't understand her, but I was positive I knew what she would do, and what she would do after that, and after that.

Or the novel may bog down because in terms of overall structure—pace, emphasis, and so on—the writer can no longer see the forest for the trees. I've often labored with ferocious concentration on a scene, polishing, revising, and tearing out; rewriting, polishing, and revising again until finally I realize that I have no idea what I'm doing, can't even recall why it was that I thought the scene necessary. Experience has taught me that, unpleasant as it is to do so, I have no choice but to put the manuscript away for a while—sometimes it takes months—and then look at it again. When the proper time has elapsed—in other words when the manuscript is "cold"—the faults stand plain. One may discover that the scene is much too elaborate in relation to scenes before and after it, or that it does not belong in the novel at all, or—this happened to me just once—that the scene is terrific but the rest of the novel has to go. It is hard even for an experienced writer to throw away two hundred pages of bad writing, or anyway it's hard if one is still close enough to the writing to remember how much time and work it took. A year or two later, taking a fresh look at those bottom-drawer pages, it is easy—even satisfying —to be merciless.

I think there really is no other way to write a long, serious novel. You work, shelve it for a while, work, shelve it again, work some more, month after month, year after year, and then one day you read the whole piece through and, so far as you can see, there are no mistakes. (The minute it's published and you read the printed book you see a thousand.) This tortuous process is not necessary, I suspect, for the writing of a popular novel in which the characters are not meant to have depth and complexity, where character A is consistently stingy and character B is consistently openhearted and nobody is a mass of contradictions, as are real human beings. But for a true novel there is generally no substitute for slow, slow baking. We've all heard the stories of Tolstoy's pains over *Anna Karenina*, Jane Austen's over *Emma*, or even Dostoevsky's over *Crime and Punishment*, a novel he grieved at having to publish prematurely, though he had worked at it much longer than most popular-fiction writers work at their novels.

So by the nature of the novelist's artistic process, success comes rarely. The worst result of this is that the novelist has a hard time achieving what I've called "authority," by which I do not mean confidence—the habit of believing one can do whatever one's art requires—but, rather, something visible on the page, or audible in the author's voice, an impression we get, and immediately trust, that this is a man who knows what he's doing—the same impression we get from great paintings or musical compositions. Nothing seems wasted, or labored, or tentative. We do not get the slightest sense that the writer is struggling to hear in his mind what he's saying, the rhythm with which he's saying it, and how it relates to something later in the book. As if without effort, he does it all at once. He snaps into the trance state as if nothing were easier. Probably only examples can suggest what I mean.

Notice the careful, tentative quality of the opening paragraph of Melville's *Omoo*:

> It was in the middle of a bright tropical afternoon that we made good our escape from the bay. The vessel we sought lay with her main-topsail aback about a league from the land, and was the only object that broke the broad expanse of the ocean.

There is, I think, nothing actively bad about this writing; but we get no sense of the speaker's character, no clear mood from the rhythm (we cannot tell how seriously to take the word "escape"), certainly no sense of prose invading the domain of poetry. If you're musical you will notice that the sentences fall naturally into $\frac{4}{4}$ time. That is:*

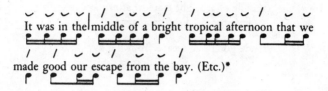

Compare what the same writer can do once he's found his booming, authoritative voice:

> Call me Ishmael. Some years ago—never mind how long precisely—having little or no money in my purse, and nothing particular to interest me on shore, I thought I would sail about a little and see the watery part of the world. . . .

That is what I mean by authority. No further comment is necessary, but notice how flowing, tricky, and finely balanced the music is. (Needless to say, another reader might analyze the rhythms differently. My notation reflects my own hearing of the sentences.)

$\frac{2}{4}$ Call me Ishmael. $\frac{4}{4}$ Some years ago—never mind how $\frac{2}{4}$long precisely—

having $\frac{4}{4}$ little or no money in my purse, and nothing particular to

interest me on shore, I thought I would sail about a little and see the

watery part of the world. It is a way I have of driving off the spleen

and $\frac{2}{4}$ regulating the circulation . . . .

* ⌣ = unstressed syllable,
/ = stressed syllable (coinciding with the musical beat).

In *Omoo* the rhythms plod and dully echo each other:

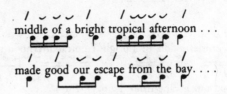

In *Moby Dick* the rhythms lift and roll, pause, gather, roll again. A few figures establish the basic pattern. For example, note the permutations of ♩♪ ♪♪♪:

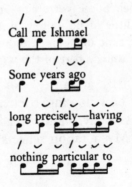

Etc.

Melville, we may be sure, did not sit down and score his rhythms like a composer, but his ear found them—found brilliantly subtle rhythmic variations, poetically functional alliteration (compare "broke the broad expanse of the ocean," in *Omoo*, with "watery part of the world. It is a way I have," in *Moby Dick*), and at the same time found orbicular rhetoric like a nineteenth-century congressman's or a Presbyterian minister's (as Mark Twain might say), and a compressed, energetic way of going for meaning. He reached authority.

Unlike a poet or short story writer a novelist cannot hope

to reach authority by frequent successes. I first declared myself a serious novelist in 1952, when I began *Nickel Mountain*; that is, I decided then that, come hell or high water, a novelist was what I would be. I published my first novel in 1966—not *Nickel Mountain*. I wrote several novels between 1952 and 1966, none of them successful even by my youthful standards. I worked, as I still work, long hours, seven days a week. As a young man I worked a regular eighteen-hour day; now I work less, but now I know more tricks and get more done in an hour. I do not mean to boast about this. Nearly all good novelists work as I do, and there are many good novelists in the world. (Besides, it can't really be called work. A famous basketball player once remarked, "If basketball were illegal, I'd be in prison for life." It's the same with novelists: they'd do what they do even if it were illegal, which, in comparison to basketball, it is.)

So—to return to the subject—a novelist is not likely to develop authority by success after success. In his apprenticeship years he succeeds, like Jack o' the Green, by eating his own white guts. He cannot help being a little irascible: some of his school friends are now rich, perhaps bemused by the fact that one of their smartest classmates is still struggling, getting nowhere, so far as anyone can see.

If the young would-be novelist is not in some way driven, he will never develop into a novelist. Most don't. Some give up, some get sidetracked. TV and film devour more brilliance and imagination than a thousand minotaurs. They need the true novelist's originality, but they cannot deal with it except in crippled form—pink slips instead of thought, and worse. I once visited a successful Hollywood producer, and he gave me a list of what "the American people don't like." They've done marketing research, and they know. The American people don't like movies with snowy landscapes. The American people don't like movies about farmers. The American people don't like movies in which the central characters are foreigners.

The list went on, but I stopped listening, because the movie I'd come to talk about concerned a Vietnamese immigrant family's first winter in Iowa. What one notices, when one hears about Hollywood marketing research, is that the only movie one is allowed to write is a cheap imitation of last year's blockbuster.

The would-be novelist can get sidetracked in many ways. He can do TV movies or "real" movies (this is not to deny that we occasionally get fine movies) or moronic TV episodes; he can become a full-time teacher of creative writing; he can move into advertising or porno or pieces for the *National Geographic*; he can become an interesting local bum; with a little popular-novel success he can become a regular on talk shows; he can become a politician or a contributor to *The New York Times* or the *New York Review of Books*. . . .

Nothing is harder than being a true novelist, unless that is all one wants to be, in which case, though becoming a true novelist is hard, everything else is harder.

Daemonic compulsiveness can kill as easily as it can save. The true novelist must be at once driven and indifferent. Van Gogh never sold a painting in his life. Poe came close with poetry and fiction, selling very little. Drivenness only helps if it forces the writer not to suicide but to the making of splendid works of art, allowing him indifference to whether or not the novel sells, whether or not it's appreciated. Drivenness is trouble for both the novelist and his friends; but no novelist, I think, can succeed without it. Along with the peasant in the novelist, there must be a man with a whip.

5

No one can really tell the beginning writer whether or not he has what it takes. Most people the young writer asks aren't qualified to judge. They may have impressive positions, even fame, but it's a law of the universe that 87 percent of all people in all professions are incompetent. The young writer must decide for himself, on the available evidence. I've given, in some detail, the evidence to think about:

Verbal facility is a mark of the promising novelist, but some great novelists don't have it, and some quite stupid novelists have it in abundance.

The accuracy and freshness of the writer's eye is of tremendous importance. But one can learn it if one hasn't got it. Usually. One can recognize that the abstract is seldom as effective as the concrete. "She was distressed" is not as good as, even, "She looked away."

Nothing is sillier than the creative writing teacher's dictum "Write about what you know." But whether you're writing about people or dragons, your personal observation of how things happen in the world—how character reveals itself—can turn a dead scene into a vital one. Preliminary good advice might be: Write as if you were a movie camera. Get exactly what is there. All human beings see with astonishing accuracy, not that they can necessarily write it down. When husbands and wives have fights, they work brilliantly, without consciously thinking. They go precisely as far as it's safe to go, they find the spouse's weakness, yet they know without thinking just when to hold back. The unconscious is smart. Writers have this brilliance in them as surely as do trout fishermen and mountain climbers. The trick is to bring it out, get it down. Getting it down precisely is all that is meant by "the accuracy of the writer's eye." Getting down what the writer really cares about—setting down what the writer himself notices, as opposed to what any fool might notice—is all that is meant by the *originality* of the writer's eye. Every human being has original vision. Most can't write it down without cheapening or falsifying. Most human beings haven't developed what Hemingway called the "built-in shock-resistant shit detector." But the writer who sets down exactly what he sees and feels, carefully revising time after time until he fully believes it, noticing when what he's saying is mere rhetoric or derivative vision, noticing when what he's said is not noble or impressive but silly—that writer, insofar as the world is just, will outlast Gibraltar.

As for the novelist's special intelligence, ask yourself whether or not you've got it. If you haven't, then knowing what it is may help you to develop it. If you dislike the novelist's special intelligence, don't become a novelist—unless, in spite of all I've said, you really want to.

Daemonic compulsiveness. If you haven't got it and you nevertheless write fine novels, I'll be the first to say, "Gentlemen, hats off!" I mention the value of compulsiveness because I would not have anyone go into the novelist's arena unarmed. There are many ways of surviving an activity not easily justified in practical terms. Thousands of Americans stand for hours in streams trying to catch fish. The novelist's work is no more visibly useless than amateur fish-catching. And I suspect most fishermen are not daemonically compulsive.

The question one asks of the young writer who wants to know if he's got what it takes is this: "Is writing novels what you want to do? *Really* want to do?"

If the young writer answers, "Yes," then all one can say is: Do it. In fact, he will anyway.

II.

THE WRITER'S TRAINING

AND EDUCATION

One of the most common questions asked by young writers is whether or not they should study creative writing and literature in college or graduate school. If the writer means only: "Will these courses help me become a better writer?" the answer is generally, Yes. If he or she means: "Will they improve my chances of supporting myself, for instance by getting a Master of Fine Arts degree and then getting a job teaching writing in college?" the answer is, Possibly. The world has far more writing teachers than it needs, and as a rule it is publication, not the MFA degree, that impresses employers, though an MA or MFA from a good school may help.

It's common for students to think of their college and/or grad school education in practical terms, as preparation for making a living. In many fields it is reasonable to think in this way, but not in the arts. European and English writers receive a good deal of support from the state, but in America, though federal, state, and local governments make feeble gestures of support (the whole National Endowment for the Arts comes to, I think, the cost of one frigate), it seems clear that nobody quite knows what to do with artists. In former times, when artists were church- or patron-supported, things were simple. Not now. Today, true, serious artists in all fields (music, visual arts, literature) are something like an alternative culture, a group set apart from all other groups, from theology to professional pornography. They sacrifice the ordinary TV-watching pleasures of their society to pursue an ideal not especially valued by the society, and if they are lucky, they bring the society around, becoming culture heroes, but even the successful pay dearly. Both in the world of grants and in the marketplace, the novelist probably has a better chance than any other artist—certainly a better chance than the serious actor, poet, or composer. But very few novelists can support themselves by their writing. The study of writing, like the study of classical piano, is not practical but aristocratic. If one is born rich, one can easily afford to be an artist; if not, one has to afford one's art by sacrifice. On this, more later.

Let us turn to the benefits and dangers of going through a creative writing program and of studying literature in college.

It is true that most writers' workshops have faults; nevertheless, a relatively good writers' workshop can be beneficial. For one thing, workshops bring together groups of young writers who, even in the absence of superb teachers, can be of help to one another. Being with a group of serious writers at one's own stage of development makes the young writer feel less a freak than he might otherwise, and talking with other writers, looking at their work, listening to their comments, can abbreviate the apprenticeship process. It cannot be too strongly emphasized that, after the beginning stages, a writer needs social and psychological support.

When a writer first begins to write, he or she feels the same first thrill of achievement that the young gambler or oboe player feels: winning a little, losing some, the gambler sees the glorious possibilities, exactly as the young oboist feels an indescribable thrill when he gets a few phrases to sound like real music, phrases implying an infinite possibility for satisfaction and self-expression. As long as the gambler or oboist is only playing at being a gambler or oboist, everything seems possible. But when the day comes that he sets his mind on becoming a professional, suddenly he realizes how much there is to learn, how little he knows.

The young writer leaves the undergraduate college, where everyone agrees he is one of the best writers there, and he goes to, say, the Iowa Writers' Workshop, or Stanford, Columbia, or Binghamton. There he finds nearly every one of his classmates was a writing star at his or her college; he finds famous teachers who read his work and seem largely unimpressed; and suddenly the young writer's feelings are mainly alarm and disappointment. Why did his undergraduate teachers so mislead him? he wonders. I'm not sure myself why undergraduate reputations are inflated even by good teachers with high standards; perhaps because outside the specialized, nationally known writers' workshops one encounters relatively few young writers of real promise; or perhaps because at this early stage of a writer's work, the teacher believes that encouragement and praise seem more beneficial than a rigorous assessment of the writer's skills.

In any event, the writer adjusts (or else he gives up). He accepts the truth that he is not as great as his teachers and classmates imagined. He recognizes that the success he hopes for will take work. What a writer in this gloomy situation needs above all is a community that values what he values, a community that believes, rightly or wrongly, that it is better to be a good writer than to be a good executive, politician, or scientist. Good writers are after all intelligent people. They *could* have been executives, politicians, or scientists. They might not like or want such jobs, but they could do them, and in some ways any one of those jobs might be easier. What keeps the young writer with the potential for success from turning aside to some more generally approved, perhaps easier path is the writing community.

No doubt the truth is that as often as not the writing community saves the writer by its folly. It is partly made up of fools: young innocents who've not yet had the experience of valuing anything other than writing, and maniacs who, having considered other things, think writing the only truly valuable thing the human mind can do. It is partly made up of born writers: people who value other human activities but have no wish to do anything but write. (Asked why she wrote fiction, Flannery O'Connor once said, "Because I'm good at it.") Some members of every writing community are there because they're snobs: writing, or just being around writers, makes them feel superior; others are there because they think being a writer (though they may not have much talent) is romantic. Whatever their reasons or reasonings, these various contingents form, together, a group that helps the young writer forget his doubts. However good or bad the writing teacher, the young writer can count on close attention from all these kinds of people, not to mention a few chemists who enjoy going to readings. The young writer writes, feels uncertain about his work, and gets praise or, at very least, constructive criticism—or even destructive criticism, but from people who appear to care as much about writing as he does himself.

It's the same in all fields, of course. A young businessman in a society of people who can see only wickedness in business cannot easily remain a young businessman. We're social animals. Few born and bred Republicans remain Republicans in a context where everyone they know and respect is a Democrat. I've said that stubbornness is important for writers. But stubbornness can carry one only so far. If you grow up in a happy family and move to a community of pessimists—for example, if you grow up on a fortunate and peaceful farm in Indiana and move to New York City—you can stubbornly hold out, but only because you have, in your memory, something real to hold out for. (The same is true in reverse. Born and bred in Manhattan, you cannot easily shift to the less cynical attitudes of rural Ohio.) I don't mean to slight the complications. You may be by nature a pessimist, even though born to a happy family in Indiana. But in hostile circumstances

—that is, in the exclusive company of optimists—you cannot easily make art of your pessimism, you can only be odd and miserable.

So the first value of a writers' workshop is that it makes the young writer feel not only not abnormal but virtuous. In a writers' community, nearly all the talk is about writing. Even if you don't agree with most of what is said, you come to take for granted that no other talk is quite so important. Talk about writing, even in a mediocre community of writers, is exciting. It makes you forget that by your own standards, whatever they may be, you're not very good yet. It fills you with nervous energy, makes you want to leave the party and go home and write. And it's the sheer act of writing, more than anything else, that makes a writer.

On the other hand, the writer who avoids writers' workshops (or some other solid community of writers) is probably in for trouble. One can be fooled by the legend of, say, Jack London, and imagine that the best way to become a writer is to be a seaman or lumberjack. Jack London lived in an age when writers were folk heroes, as they are not now, and an age when technique was not quite as important as it is now. Though a tragic and noble man, he was a relatively bad writer. He could have used a few good teachers. Hemingway once remarked that "the best way to become a writer is to go off and write." But his own way of doing it was to go to Paris, where many of the great writers were, and to study with the greatest theorist of the time, and one of the shrewdest writers, Gertrude Stein. Joseph Conrad, though we tend to think of him as a solitary genius, worked in close community with Ford Maddox Ford, H. G. Wells, Henry James, and Stephen Crane, among others. Melville had Hawthorne and his circle. Great writers are almost always associated with a literary dynasty. It's hard to find an exception. (Incredibly, even Malcolm Lowry was part of a group.) So for psychological reasons, if for no other, even a bad workshop may be better than none.

If a bad writers' workshop is worth attending, a good one is more so. If I could, I would tell you what the good workshops are. Iowa, being the oldest and best known, always attracts good students and sometimes has fine teachers. Binghamton has a good program in fiction, which is why I teach there. I've already mentioned others I consider dependable— Columbia and Stanford; and the list might easily be expanded. But it's hard to give sure advice. For one thing, workshops change from year to year, as skillful writing teachers come and go; and for another, what makes a good workshop for one writer may be a disaster for another. I myself am not very interested in so-called experimental writing, though I do it sometimes and have occasionally been moved or delighted by works of fiction by William Gass (who does not normally teach writing) or Max Apple (with whom one can study at Rice). When I find I have in one of my writing classes a student who has no interest in the more or less traditional kind of fiction I favor, I know that both the student and I are in trouble. Much as I want to help him, I am the wrong kind of doctor. On the other hand, John Barth, who heads the writing program at Johns Hopkins and has gathered around him an interesting group of writers who, like himself, favor the new and strange, can have a crippling effect on the young realist. What all this suggests, of course, is that the student should select his writing program on the basis of its teachers, hunting out those whose interests seem closest to his own.

One of the things that make a good writers' workshop beneficial is that it has at least one or two brilliant students (also five or six solid, sensible ones, and then several who are either pretentious or ploddingly conventional). Even in the best writers' workshop one is likely to learn more from one's fellow students than from one's teachers. A workshop perceived to be better than most attracts good students, and because they are at the apprentice stage, these people can be counted on for careful scrutiny of one's work, for encouragement, and useful criticism. Teachers in the well-known workshops may or may not prove helpful. They tend to hire the more famous writers, but not all famous writers are good teachers. Moreover, the main commitment of famous writers is, as a rule, to their own work. However deeply they may care about their students, their main business is to work on a form that takes a great deal of time. Often their solution is to concentrate on the very best of their students and give the rest short shrift. There is no doubt, I think, that good teachers can be helpful to the young writer; but in practice it turns out that the student either encounters good writers who teach on the side and do not work as hard as they might at it, or good teachers who are not very good writers, so that what they teach is partly wrong, or good writers who cannot teach at all.

Whatever the quality of their teaching, famous writers do a good deal for writing programs. Perhaps the chief value of the famous writer is his presence, his contribution as a role model. Just by being around him day after day, the young writer learns how the famous man reads, and what he reads; how he perceives the world; how he relates to others and to his profession; even how he schedules his life. The famous writer's presence is vivid proof that the young writer's goal is not necessarily unreasonable. If the student is extraordinarily lucky, the famous writer may also be a good teacher: he not only knows what real art is but can explain it.

I must add that at some of the creative writing programs where I've visited or taught I've found excellent teachers who are not creative writers at all, really, though they may have published a story or two, or one novel years ago, or several mediocre novels. Some people can catch mistakes in student writing that they cannot see in their own, and some writers who have excellent minds write, by some quirk of personality, books unworthy of them. Sometimes the excellent writing teacher is a critic rather than a fiction writer; sometimes he is a person without literary credentials, perhaps a freshman English teacher who, drafted to teach a lower-level creative writing course, has proved to have a gift for it. How to find such teachers only luck or the grapevine can tell you. One can ask writers one admires where they would go if they were just starting out; or one can simply set out for a generally respected university and hope. The odds are good that one will find, in any major university, someone who can help.

One of the oddities of creative writing courses is that there exists no standard theory on how to teach creative writing. Many people ask—even some creative writing teachers—"Can writing really be taught?" No one asks that about painting or musical composition. Writing has been identified so strongly with "genius" or "inspiration" that people have tended to assume that the art cannot be passed on by such methods as the other arts have used. That perception may be partly right; the writing of fiction may be a less specific, detectable skill than painting or musicianship. But the reason for doubt that writing can be taught is also, I think, at least partly historical. From early times, schools of painting and music directly served religious and political functions in a way writing poetry or fiction did not. Since the church and city-state of Florence needed Giotto's skills, Giotto taught his methods; his near contemporaries Dante and Boccaccio worked, respectively, at politics and the teaching of literature. In any case, within the past twenty or thirty years, with the rise of creative writing programs in the United States, a pedagogy for the art has begun to develop, and with every passing year the general level of teaching improves. There are those who deplore this fact, claiming it as the main reason for the dreary sameness of so much of our fiction and poetry; and no doubt there is something to be said for that view. But at least at the technical level, it seems to me, fiction has never been better off. Probably the truth is that in any age there are only so many writers of genius, and teaching a writer not to make mistakes—teaching him to avoid those forms of vagueness or clumsiness that impair the vivid and continuous dream—cannot make him a more interesting or original person than he is. Perhaps the one great danger that the student in a good creative writing course ought to guard against is the tendency of good technical theory to undermine individuality and the willingness to take risks.

A bad workshop in creative writing has one or more regular features. If the student notices several of them in the workshop he has chosen, he should drop the course.

In a bad workshop, the teacher allows or even encourages attack. It is common in writers' workshops for the student to read a story (usually one he's gone over beforehand with the teacher), then get comments from his teacher and classmates. In a good workshop, the teacher establishes a general atmosphere of helpfulness rather than competitiveness or viciousness. Classmates of the writer whose work has been read do not begin, if the workshop is well run, by stating how *they* would have written the story, or by expressing their blind prejudices on what is or is not seemly; in other words, they do not begin by making up some different story or demanding a different style. They try to understand and appreciate the story that has been written. They assume, even if they secretly doubt it, that the story was carefully and intelligently constructed and that its oddities have some justification. If they cannot understand why the story is as it is, they ask questions. A common fault poor teachers inculcate in students is the habit of too quickly deciding that what they have failed to understand makes no sense. It takes confidence and good will to say, "I didn't understand so-and-so," rather than, belligerently, "So-and-so makes no sense." It is the nature of stupid people to hide their perplexity and attack what they cannot grasp. The wise admit their puzzlement (no prizes are given in heaven for fake infallibility), and when the problem material is explained they either laugh at themselves for failing to see it or they explain why they couldn't reasonably be expected to understand, thus enabling the author to see why he didn't get his point across.

Good workshop criticism, in other words, is like good criticism anywhere. When we read what is generally acknowledged to be a great work of art, we try to understand, if we have sense, why intelligent people, including the writer, have thought the work aesthetically satisfying. In a good fiction workshop one recognizes that even if a work seems bad at first glance, the writer sat writing and thinking about it for a fair amount of time and deserves a generous response. It is true, of course, that some of the fiction one hears read in a workshop is bad, and often there is no real question about its badness. The story is patently melodramatic, vague, pretentious, inadequately thought out, overloaded with detail, sentimental, uninterestingly vulgar. I myself think really bad fiction should never reach a reading in the workshop; it cannot teach much or sharpen students' critical skills, and it is likely to embarrass the writer. If bad fiction does reach the workshop, it should be dealt with quickly and politely, its mistakes made clear so that neither that writer nor any other in the workshop is inclined to repeat them, and its virtues acknowledged. But in most fiction that reaches workshop reading, the badness is not so obvious. The business of the teacher and the writer's classmates is to figure out (or if necessary ask) the purpose and meaning of the piece and only then to suggest carefully, thoughtfully, why the purpose and meaning did not come through.

A writer does not become better by being scorned. It is helpful if a class, as it listens to a writer's story, makes careful notes of apparent mistakes or weaknesses and reads them to the writer after the story has been read, but it is helpful only if the class generally understands that anyone's work could have similar shortcomings. If a class regularly attacks its members, and the teacher allows it, the course is counterproductive. The only final value of class criticism is that it teaches each member of the class to criticize and evaluate his own work and appreciate good fiction different from his own. Often class criticism can show the writer that he has at some specific point written misleadingly or has failed to evoke some important element of a scene—mistakes the writer could not catch himself because, knowing what he intended, he thinks his sentences say more than they do. He may imagine, for instance, that the bulge in his female character's coat clearly indicates that she is carrying a gun, whereas a listener not privy to the writer's mental image may imagine that the woman is pregnant. Seeing the effects of his mistakes makes the writer more careful, more wary of the trickery words are capable of. Or again, class criticism may make a writer aware of his unconscious prejudices, for instance his notion that fat people are easygoing, or that all hellfire fundamentalists are mean, or that all homosexuals try to seduce boys. The wide range of opinion a class affords increases the writer's chance of getting a fair hearing—especially the writer whose style, goals, and attitudes differ radically from his teacher's—and the focus of the whole class on the writer's work increases the odds that most of his mistakes or ineffective strategies will be noticed. At its best, class criticism can help everyone involved, as long as that criticism is basically generous. Vicious criticism leads to writer's block, both in the victim and in the attacker.

In a bad workshop, the teacher coerces his students into writing as he himself writes. The tendency is natural, though not excusable. The teacher has worked for years to figure out his style and has persistently rejected alternatives. The result is that if he is not careful he is likely to be resistant to writing markedly unlike his own or, worse, written in a style opposed to his own, as in the case of the elegant stylist confronting a rough, demotic prose. The teacher's purpose ought to be to help students find their *own* way. This is the point teacher and poet Dave Smith is making when he says, "My object is to catch right now what will embarrass my students when they look at their poetry ten years from now." His object, in other words, is not to impose some strictly personal standard but to notice, within the implicit laws of the student poet's standards, what will not stand up in time. The poetry teacher who by force turns a light, anapestic, lyrical poet into an ode writer in stern Anglo-Saxon rhythms, the fiction teacher unwilling to tolerate experimental writing of a kind he himself hates to read —the teacher who consciously or unconsciously seeks to make fundamental changes in his student's personality—is, at least for that student, an inadequate if not a destructive teacher.

In another kind of bad workshop, there are no standards of goodness. I mentioned earlier one common set of standards for good fiction—creation of a vivid and continuous dream, authorial generosity, intellectual and emotional significance, elegance and efficiency, and strangeness. Another teacher of writing may have other aesthetic values—though I hope most teachers would admit the general validity of these. If the teacher has no basic standards, his class is likely to develop none, and their comments can only be matters of preference or opinion. Writers will have nothing to strive toward or resist, nothing solid to judge by. As I've said, undue rigidity can be destructive; but even a rigid set of standards, if it's clear and at least more or less valid, can be useful in giving the student something to challenge. An individual style is developed as much by resistance as by emulation. Students of a teacher who refuses to set standards are in danger of falling into the philistine persuasion that all literary success is luck or public whim. In that class, the student who writes an excellent story about fishermen and dolphins will be open to the objection that some particular classmate hates all stories of the sea. This is not to say that standards cannot change, adapting themselves to new successes. The moment I propound my principles, I can count on it that some clever student will consciously, perhaps even brilliantly, defy them. In that case, as a serious teacher I must determine without guiding rules—nothing but my honest thought and emotions—whether or not the story works, that is, interests me and moves me. The workshop teacher who has no basic theory, no set of aesthetic values conscientiously worked out, is probably doomed to mediocrity, as is his class. There is in the end no substitute for a critical understanding of fiction—which is not to claim that fiction is philosophy.

No experienced teacher underestimates how hard it is to see a student's work in its own terms. Since I generally teach fairly advanced courses, mainly graduate school level, I've often seen student work I thought to be quite bad and then later learned that the same piece was singled out for praise or even publication by other teacher-writers I respect. Recently I was given a story (a work sample on the basis of which I was to decide whether or not the student should be admitted to my course) that had been praised by two earlier writing teachers, both of them firmly established writers reputed to be good teachers. I did admit the student; the energy and vividness of the work were undeniable. But I thought the story execrable. It was a first-person story told inside the head of a madman, a tour de force of violence and scatology, seething with malice, frighteningly cynical, ending in the same place it began. It did none of the things I think art ought to do, except that it was vivid and (in a nasty, discomforting way) interesting. And the sentences were carefully made. When I said, with restraint, that I did not like the story very much, the student sighed and confessed that he didn't like it, either. Some of the verbs were too low-key, he said, and when he tried to put in more lively verbs they seemed to call undue attention to themselves. At this point, of course, I saw that I hadn't been thinking well. The student really was a gifted writer, fully conscious of what he was doing, earnestly looking for help from a teacher whose standards are about as applicable to his project as the rules of pinochle or the gladiator's oath.

One forgets the extent to which aesthetic standards are projections of one's own personality, defensive armor, or wishful thinking about the world. If there are objective laws of aesthetics, not all of them apply in every instance, and none of them finally have to do with purpose. One can argue, as I've done elsewhere, that—descriptively speaking—the fiction that lasts tends to be "moral," that is, it works with a minimum of cynical manipulation and it tends to reach affirmations favorable rather than opposed to life. One can argue on this basis that a writer is generally unwise to fake despair and nihilism he does not really feel. One cannot argue that the writer's purpose should be the creation of moral fiction, or any other kind; one cannot even argue that his purpose should be to create something beautiful or pleasing or even honest or universally interesting. A given writer may wish to set such standards for his students; but insofar as he means to be a teacher, he must leave room for intelligent rebellion.

In a bad workshop, the teacher takes the place of the student's critical imagination. This is the one great danger in a workshop where the teacher is not only an impressive writer but also a skillful and articulate teacher, one who can figure out narrative or stylistic problems, solve them, and make his mental processes clear to students. This fully articulate teaching implies, of course, a close teacher-student relationship—not just one in which the teacher jots an occasional comment on the student's writing but rather one in which the teacher goes over each of the student's works with meticulous care, missing neither the virtues of the piece nor the defects. How it is that the best teacher's help and concern can impede the student's progress—how the virtue of showing students ways of evaluating and correcting their fiction can pass over into the defect of making student minds clones of the teacher's—is a matter both teacher and student need to become sensitive to.

The best kind of writing teacher, it seems to me, not only meets his regular workshop classes but deals with each student individually, half an hour or an hour each week or so, in tutorial sessions, like a violin instructor. The teacher closely analyzes the student's work and shows him, not on the basis of the teacher's own personal preferences but in terms of the inherent logic of the student's fiction, what is right and wrong and what needs to be done. This is not a matter of opinion or individual feeling. In any true story, certain things have to be shown dramatically, others can be summarized or implied. In general the rule is simply this: Anything necessary to the action's development must be shown dramatically. For instance, if a man is to beat his dog, it is not enough for the writer to *tell* us that the man is inclined to violence or that the dog annoys him: we must see how and why the man inclines to violence, and we must see the dog annoying him. For young writers it is sometimes hard to recognize what has to be dramatized or how it can be done. And here the problem arises.

Nothing is easier than to give the student specific actions, even specific sentences, that will solve his story's problems; and at a certain point in the young writer's development it may perhaps be valuable to do such things, so that the student can get the hang of it. But basically what teachers need to teach students is not how to fix a particular story but how to figure out what is wrong with the story and how to think about alternative ways of fixing it. At the Bread Loaf Writers' Conference I've frequently worked with writing assistants—young writers with successful first novels—whose inexperience as teachers led them to focus on finding the best solution to problems in the writing placed in their care, led them, in other words, to show the student writer what to do to make his fiction work. In case after case, when I myself looked at the student's work later, I felt there were a number of possible solutions to the problems—alternative solutions whose relative value must depend on the student writer's preferences—and that in suggesting only one solution, the one he himself would choose, my assistant had done an unwitting disservice to the student. What the beginner needs to learn is how to think like a novelist. What he does not need is a teacher who imposes his own solution, like an algebra teacher who tells you the answer without showing how he got there, because it is *process* that the young writer must learn: problems in novels, unlike problems in algebra, may have any number of solutions. At some point —the sooner the better, some would say—the teacher's job is simply to say, "Not good enough," and vanish.

Finally, a bad fiction workshop is "workshoppy." It tends to emphasize theme and design over feeling and authentic narrative. Working too much with too many young writers, or having no teaching talent in the first place, the teacher may slide into simplifying his work by forcing original ideas into what all good editors immediately recognize as workshop formulas. The evil is perhaps most easily described in the case of poetry: rather than helping the student poet to feel out the natural development of his poem, the writing teacher may rest on some simpleminded habit of design—for instance, the notion of "orchestration," the idea that the end of a poem should somehow bring back, like a musical comedy, all its main ideas and images in a final stanza. The same mistake is possible in fiction. Beware of the teacher who cries, "Reprise! Reprise!" The reader who encounters a reprise ending—if he's not very good at reading poetry or fiction—feels a superficial thrill of recognition. The more experience he gets, the more annoyed he is by such foolishness.

A story may be "workshoppy" because the writer (or the teacher) has too often thought from the literature student's point of view rather than from the writer's, so that instead of working like a storyteller, beginning with what happens and why, and only gradually moving (in his thought process if not in the actual writing) to the larger issues (how this story is in some way every human story, an expression of a constant or universal theme), the student writer begins with theme, symbolism, etc., in effect working backward from his imagined New Criticism analysis of a story not yet in existence. One can quickly spot this tendency in a workshop. Class discussion of a story begins in the wrong place, not with the immediate virtues of good fiction (an interesting and original but not distracting style, a clear and well-designed plot, vivid characterization and setting, an interesting and expressive use of a particular genre) but with the kinds of things normally central to a class in literature (theme and symbol). It is of course true that in a given story these less immediate matters may be the appropriate starting point; indeed, one mark of the first-rate writing teacher is his ability to move discussion swiftly to what happens to be the most important ground for judgment of the story at hand.

Another reason workshops become "workshoppy" is that often teachers slide unconsciously into overprizing the kind of narrative writing that teaches well, undervaluing and even dismissing work that does not. This sometimes gives an advantage to, for instance, the symbolic or allegorical story over the straightforward, well-crafted realistic story, and to almost any short story over the more sprawling prose of a novel-in-progress. For the teacher, a well-made allegorical story is a delight, a puzzle he and the class can, if they wish, play with for hours. In the fiction workshop I am teaching this semester I encountered a story entitled "Jason," which I hope soon to publish in the magazine I edit, *MSS*. Early in the story, a child, Jason, loses one shoe; much later in the story, we come to a huge old Vermont inn, many-storied and circular, whose hallways wrap around like the coils of a snake (the idea is better expressed in the original). The story is told so cunningly, with such realistic detail, that only one member of this well-read graduate class caught on to the writer's use of the Jason and Medea myth. Once the secret was out, the class pounced on one allusion after another, and after that members of the class delighted in turning over, with subtlety almost equal to the writer's, the story's deconstructionist (or revisionist) tricks. I think no one who attended the class or has read the story would deny that it's an interesting and effective piece. But the point is, the first chapter of Tolstoy's *Anna Karenina* probably could not have stirred such lively discussion.

Short fiction in the symbolic or allegorical mode can no

more compete in the arena of well-constructed full-length novels than a bantamweight can hope to compete in the ring with a skillful heavyweight. (It goes without saying that each has its/his place.) But in the writers' workshop the heavyweight may not fare well. For practical reasons (the fact that young novelists try out their wings on the short story, for one thing) most creative writing workshops are oriented toward short fiction. For the young novelist, this can be troublesome. His talent may go unnoticed: his marathon-runner pace does not stir the same interest as the story writer's sprinter's pace; and the kinds of mistakes workshops focus on are not as important in a novel as in a short story. Poets and short story writers must learn to work with the care of a miniaturist in the visual arts. Novelists can afford to stand back now and then and throw paint at the wall. Granted, they must throw well; but there can be no comparison between the skillful paint thrower and the Japanese master who touches his brush to the surface between heartbeats. Sometimes it happens that the young novelist distorts his art in an attempt to compete with the short story writers in his class. He tries to make every chapter zing, tries dense symbolism and staggeringly rich prose; he violates the novelistic pace.

Ideally, he belongs in a novel-writing workshop. The young novelist is as different from the young short story writer as the young short story writer is from the poet. The aesthetic problems he must work out are different from those that confront the story writer, and the novelist's whole character and way of working are different. (Granted, some people write both good novels and good short stories. I am speaking of extreme examples of the two types of writer.) Every three or four years I run a novel workshop (the rest of the time I teach workshops for anyone who wants to come and can already write well enough to get in). The novel workshop is, one soon learns, serious business. The people who become my students wait like hill-country outlaws for the course to be given, and then, when it is finally announced, strike like snakes.

In the last workshop I gave I had ten students. I asked that they work up a novel outline, which we would go over in class, and then that they present me, each week after that, with a new chapter and also a revision of the former chapter (revised in the light of our conference discussion of it). I didn't believe anyone could really hold to this schedule; I presented it only as an ideal to work toward, pointing out that the farther they were able to get on their novels, the more I would be able to show them about episode rhythm, overall construction, and so on. All but one of the students kept to the schedule. The exception, a town woman with a full-time job, was hospitalized as a result of overwork. I pushed these students no harder than I push students in other workshops. (In fact, I hardly push at all. If the student doesn't feel like writing, I don't have to read his work.) The novelists pushed themselves, as novelists characteristically do. The true young novelist has the stamina, patience, and single-mindedness of a draft horse. Those novel-workshop students who were involved with other college courses that semester dropped those other courses. Of the ten students in the course, eight later published their novels.

Students like these have no very comfortable place in the elegant, leisurely world of poets and short story writers. In the usual creative writing course, the potentially fine young novelist may even look rather dull. One of the best young novelists I ever taught, now a successful writer, got bad grades in high school and entered college (as a rugby player) with one of the lowest verbal aptitude scores on record at that university. His grammar was awful and his social adjustment was less than might have been desired. He stands for me as a kind of symbol of the young novelist, even though some are in fact witty, classy, and petite.

You know you're in a good writers' workshop if nearly everyone in the class is glad to be there, if writing and talk about writing become, in the course of the term, an increasingly exciting business, and if the writers in the workshop become increasingly effective as writers. The chief mark of a bad writing class is teacher meanness. Beware of the teacher who scoffs at "little magazines," claiming that they promote and proliferate mediocrity: you are dealing with a snob. Beware of the teacher who loves little magazines and hates *Esquire*, *The New Yorker*, or the *Atlantic*. You are looking at the same snob in drag. If you feel miserable in your writers' workshop, you should talk about your misery in private with the teacher, and if things don't improve, you should quit. A bad writing class doesn't only fail to teach writing, it can make one give up.

It is of course possible to become a good writer without a college education or, more specifically, without courses in literature. One does not have to be college-educated to be a sensitive and intelligent human being; in fact, there are some advantages to remaining one of the so-called common people, and thus avoiding the subtle social distancing higher education imposes. Writing ability, however improvable by teaching, is in large part a gift. If one cannot get to college, one need not despair of being a writer.

On the other hand, a college education gives advantages not to be lightly dismissed. The uneducated writer may successfully tell the stories of the people around him, may set down their longings and sufferings in comic or deeply moving or awe-inspiring ways; and if he is a self-educated writer, one who reads books, goes to good movies, and listens intently to the stories he hears among his friends and fellow workers, he may even become a subtle and original storyteller. But he will almost certainly remain a sort of primitive, that is, a kind of folk writer; he has difficulty becoming a virtuoso, one of those writers whose fictions impress us not only by their truth to life but also by their brilliance, their value as performance.

It's hard to explain the difference between a well-educated writer, one who understands from inside the beauty of a play by Shakespeare, the strange genius of James Joyce, Andrei Bely, or Thomas Mann, and an equally intelligent writer who knows only "the world" or, at best, knows only the world and the popular books he can get from his local drugstore, from a book club, or at a nearby branch of Waldenbooks. The uneducated writer is, for one thing, locked in his own time and place. Not knowing (not really knowing) about Homer or Racine or the contemporary fiction of South America, not knowing the many different ways in which a story can be told, from the rough-hemp tale-spinning of the saga poets to the dandified French allegorical tricks of the Middle Ages to the strange ways of India and China or avant-garde contemporary Africans, Poles, or Americans, he is like a carpenter with only a few crude tools: a hammer, a knife, a drill, a pair of pliers. He has no knowledge of the cunning tools of other times and places, with the result that when he asks himself what the best way of telling a given story might be, he has only two or three answers available. Or to put it another way, he has very few models for his work. He may use superbly the models he knows, becoming the literary equivalent of a maker of fine Shaker chairs; but what he might have done had he known other ways and means we will never find out.

What the writer should study if he goes to college is debatable. A good program of courses in philosophy, along with creative writing, can clarify the writer's sense of what questions are important—in other words, what worries and obsessions may give real importance to the writer's fiction. There are obvious dangers. Like any other discipline, philosophy is apt to be inbred, concerned about questions any normal human being would find transparently ridiculous. If one reads major journals on aesthetics, for instance, one cannot help but notice that most of the people who write about the arts seem never to have noticed how the arts really work. With solemn jargon and diagrams, professional aestheticians seek to demonstrate that fiction does or does not actually arouse feelings in the reader; or with great shows of learning they seek to demonstrate that fiction does or does not have, in any real sense, "meaning." All human thought has its bullshit quotient, and professional thought about thought has more than most. Nevertheless, the study of philosophy, perhaps with courses in psychology thrown in, can give the young writer a clear sense of why our age is so troubled, why people of our time suffer in ways different from the ways in which people of other times and places suffered. Though the ordinary housewife, politician, or ballplayer, as well as most academics, may never have read Nietzsche, Wittgenstein, or Heidegger, the ideas of those philosophers help make clear—or helped to cause—the problems of ordinary modern people. Moreover, for a certain kind of writer philosophy is interesting in itself. Writers always write best about what they most care about. The writer who cares more about philosophy than about anything else (except writing) should study philosophy.

For another kind of writer, the most valuable course of study may be one of the hard sciences. This is especially true, obviously, of the serious writer whose chief literary love is sophisticated sci-fi. Though it is true that most science fiction is junk, some of it is excellent. Certain books spring immediately to mind—some of Ray Bradbury's work or Kurt Vonnegut's, certain modern classics like *Brave New World* and *1984*, not to mention works of obvious high-class intent, such as Thomas Pynchon's *Gravity's Rainbow*, William Burroughs's *The Ticket That Exploded*, or the work of major writers outside America, like Kobo Abe, Italo Calvino, Raymond Queneau, or Doris Lessing. The number of aesthetically valuable works of science fiction is greater than the academy generally notices. One finds intelligence and emotional power in, for instance, Walter Miller's *A Canticle for Leibowitz* (mentioned earlier), the fiction of Samuel R. Delaney, some of Robert

Silverberg, Roger Zelazny, Isaac Asimov, and, when he holds in the fascism, Robert Heinlein. One finds a fair measure of literary merit in Algis J. Budrys's *Michaelmas* or the work of Robert Wilson, whose novels (for instance, *Schrodinger's Cat*) out-Barth John Barth without sacrificing the primary quality of good fiction, interesting storytelling. And science fiction is the domain of one of the greatest living writers, Stanislaw Lem.

I don't mean to say that a scientific background needs to lead the writer to science fiction. Many writers—Walker Percy and John Fowles, for example—put their scientific knowledge to work in writing fiction of the here and now, thereby enriching their art. More and more, as we look around, we see science and literature coming together—Nabokov's moths, Updike's symbolism drawn from, among other sciences, astronomy and botany, Philip Appleman's Darwin poems, and so on. As twentieth-century science becomes increasingly the basis of our life metaphors—relativity, uncertainty, entropy, infinite transformation—and as technology becomes the very ground we stand on, whether we live in skyscrapers or on space stations, a background in science looks better and better as a springboard into writing. A science background cannot help the writer develop the literary skills that change an ordinary work into a fine one, but like any other discipline, it can give the young novelist, insofar as he cares about that discipline, important subject matter.

I will not go on to discuss the advantages and disadvantages of studying the social sciences, history or law, and so forth. A good writer may come out of any intellectual discipline at all. Every art and science gives the writer its own special ways of seeing, gives him experience with interesting people, and can provide him with means of making a living—supporting himself while he writes. Since only a few novelists, including very good ones, earn enough by their fiction to take care of themselves and their families, and since after a day of hard manual labor or taxing white-collar office stress it is hard to sit down and write fiction, the young novelist is wise to train himself in some profession where, if he likes, he can ease up a little, take some of his time for writing. Some novelists (Al Lebowitz) practice law part-time; some (Frederick Buechner) are ministers; some are doctors (Walker Percy); a great many are teachers. The trick, of course, is to find a profession you like and one that will also feed your writing, and not eat up all your time.

It is not necessary—or perhaps not even advisable—that the young writer major in literature. It *is* advisable that he take as many good literature courses as he's able to work in. Only the close study of the great literature of the past, in whatever language, can show the writer clearly what emotional and intellectual heights are possible. And only the study of literature can awaken the writer to those techniques which, if he reads only modern literature, he would never know the existence of. Very good young writers invariably become so by exposing themselves to good models, usually by getting a good teacher's help as they explore fiction of the far and near past. Sooner or later they learn the techniques of the so-called New Criticism (expressed in such books as *Understanding Fiction*, by Cleanth Brooks and Robert Penn Warren, *Reading Modern Short Stories*, by Jarvis Thurston, or *The Forms of Fiction*, by Lennis Dunlap and John Gardner; more recent books, such as *Fiction 100*, 2nd Edition edited by J. Pickering, give less emphasis to close analysis but tend to achieve the same thing, an ability to read closely). Learning to read a literary text well helps the student create more complex and interesting fiction. Insofar as possible, the young writer should choose courses dealing with the greatest literary figures available. And he should never study what he can easily figure out on his own. Most survey literature courses, by this rule, should be avoided.

Whatever the student majors in, and whatever he selects for elective courses, college work is enriching, probably more stimulating than anything else the young person can do at this period of his life. If he can, the young writer should give at least glancing attention to as many as possible of the major fields of study: a foreign language, history, philosophy, psychology, one or more of the hard sciences, fine arts. Glancing attention to these fields will enable the student to pursue them further on his own whenever he—or one of his characters—needs information. After his undergraduate years, the young writer who has played the field will find himself drawn naturally to additional interests, picking up paperback books about UFOs, botany, or the Russian Revolution, or falling into intense conversation, at parties, with morticians, go-go dancers, and dog trainers. Even a weak education opens up new worlds. Most writers, one may as well admit, get weak educations. Their minds are too much on their writing, and they lack proper respect. The writer ought not to be too proud of this. At the very least, he should learn to spell.

III.

PUBLICATION
AND SURVIVAL

Some writing teachers claim that the student writer should never think about publishing but should simply work hard at learning his craft—presumably on the assumption that if the student learns his craft well enough, publication will take care of itself. The assumption is probably right, but I'm suspicious of those who argue it: I suspect the teacher's main motive is the wish not to be bugged by students about publication. And in any case, though it's generally true that one ought not to publish until one has work worth publishing, and that when one does have such work, publication is not likely to prove inordinately difficult, it is nevertheless a fact of life that young writers do want to get published, and to tell them "Hush and eat your spinach" is to evade real problems.

Young writers want to publish because they're unsure of themselves. However talented they may be, they cannot go on writing for long (as a rule) without some reassurance beyond their fellow students' praise and the teacher's A minus. Part of the good young writer's virtue is his wish that "real" people like his work—some editor who does not know him, some casual reader in Lost Nation, Iowa. It is perhaps unreasonable to ask the writing teacher to make a special effort to get his competent students published; he has enough to do already— far more than the ordinary teacher of literature, who can meet his classes, grade two or three sets of papers a term, and spend the rest of his time fishing. (I speak as a teacher who has done both.) But the teacher should at least recognize that the student's wish is legitimate and healthy; and if the student's work really is good enough to publish, the teacher ought not to scorn the student's wish. Some widely respected writing teachers—for instance, the novelist Robert Coover—are famous for the energy and relative success with which they push their students' work on appropriate editors. Since students need confidence to write at all, and respectable publication is one of the roads to confidence, the teacher does well to offer what help or encouragement he can.

More important, of all the hard things a student needs to learn in order to become a professional writer, nothing is more self-preserving than learning the ropes of publication, so he might as well start learning while still in school. In some ways the young writer may need as much guidance in the matter of publication as he needs in the development of writing skills. Letters of rejection from even the most respectable magazines may be wise and helpful but are more likely to be perfunctory. I have seen editors complain of "too obvious symbolism" in a story no one else would call symbolic, and recommend cutting what any sane reader would instantly recognize as the best moment in the story. The editor may complain of sentimentality in a story I myself would call not sentimental but authentically moving; or he may, after skimming a story too quickly, complain that the plot is unclear, though in fact it's clear as day. Getting any letter at all from an editor is of course a mark of interest—it shows he thinks too much of the writer to send out a printed rejection slip—but the writer must learn not to take such letters of rejection too seriously. For the young writer, that is a hard thing to learn. The editor has power; surely he's smart. And the editor liked the story enough to send a letter; perhaps with just a few changes—even if they seem senseless —he'll accept the story and print it.

The writer sends out, and sends out again, and again and again, and the rejections keep coming, whether printed slips or letters, and so at last the moment comes when many a promising writer folds his wings and drops. His teachers and classmates praised him, back in school, his spouse is baffled by the rejections; but the writer's despair wins out. It's a terrible thing to write for five or even ten years and continue to be rejected. (I know.) And so at last, down goes another good writer. (Let no one tell you that all good writers eventually get published.) At this precarious moment when he's ready to give up, the writer needs three things: trustworthy reassurance that his work really is of publishable quality; a clear understanding of how editing works, so that the editor's damage to the writer's ego is minimized; and the strongest possible support from teachers and friends. It will not hurt, of course, if he can get one thing more: a contact—some writer or agent or famous critic who can help. Let me pause a moment on these three things, or rather four, that the young writer needs as he approaches his hour of despair.

Most rejected fiction is rejected because it's not good. Not all is rejected for this reason, as I've said: some is rejected because it was sent to the wrong kind of publisher, or because it never got past the slush-pile reader, who's tired and maybe not too bright, or because the publisher has a backlog, or because the editor cannot stand stories about cows. But most rejected fiction is rejected because it's bad. The writer, in this case, needs to find a better teacher, or if he can't get a teacher he should study the various books about writing—though for the writer who's worked for years and is still just plain bad, neither courses nor manuals are likely to help.

Sometimes good writing gets rejected by the very editor who ought to have recognized its worth. One should fight like the devil the temptation to think well of editors. They are all, without exception—at least some of the time—incompetent or crazy. By the nature of their profession they read too much, with the result that they grow jaded and cannot see new talent though it dances in front of their eyes. Like writers, they are under insupportable pressures: they have to choose books that will sell, or at least bring the publisher honor, so they become hypercritical, gun-shy, cynical. Often they are consciously or (more often) unconsciously guided by unspoken policies of the publishing house or magazine they work for. *The New Yorker*, for instance (to mention one of the best), has from the beginning been elegant and rather timid, a perfect magazine for selling expensive clothes and fine china, and its fiction editors, probably without knowing they do it, regularly duck from strong emotion or strong, masculine characters, preferring the refined and tentative. Alfred A. Knopf, one of the most respected publishers of novels, tends to resist publishing a profoundly pessimistic book. It is useful, in short, for young writers always to think of editors as limited people, though if possible one should treat them politely.

Understanding editors, one will recognize that at certain points one can stop thinking of them as enemies and begin to consider them friends. Although they're skittish and sometimes blind to real talent, they are often ambitious idealists; they would like nothing better than to discover and publish a great book—or even a moderately good one. This means they can be worked. They would *like* to publish a certain young writer's book, but they're unsure of themselves, so the thing for the young writer to do is win prizes and honors, fellowships and grants. If other people have admired the young writer, the editor feels more comfortable doing the same. (The editor is happiest when he can bet on a favorite while at the same time appearing to have discovered him.) Publication in one magazine makes publication in the next one much easier, as long as the writer is a good writer in the first place. And publication in several magazines—especially one or two reputedly good ones, like the *Georgia Review* or the *Atlantic* or *The New Yorker*

—increases the odds that when one is ready with a novel, it will be taken.

Once the editor has made up his mind to take a chance on the writer, some trick of the mind makes him sure he was right, and from that moment on, all the editor can see in the writer is good and more good. He may give advice, may even make annoying changes in the writer's manuscript, but essentially not even the writer's mother can love the writer as that editor does. He tells everyone he can find—his wife and children, his friends who write reviews, his fellow editors—and as the publication date nears, the editor's whole world, not to mention the writer's, begins to vibrate with panicky joy. If the writer is savaged by reviewers, the editor will be at least as angry as the writer, and the next book the writer sends in, the editor will fight for, partly because he likes it, partly because he has bet his credibility on the writer's career. Editors, at this point, are the bravest, most wonderful people on earth. A newly discovered writer has to go far out of his way—some writers do manage it—to turn his editor against him.

Let me pause for a few words on what the editors of novels do. Either by way of an agent (on which more in a moment) or "over the transom"—that is by direct submission from the writer—the novel arrives at the editor's desk. Normally a note comes with it, partly because mention of the writer's previous publications may help sway the editor (so the writer or agent hopes), and partly because sending a note is common politeness. If the note is from an agent, it is sure to address a particular editor by name, since a given book is likely to be of more interest to one editor than to another. The young novelist living in Filer, Idaho, or St. Joseph, Missouri, may have a hard time getting a specific editor's name and may have no idea which editor would like what. If so, "Dear Editor" will do, though obviously that writer would be better off with an agent. (Magazine submissions, like submissions to publishing houses, should also go, ideally, to a particular editor.)

As soon as he possibly can, depending upon how many manuscripts he's received that day or week, the editor reads the manuscript. At major publishing houses this is usually not a long-drawn-out process. Little-magazine editors are often not paid for their editorial work, have other responsibilities such as teaching, and in any case are so deluged with manuscripts they can't possibly be prompt; but at publishing houses the selection process is usually efficient. It may be, in a given house, that slush-pile readers cull out the obviously bad work, then pass on the better manuscripts to more senior people. One way or another, the better manuscripts reach a senior editor, who, as I've said, reads it fairly quickly and, in my experience, as conscientiously as he knows how. He thinks about various things as he reads, notably: Is this a book that is likely to sell or bring the house prestige? Is it the kind of book that's suitable to this particular house? (Publishers have various specializations, and the editor who pushes for a book too far outside the specialization of the house knows he's running a number of risks. In a house where final decisions are made by an editorial committee—the usual case—he may lose his fight with the other editors. In smaller houses, where one or two senior editors make the final decision, he may not only lose his fight for the book but also lose credibility with the boss or bosses. Or if he wins his fight for a book that is not within the usual range of his house, the sales force may misunderstand or fail to push the book. The salesmen for a publishing house have large districts to cover, a great many bookstore owners or managers to visit. Except in those rare cases—and they do occur—when the salespeople believe strongly in an unusual book, one that requires them to take extra time making a special presentation to the buyer, they tend to mention the unfamiliar book and, getting no reaction, hurry on. Editors, knowing this, do not often push hard for a book they believe most of the sales force will find an annoyance.) But the main thing the editor asks himself is: "Do I really *like* this book?" Experienced editors have a keen eye for what is, according to some standard (commercial or aesthetic), good. They are good readers; that is, when a novel ends disappointingly, or has lumpish spots, or will annoy readers in an unjustifiable way, they know it.

If a book is generally well written and intelligent (given its intended audience) but seems to the editor finally unsuccessful, the editor writes what he means to be (and what sometimes is) a thoughtful, helpful letter to the writer or his agent. He explains what he likes and what he doesn't like, where the book succeeds and where it fails. The writer who gets such a letter should understand that the editor is interested in his work (otherwise, of course, he'd fire off a printed rejection slip, or no comment at all). If the writer agrees with the editor's comments (after a suitable period of calming down, getting rid of his anger or depression), he is wise to revise his book and submit it again to the editor who signed the letter. If the writer doesn't agree, he should of course try elsewhere. The editor reads the resubmitted book and either decides to take it or sends further (or new) objections. Again, if the writer comes to feel that the editor is right, he should again revise and again resubmit. It is probably true that his odds are going down— he can gauge this by the tone of the second rejection letter. Sometimes when an editor rejects a book more than once, each time with a carefully reasoned letter, he's rejecting the book for reasons he's not fully conscious of. Nonetheless, as long as the editor's comments seem right to the writer, on due reflection, his best course is to keep revising. He may never convince this particular editor, but the writer is wise to take good advice wherever he can find it: as long as the editor is willing to keep commenting, he's of use. Writers often feel—especially writers prone to dejection—that repeated rejections accompanied by reasoned letters mean that in the end there's no hope. This is simply not true. All editors want to publish (within the boundaries of their profit requirements) excellent books, and they are willing to help the promising writer achieve those standards.

None of this is to say that the writer should make changes that he does not believe in. But he should make sure he has understood the objections. It is sometimes supposed that editors suggest changes in a good writer's book to make the book more commercial. In my experience this isn't true, and a recent questionnaire asking successful writers their opinion on the matter showed that their experiences are mostly like my own. If you write a thriller, the editor will try to make it the best possible thriller. If you write a serious work of art, he will try to make it what it is meant to be, and not make you turn it into a thriller or a Harlequin romance. If you have ever worked as an editor or a sub-subeditor of a magazine, you know that all second-rate stories submitted tend to sound alike. Certain devices that the ordinary writer could not guess to be old hat—such as a compulsive use of the third-person-limited point of view, or the habit of starting every story with the weather ("It was unseasonably cool that morning," or "The sun hung directly overhead")—prove so commonplace that one feels compelled to avoid them in one's own fiction. Editors' experience makes them sensitive to these clichés, and one is wise to listen as objectively as possible. If it seems to the writer that the editor's comments on his novel are wrong, my advice is that he write back and defend himself. If the writer's defense is foolish or petty (if it reveals a personality much worse than the editor guessed from the novel), the editor is likely to drop the novelist. Who needs a crank pen pal? But if the writer is correct and states his case intelligently, the editor is likely to pay attention.

The first editor to look with a certain amount of interest at my work was Bob Gottlieb at Knopf. I went unpublished for a long time, as I've already mentioned, so I had a number of novels waiting for someone to notice them. When I sent *Grendel* to Gottlieb he was puzzled by it and wrote a letter full of reserved admiration and doubts. Being young and foolish, I assumed he was giving me the brush-off, so I sent the book elsewhere, to no avail. Later I sent him *The Sunlight Dialogues*, which he suggested that I cut by a third. I responded with a postcard: "Which third?" (He didn't answer.) A few months thereafter, the late David Segal, then at New American Library, read my work; he was partly influenced by William Gass, who had recommended me (and was then publishing, under Segal's editorship, *Omensetter's Luck*), and partly influenced by my arrival at his office in a black leather motorcycle jacket, carrying a shopping bag full of manuscripts—*The Resurrection*, *The Wreckage of Agathon*, and *Grendel*. (The rest of the story is embarrassing but I'll tell it anyway.) I placed on Segal's desk the three novels I'd biked into town with and said, "Mr. Segal, I'd like you to read these novels," and then, after a pause, "Now." David Segal was a kind man, though not really one to be bullied. He began to read, went through two or three pages, then said, "Mr. Gardner, I can't read your fiction while you're watching." So I left. When he arrived at his office the next morning at ten he told me he was taking all three novels. He published one at New American Library, then moved to Harper and published one there, then moved to Knopf, where he was in the process of publishing *Grendel* and *The Sunlight Dialogues*, which he'd subsequently accepted, when, to this world's great loss, he died.

David Segal's style was probably unusual in the publishing world. He accepted my books on the basis of the merit he saw in them and only then told me what he thought wrong. I have a long letter from him about *The Sunlight Dialogues* in which he tells me where the symbolism has gone amiss, where the language is excessive, and so on. (Though he did not say it, one implication of his letter was that I should cut the book by a third.) Because he approached me as he did, treated me as a serious novelist and attacked the work on its own grounds, I found it easy to listen. Later, after he died and I began to work with Bob Gottlieb, I came to understand that they both knew the same things; the difference was one of style. Bob Gottlieb hints at what's wrong, sometimes stating the problem meta-phorically. (The novelist Harry Crews once wrote a scathing *Esquire* piece mocking Bob Gottlieb for saying Crews should let his novel "breathe." Some who have read Crews's work would say Gottlieb was right.) Other editors work in other ways. Some write long, thorough letters after the first reading; some prefer to talk informally with the writer; some make almost no comment but take the book as it stands (these last are rare). All of them, though they may at times be off the mark, are serious, careful people.

Once the novel is accepted, the editor goes through the manuscript again and marks it up, suggesting cuts, improvements, expansions, reworkings. I have found that some editors edit with a light hand, while others question almost every line. Usually I'm happy with either kind of editing. On rare occasions one hits a stubborn, wrongheaded editor, and then one is in trouble. The editor of one of my novels (not Gottlieb or Segal) insisted on changing my punctuation, forcing it to conform to some rule he learned at Yale and denying absolutely the notion that punctuation can be an art. One of the characters in the novel was unable to remember people's names and used any name that came into his head. The editor fixed all this. When I howled, he said nothing, and he refused to change anything back. I don't know what the writer is supposed to do in a case like this—probably withdraw the manuscript. Certainly don't go to that editor again. That kind of experience is rare, or at least it has been rare for me. On the whole, editors are flexible and respect the author's wishes.

Now the manuscript goes through copy editing. The writer's literary editor turns the book over to another kind of editor, a maniac for details, who goes through the book checking spelling, accuracy of statement, consistency of style, and so on, and giving any necessary instructions to the typesetter. When the job is finished, the copy editor sends the marked-up manuscript back to the writer with pink slips of paper attached, giving the copy editor's queries. The writer takes or rejects each of the editor's corrections, and the manuscript goes to the typesetter. After a short while (a few weeks, in my experience), the writer gets the galleys—long pages from the typesetter, marked up by the proofreader for typographical errors. The writer rechecks what the copy editor has checked, notes mistakes, sends the galleys back, and waits for the book. Sometimes writers are still rewriting at the galley stage. Changes at this point cost money, and the writer who suddenly has a major new vision of his novel is sure to make his publisher unhappy. If the book is high art, or if it's one the publisher is sure will make a fortune, galley changes may not be a matter for concern. But ordinarily one should alter galleys sparingly.

After the book arrives in the writer's mailbox, and after it has finally reached the bookstores, the writer wrings his hands over a new problem: promotion. Writers are almost never satisfied with the promotion job their publishers do. There's nothing wrong with complaining and exerting any pressure one can to get more, bigger, and better ads, nothing wrong with getting the publicity department to try to arrange TV interviews and so on; but the writer should understand that the game is now pretty much out of his hands. Publishers generally know what kinds of books will benefit from aggressive promotion and what kinds of books, no matter how hard you push them, won't take off. Like other businesspeople, publishers invest where they expect their investment to pay. The masterful promotion job done on John Irving's *The World According to Garp* (jackets in various colors; large ads in major papers and magazines; for all I know, T-shirts and bumper stickers) obviously paid off; but the same campaign used on another novel, even an earlier novel by John Irving, might have been a waste of time and money. *Garp* is one of those novels that can be viewed either as a serious work of art or as a book for a mass audience, containing, as it does, the requisite sex, strange violence, and concern with great questions of the moment (e.g., feminism). If the book had not in fact had the kind of appeal its promoters claimed for it, the publisher's credibility would have dropped, readers and bookstore managers would have been angry, and John Irving would have done less well on his next novel. Since promotion departments are usually efficient, it is probably not very beneficial to yell and scream at them, or to insist on the publisher's writing into the contract the amount of money guaranteed for promotion. (If he gives the writer more money for promotion, he'll take it away elsewhere, for instance lopping off part of the advance. And if the publisher is right about how much promotion to use and where it will become a matter of diminishing returns, the writer who demands more promotion and accepts a lower advance to get it is robbing himself.) As for TV interviews and the like— things that cost the publisher nothing—the writer can choose to do as many as he pleases or can get. (He may get none, of course.) His publisher's promotion department can try to arrange, in various cities, book-and-author luncheons, or get the writer onto all-night radio talk shows. If the writer proves extraordinarily charming, such strategies may do wonders.

So much for the writer's relationship with his publisher. Let me turn to the writer's need for the support of those around him. However tough the peasant in his heart, every writer needs people who believe in him, give him a shoulder to cry on, and value what he values. If the writer doesn't get it, he might try changing friends. Above all, I think, it pays to seek out other writers—taking a writing class, going to readings if there are any he can get to, attending a summer writers' conference.

Summer conferences sometimes offer beginning writers a good chance to meet editors and agents, get their fiction evaluated by famous older writers and fast-rising younger writers, and meet other serious beginners suffering some of the same troubles they have, aesthetic, psychological, and social. The writing community encountered at such a conference does not end, for many people, when the conference ends. It is common for conferees to write to one another through the year, meet once or twice in some convenient city, and look for help, long after the conference, from conference instructors. One hears the complaint that conferences lead to a kind of writer incest: we find one instructor praising another's book on the book jacket, or reviewing it in *The New York Times*, and so forth. What is really involved is almost always a senior conference instructor giving help to the book of a younger instructor or a conference student. Friendships (not to mention love affairs) can be intense at conferences. No doubt this has to do with the frenetic atmosphere bred by the brevity of the conference—the student's hunger to learn everything he can, the teacher's responsiveness to it, and the occasional escapes into pressure-relieving revels. From every point of view, except in the instance of the bad writer who goes away feeling ignored by his teachers and fellow students—that is, goes off psychologically less strong than when he came—writers' conferences are wonderful ego boosters for young writers.

Professionally, the young novelist's most valuable support is his agent. Poets and writers of short stories don't need an agent as badly and probably can't get one anyway: there's ordinarily not enough money in poetry and short stories to make the agent's expenditure of time worthwhile. If the short story writer prints a few stories in high-paying magazines like *The New Yorker*, he may be able to attract an agent, but he obviously doesn't need one. He can sell his own stories, and with a magazine one can't use an agent to jack up the price. But for a young novelist, an agent is all but indispensable, even if, thanks to powerful friends or freaky good luck, he's able to sell his novel on his own. A good agent knows what the going rates are, knows editors personally and can accurately gauge how hard a given one can be pushed. The innocent writer can be eaten alive by a publisher's contract. It's common for publishers to try to take a share of movie rights, foreign rights, anything they can grab. Only an experienced agent knows when to make a canceling sweep of the pen.

Agents are also of value, of course, in getting the writer's work sold. Agents may not work as hard at selling as the writer would do himself. They have a stable of writers to work with, and no personal urgency; they know from experience that the good fiction that comes into their office will probably sooner or later be bought. Ordinarily they don't mind if the writer tries to sell things on his own (they get their ten percent anyway) and if the writer has the proper temperament he may want to do some of the selling, keeping the agent in reserve for contract negotiations. On the other hand, an agent can take pressure off a writer. Whereas after a certain number of rejections the writer is likely to give up on a story or novel, the agency goes on, impartial as a pulsar, sending out the fiction, getting it back, sending it out again. (Agents usually know better than writers do when to give up.) And whereas the writer is likely to be humbled or enraged by letters of rejection, with all their perhaps foolish advice about how to fix the book, agents tend to be unimpressed. At the writer's instruction, the agent will tell him nothing of what editors advise—except if some editor comes up with a suggestion that seems to the agent important. While writers may feel self-doubt—after twenty published books, I still often ask myself if I'm really a writer —and while editors have grievous responsibilities, the agent deals in simple yeses and noes, more dollars or less dollars. As long as he has reason to trust his own judgment (from repeatedly selling his clients' books), he expects editors to pay attention to his judgment, and the force of his conviction helps make it happen. An agent, in short, is a good person to have on your side.

Getting a good agent can be almost as hard as getting a publisher. One should avoid dealing with an agent who charges a reading fee. It's usually against the policy of the literary agents' associations and suggests that the agent may be in the business of fleecing amateur writers. (If one takes in enough reading fees, one never needs to sell a book.) For information on reliable agents, or to contact an agent, write to ILAA (Independent Literary Agents Association), Box 5257, FDR Station, New York, N.Y. 10150. This organization includes younger agents, the kind most likely to take on a new writer, if the writer does not have strong recommendations from someone famous. Or write Society of Authors' Representatives, P.O. Box 650, Old Chelsea Station, New York, N.Y. 10113. Tell the agency head in brief, clear terms what kind of writer you are and what kind of book you want to sell. (If the agency doesn't answer your letter, fine; that's one agency you don't want.) You need to write a smart letter, of course. If the letter contains bad writing (tiresome chattiness, jargon, crabbed syntax), the agent will know he doesn't want you. With agents as with anybody else, name dropping helps. If you've studied with famous writers, mention them. If you've published stories or won prizes, mention that.

In the normal course of things, one or more agencies will write back asking to see your work. Send it. (Neatness counts. Nobody, including agents, wants to labor through a manuscript that's barely legible.) If every agency in the end turns you down, you will know you're either not good enough or too good. If you're too good, keep writing, keep your contacts with the writing community available to you, and eventually your day will come.

One last word on this subject. Rejection by an agent means more, usually, than rejection by an editor. Agents seldom explain in detail why they've rejected a writer, but they have, invariably, only one reason: they do not think they can sell the writer's work. They may think it's wonderful, they may think it's awful; but they don't think they can peddle it. The only agent you want is the one who wants you. As I've said, it may help if a famous writer introduces you—certainly the young writer should tug the coattails of every famous writer he can get near without making him angry—but in the end, agents trust no one but themselves. That's why they prosper, and why their clients prosper.

While one is learning one's craft, then practicing it and hunting for an agent, then waiting for mail with the agent's return address, one must somehow make a living. Every writer hopes, like a medieval Christian, that after his period of honorable suffering, bliss will follow as a reward. So the writer takes some miserable part-time job, or lives off his parents or spouse, and writes and prays and waits. One day, the writer tells himself, the big break will come, and his money troubles will be over.

It's not true. At any rate, it's not true for the serious writer. Maybe one in a thousand serious novelists ever become self-supporting by means of their art. The writer, for all his childishness, needs to face this fact and deal with it.

Through the centuries writers have found various tricks for survival. Ancient poets begged or attached themselves to kings. There are still, here and there in the world, decent rich people who will give financial help to the promising writer, knowing they will probably never get paid back. The usual means by which the rich give help to the noble poor is through foundations—the Guggenheim, for instance. Or the writer may seek public support, from the National Endowment for the Arts or the arts councils in the various states. The extremely good writer has a chance with such organizations, especially if he knows well-known writers who can testify to his worth. But there is inevitably a certain amount of crookedness in foundations and grant programs. Somebody has to judge the writer's merit, and judges have friends whose work friendship causes to shine more brightly than it otherwise might. The writer without friends may be at a disadvantage. Or the judges on foundation boards may have some particular kind of fiction they like, so that even if they recognize an applicant as out-standing, they give their money to someone else. If the young writer can get some rich individual to back him, he should swallow his pride and do it. For organizations that can help the young novelist, locate good teachers, get advice on fellowships, and so on, write or phone Poets & Writers, 201 West 54th Street, New York, N.Y. 10019 (phone [212] 757-1766). The magazine published by Poets & Writers, *Coda* (annual sub-scription rate, $10), has complete, up-to-date information on contests, fellowships, and money available to writers through arts councils and foundations.

More likely, the writer will have to find a job. Almost all full-time jobs are hard on writing, even office work where one has practically nothing to do. I myself cannot write with peo-ple around me—I need solitude both for concentration and for the freedom to go through without embarrassment the kind of gesturing, wincing, and mumbling I often need to get a scene right. Also, I cannot work on a novel if I do not have long time blocks for writing—fifteen hours straight is for me ideal. Try-ing to nickel and dime your way through a five-hundred-page novel can drive you crazy. Some writers, in hopes of solving such problems, take work as fire watchers and sit alone in high lookout posts, occasionally glancing at the horizon. Theoreti-cally that ought to be an ideal situation, but in practice it's a pain, mainly because the CB never quits. Jobs as night watch-man or night hotel clerk are not much better, and trying to earn a living by teaching high school is much worse—nothing is more draining, even for a teacher not overburdened by a sense of responsibility. Journalism may be a better option, but it may undermine the writer's prose and sensibility.

One of the favorite jobs of writers in recent years has been college teaching. College teachers get the summer off and even in winter are likely to find more time for writing than almost anybody else except the full-time hobo. One teaches, say, three classes, each three hours a week, sees students for several hours each week (with luck, one can bunch up appointments so they all come on Tuesday or Wednesday), spends a few hours preparing classes (if one is unusually conscientious), and the rest of the time is his own. For the writer of suitable temperament, university teaching may be an excellent solution. The trouble is that there are fewer and fewer jobs. MFA and PhD programs turn out far more writers looking to teach than the market can absorb. That fact perhaps need not be utterly discouraging. The extraordinary student is still employable. His strong recommendations from professors and his fine record of publications, whether in fiction or in his chosen academic field, may pry open doors that to others seem rusted shut. And for another, a PhD in any respectable field—English literature, for instance, or even philosophy—helps to crack doors elsewhere, for instance in government, advertising, or business.

The writer who survives by teaching writing may discover, however, that his teaching hurts his art. Dealing day in and day out with beginning writers, he finds himself forced continually to think in analytical fashion about problems he would normally solve in other ways. To make his student see clearly what is wrong in his or her fiction, the writer-teacher has no choice but to work in a fully conscious, intellectual way. Every writer at some point must go through an analytical period, but in time he must get his own characteristic solutions into his blood, so that when confronted by a problem in a novel he's writing he does not consult his literary background. He *feels* his way to the solution; rather than drawing back from the fictional dream to look at what he's doing, he solves the problem by plunging deeper into the dream. For the writing teacher, the habit of intellectual analysis may become crippling.

He may encounter other problems. As the teacher sees more and more talented students, he may consciously or unconsciously begin to set himself increasingly difficult tasks, distancing himself from his best students' work by tour-de-force showmanship, pyrotechnics, and subtlety beyond his students' means. He becomes precious, arty, academic. And because it is necessary for a teacher to awaken his students to the various possibilities of contemporary fiction, so they don't all write alike, as if Donald Barthelme were the only writer who ever lived (or Hemingway or Salinger or whoever is most influential in a given class), the teacher may become unduly influenced by other writers of his time, or unduly concerned with theory. No doubt, for some teachers of writing this never happens; but one hears it as a common complaint.

However he goes about it, what the writer must do, assuming he's not independently wealthy, is to find some kind of congenial work that will not eat up all his energy and time. For example, delivering rural route mail is terrific (one can get off by noon). And for the sake of his art he must learn to live within the limits his odd existence sets. If the writer wants everything he sees on TV, he'd better quit writing and get serious about money or else give away his TV to the poor in spirit.

The most obvious escape from the debilitating effects of one's competitive, ware-hawking culture is to move out of it —go to Mexico or Portugal or Crete. This is exactly what many writers do, but the cost of living cheaply may be greater than one at first imagined. Also, by leaving one's culture one may lose one's material. Expatriation may be all right for the fabulist, the nonrealistic writer. But again and again through history, writers have found that in leaving the people they know best—the specific kind of culture they come from—they leave the wellspring of their art. So the English novelist Arnold Bennett, when he left his country origins for London's brighter lights, found himself a weakened writer. Such examples might be multiplied. Some writers thrive on transplanting, of course. Leslie Fiedler claims that Missoula, Montana, was the very best place for him to live for twenty years because all the differences between Missoula and New York stimulated his imagination; also, the nights were long and there wasn't much for him to do except write. The shock of an unfamiliar culture was equally beneficial to Malcolm Lowry, Graham Greene, and Henry James, not to mention Dante. But the risk is there; one should be ready for it. Many writers feel they suffer from being set down in a region—usually because of a teaching job —so different from their appropriate milieu (New Englanders in Southern California, Texans in Cleveland) that they feel diminished, unreal to themselves. A special case of this general problem is the transplanting of the lower-class writer to some setting, especially the university, where gentrification undermines his language and values or otherwise denatures his experience of the world.

The best way a writer can find to keep himself going is to live off his (or her) spouse. The trouble is that, psychologically at least, it's hard. Even if one's spouse is rich, it's hard. Our culture teaches none of its false lessons more carefully than it teaches that one should never be dependent. Hence the novice or still unsuccessful writer, who has enough trouble believing in himself, has the added burden of shame. That's one reason writers, like other artists, have so often chosen to live off people that, at some conscious or unconscious level, they need not respect—generous prostitutes, say. It's hard to be a good writer and a guilty person; a lack of self-respect creeps into one's prose. Yet for all that may be said against it, living off one's spouse or lover is an excellent survival tactic. For some businessmen, nothing gives more satisfaction than a wife or lover's artistic achievement; and some women, in a way that only a cynic would call morbid, derive pride and satisfaction from enabling an artist husband or lover to do his work. I do not mean that the writer should seek out someone on whom he can feed like a vampire. But if a writer finds himself living, for honest reasons, with someone glad to support his art, he or she should make every effort to shake off the conventional morality and accept God's bounty, doing everything in his power to make the lover's generosity worthwhile.

With luck, the writer may eventually make money. A novel may be taken by the movies, or by the Book-of-the-Month Club, or may for some reason win the hearts of the young. But one ought not to count on it. Most novelists, including very good ones, never make a living from their art. The average income of professional writers is, I think, something like five or six thousand dollars a year. A young novelist can hardly help hoping that someday he will be published and will find himself free of guilt and debt, but—statistically, at least—shattered expectations are part of the game. One study showed that about seventy percent of those who published a first novel in a given year never went on to publish another. If one is unwilling to write like a true artist, mainly because one needs to, one might do well to put one's energies somewhere else.

IV.

FAITH

In my experience, the single question most often asked during question-and-answer periods in university auditoriums and classrooms is: "Do you write with a pen, a typewriter, or what?" I suspect the question is more important than it seems on the surface. It brings up magical considerations—the kinds of things compulsive gamblers are said to worry about: When one plays roulette, should one wear a hat or not, and if one should, should one cock it to the left or to the right? What color hat is luckiest? The question about writing equipment also implies questions about that ancient daemon Writer's Block, about vision and revision, and, at its deepest level, asks whether or not there is really, for the young writer, any hope.

1

As every writer knows—both the experienced and the inexperienced—there is something mysterious about the writer's ability, on any given day, to write. When the juices are flowing, or the writer is "hot," an invisible wall seems to fall away, and the writer moves easily and surely from one kind of reality into another. In his noninspired state, the writer feels all the world to be mechanical, made up of numbered separate parts: he does not see wholes but particulars, not spirit but matter; or to put it another way, in this state the writer keeps looking at the words he's written on the page and seeing only words on a page, not the living dream they're meant to trigger. In the writing state—the state of inspiration—the fictive dream springs up fully alive: the writer forgets the words he has written on the page and sees, instead, his characters moving around their rooms, hunting through cupboards, glancing irritably through their mail, setting mousetraps, loading pistols. The dream is as alive and compelling as one's dreams at night, and when the writer writes down on paper what he has imagined, the words, however inadequate, do not distract his mind from the fictive dream but provide him with a fix on it, so that when the dream flags he can reread what he's written and find the dream starting up again. *This and nothing else is the desperately sought and tragically fragile writer's process: in his imagination, he sees made-up people doing things—sees them clearly—and in the act of wondering what they will do next he sees what they will do next, and all this he writes down in the best, most accurate words he can find, understanding even as he writes that he may have to find better words later, and that a change in the words may mean a sharpening or deepening of the vision, the fictive dream or vision becoming more and more lucid, until reality, by comparison, seems cold, tedious, and dead.* This is the process he must learn to set off at will and to guard against hostile mental forces.

Every writer has experienced at least moments of this strange, magical state. Reading student fiction one can spot at once where the power turns on and where it turns off, where the writer wrote from "inspiration," or deep, flowing vision, and where he had to struggle along on mere intellect. One can write whole novels without once tapping the mysterious center of things, the secret room where dreams prowl. One can easily make up characters, plot, setting, and then fill in the book like a paint-by-numbers picture. But most stories and novels have at least moments of the real thing, some exactly right gesture or startlingly apt metaphor, some brief passage describing wallpaper or the movement of a cat, a passage that some-how shines or throbs as nothing around it does, some fictional moment that, as we say, "comes alive." It is this experience of seeing something one has written come alive—literally, not metaphorically, a character or scene daemonically entering the world by its own strange power, so that the writer feels not the creator but only the instrument, or conjurer, the priest who stumbled onto the magic spell—it is this experience of tapping some magic source that makes the writer an addict, willing to give up almost anything for his art, and makes him, if he fails, such a miserable human being.

The poison or miraculous ointment—it can be either one or both—comes at first in small doses. The usual experience of young writers is that during the process of writing the first draft they feel that all they write is alive, full of interest, but then when they look at the writing the next day they find most of it dull and lifeless. Then comes one small moment qualita-tively different from the rest: one small dose of the real thing. The more numerous those moments, the more powerful the resulting addiction. The magic moment, notice, has nothing to do with *theme* or, in the usual sense, *symbolism*. It has nothing to do, in fact, with the normal subject matter of literature courses. It is simply a psychological hot spot, a pulsation on an otherwise dead planet, a "real toad in an imaginary garden." These queer moments, sometimes thrilling, sometimes just strange, moments setting off an altered state, a brief sense of escape from ordinary time and space—moments no doubt sim-ilar to those sought by religious mystics, or those experienced by people near death—are the soul of art, the reason people pursue it. And young writers sufficiently worried about achieving this state to know when they've done it and feel dissatisfied when they haven't are already on the way to calling it up at will, though they may never come to understand how they do it. The more often one finds the magic key, whatever it is, the more easily the soul's groping fingers come to land on it. In magic as in other things, success brings success.

But it is not all magic. Once one knows by experience the "feel" of the state one is after, there are things one can do to encourage its onset. (Some writers, with practice, become able to drop into the creative state at any moment; others have difficulty all their lives.) Every writer must figure out for himself, if he can, how he personally works best.

Let us go back to the matter of the pen, pencil, or typewriter. There is of course no right answer to the question: "Should one write with a pen or a typewriter or what?" nor is the question worth answering except insofar as it reveals something about the creative process. Think for a moment about the very young writer, the writer of high-school or early college age. Not yet a good typist, he sits staring at the paper in his typewriter, distracted by the look of the type on the page, distracted by the fact that the paper's not quite centered, distracted by the unmanageability of the keys and, if the typewriter's electric, the impatient, henpecking hum. The writer knows that if he can ever get good at typing, writing on a typewriter will be faster, but in the meantime he seems unable to write at all. At last he tears the paper out of the typewriter, crumples it in his fist, and throws it in the wastebasket, then starts over with a pen. He begins to get into the scene he means to write—he begins to see people moving around as they're supposed to do, getting themselves into trouble as his idea for the story requires—and then, as the writer glances over what he's written, trying to get a "run" on the place where he has gotten stuck, he notices that the ink is smudged. He tries to ignore it, throwing himself back into the fictive dream, but that smudge keeps nagging. At last he copies over what he's written onto clean paper, then once more reads from the top, trying to throw himself into the dream so that when he comes to the point where his imagination failed, the dream will keep going of its own momentum, he'll "see" what the characters must do next.

The trouble, he discovers, is that handwriting, like speech, is full of gestures. We don't normally think about that fact, unless we're amateur analysts of handwriting. Nevertheless it's the case: just as when we're speaking we give conscious or unconscious signals of our feelings, accidentally curling the lip or glancing away evasively, so, too, our writing gives off second-by-second signals of our happiness or uncertainty or weariness or secret dishonesty and bluff. We do not necessarily know all this as we look over what we've written, but we find ourselves noticing the penmanship; it begins to stand like a stone wall between us and the fictive dream. We do not see a dog rummaging through garbage cans but, instead, individual words: A   dog   was.

I don't know whether any very young writer besides myself ever really suffered the woes I've been assigning him (perhaps not, except for the part about the typewriter: I had a terrible time learning to write on one, and I know many writers who've never managed it); but what I'm saying about the distracting quality of mechanics is meant to illuminate by analogy a darker problem, the distracting quality of words. Even for the expert writer, and much more noticeably for the relative beginner, language is, like an unfamiliar typewriter, a complicated, overawing, clumsy, and impatiently nagging machine. You stare at the fictive dream, you try to get it down in words, and you find language resisting you. You want to say: "She intended to tell him so-and-so"; you decide she should *go* to him and tell him, so you shift to: "She intended on going to him and . . ." but one can't say "intended on"; and you're pulled out of the dream. It's a trifle, this recalcitrance of language (especially in the example I've given, since the problem is too easily solved), but the nuisance is real. Most of the young novelists I've worked with had problems initially with idiomatic English. Which is correct for an authorial, non-dialectal voice: "She thought that she should tell him" or "She thought she should tell him"? Is it correct to say: "She'd anticipated that he would be angry"? (Should one say: "She'd anticipated his anger"?) Most writers for some reason come from the middle or lower middle class, at least in America, and very few lack quirks of speech that betray their origins; such oddities as, for instance, the New York City middle-class substitution of "bring" for "take," or "came" for "went," or the idiom "stood on line" for, as the rest of the country says, "stood in line." As long as one clings to the safest approaches (first-person narration, or third-person-limited), linguistic quirks may be texturally enriching; but as soon as the writer tries something more august—omniscient narration, or first-person narration by Bismarck or the Virgin Mary—the quirks make the writer look ignorant. Fiction in dialect has its interest, and as writers like Faulkner prove, it is possible to write large, deep-breathing fictions without unlearning one's dialect. (Instead of the usual king's English spoken by most omniscient authors, Faulkner uses a distinct Southern voice, one that does not distinguish between "infer" and "imply.") But whatever the beauties of dialect, few writers possessed of the ambition that characterizes the novelist want to be barred forever from the high tone of a Mann or Proust or Melville. So there stands language, difficult and intimidating, throwing roadblocks in the way of the writer's attempt to get the fictive dream onto the page.

And as smudges on the page written in ink, or gestural signs in the writer's handwriting, distract our hypothetical young writer from what it is he is trying to say, so blurs and the uncontrolled secondary meanings of words distract and impede. If a character in a story tells us that some thoroughly incompetent, feeble king now being carried to his grave "was born dead," meaning that the king was never really alive at all, the word "born" puns on "borne" (carried), and—unless we understand that the speaker means to be witty—we are distracted. Every writer can give examples from his own experience of how language slips and slides, turning serious moments cheap, making the writer look silly ("a two-headed lady's snake ring"), obfuscating meaning, or slyly turning the writer into a hypocrite or pretentious fool. So the writer copies down his fictive dream, then looks at the words he chose with such care and blushes like one willfully misunderstood, betrayed. Or the words say exactly what he meant, but so carefully that they make him seem prissy and self-conscious.

The trouble is not that the writer can't start up the fictive dream in his mind. If that were the trouble he wouldn't have written any words at all. The trouble is that having started up the dream and written some of it down, he's become suddenly self-conscious, self-doubting. The dreaming part is angel-like: it is the writer's eternal, childlike spirit, the daydreaming being who exists (or seems to) outside time. But the part of the writer that handles the mechanics, typing or writing with pencil or pen, choosing one word instead of another, is human, fallible, vulnerable to anxiety and shame. Making mistake after mistake, the beast in the writer begins to sweat and grind its teeth, longing to be raised up once more by the redeeming angel within—but miserably unworthy, shy in the presence of the holy, and afraid of heights.

So far, all I've said treats language as a recalcitrant and passive medium, the indifferent clay to be shaped into a figure, or the lead on which the image is to be stamped. Actually, language plays a far more active role in the creative process. No doubt it is sometimes true that the writer has an intuition of what it is he wants to say and, after a struggle, finds just the right words to express the meaning he knew was there waiting to be expressed. Just as often—probably more often—language actively drives the writer to meanings he had no idea he would come to. This process is easier to show in poetry than in prose, though I'll try to show it in both. Let me start with a poem of my own, not because I claim skill as a poet but because it seems to me an adequate poem of its kind and, more important, I know exactly the process by which it took the shape it has.

> Lovely, spooky, dark blue Gentian,
> Inner walls like speckled snakeskin,
> Trumpet shaped, fit for a small
> Angel's grimly puckered lips
> Set on the Last Day to call
> Ants and bees to Apocalypse,
> What sins too minute to mention
> Wouldst thou bring to man's attention,
> Lovely, spooky, dark blue Gentian?

I will not dwell on my various false starts in trying to get this poem down but will simply explain the choices I finally made. Having a heavy teaching load and numerous nonfictional writing responsibilities (including this book), and having therefore no time to write fiction, I decided to write a poem, a flower poem since I thought I might someday publish a book of children's flower poems to match an earlier children's book of mine on animals. I found a picture of the dark blue gentian and looked at it to see what one might say. The main things I could think of to say, at least in the light of this particular photograph, were that the flower was pretty and that it looked ominous, the luminous dark blue of nightmare. My mind stumbled around in search of a suitably gloomy rhythm and possible words to fit with it and so came up with the first line. Obviously the gloom is slightly tongue-in-cheek (flowers usually aren't good candidates for the truly scary), hence the word choice "lovely," a word one can never take quite as seriously as it would like to be taken, and "spooky," a kid's word that, in a thudding trochaic rhythm, gets drawn out a little, inflated as it would be in a ghost story told orally to kids at camp. It's this same tongue-in-cheek seriousness that made me decide to capitalize "Gentian," giving it a faintly old-timey, Romantic quality (the Romantics were nothing if not naively earnest, as some of them, like Blake, at times understood).

Once the first line was down, I looked back at the picture for a clue to the second line (What else can I say?), knowing this line could rhyme or not, though rhythmic possibilities were limited slightly (the line must satisfy the ear as consonant with the line already in existence); and I saw immediately the odd fact reported in the second line, that the throat of the flower has a speckled, waxy sheen like snakeskin—and noticed in the same instant that "snakeskin" rhymes with "gentian," or anyway comes close enough for government work. After a little muddling in search of solemn trochees meaning "throat," I came upon "inner walls" and the line fell into place. Looking back at the picture for what more I might say, I noticed the most obvious thing about the flower, that it's trumpet-shaped, and wrote that down. Where to go from there? Perhaps some-one suitably ominous (in keeping with the choices I'd made so far) might be imagined as playing the trumpet. (If I'd said "bell shaped," another legitimate trochee, the idea of a small instru-mentalist would probably not have come up.) My childhood interest in—and slight uneasiness about—religion came to my rescue, as it so often does in my writing, and I thought of the Doomsday angel. Since after many years of practice I've learned—so that I no longer have to stop and think about it—that every character who enters a fiction needs vivid rendering, I chose words that would make my angel individual ("grimly puckered lips"; this angel of doom is personally *involved* in his work, no mere functionary); and now the natural requirements of drama raised the next question: If the angel is so concerned, whom or what is he behaving so sternly toward—elves? small children? The answer simply came to me; that is, I saw it in the fictive dream: bugs of some kind (natural inhabitants of the garden's small world, and enemies of flowers). I chose ants and bees partly because those creatures have, for me, a certain inherent nastiness, and partly because the word "ants" has a hard, nasty sound, as does "bees," to a lesser extent, but the effect is nonetheless there, especially if you push the z sound. I now had a mock-solemn set of lines in an old, easily recogniz-able literary tradition, the Moralizing Verse. What solemn lesson could I squeeze out of my setup? It occurred to me that the question was absurd, that maybe the whole Moralizing Verse tradition was at least just a little absurd, a way of bullying the young, so that what was needed was a comically senten-tious close—chiming rhymes, the mock formality and churchi-ness of "Wouldst thou bring," and the preacherly rhetoric of the last line's echoing of the poem's first line—a device that especially pleased me because, in the orthodox view, Dooms-day brings Christian history full circle.

Lest my main point here be lost in my argument's details, let me reiterate it: words not only serve but help to shape the fictive vision. I had no inkling, when I started the poem, that I would write about a tiny angel or Doomsday as it applies to ants and bees, or, ultimately, the way grownups bully children with fables.

Poems "write themselves" more visibly than short stories or novels do, since it's a little difficult, though by no means impossible, to write a short story without some idea of the plot, and extremely difficult to write a novel without a carefully constructed, though tentative, plan. But the process I've been describing in relation to poetry does operate, and not just occasionally, in one's writing of a novel. The following passage occurs near the end of one of my novels, *October Light*.

> The two ancient creatures stared at one another, both of them standing more or less upright—the bear considerably more up-right than the man—the old man unable to do a thing to defend himself, too weak-kneed to try running or even jump for the gun, his heart so hammering at the root of his throat that he could not even make a sound. He often thought, going over it later, how that Britisher must have felt when he looked up at the top of the wall by the cliff, there at Fort Ticonderoga, and beheld that stone man Ethan Allen towering against the stars and gray dawn, filling the sky with his obscenities. He, the Britisher, had been an ordinary man, as James Page, here among his hives, was only an ordinary man. Ethan Allen had been put upon the earth, like

Hercules, to show an impression of things beyond it. So it was with this enormous old bear that stood sniffing at the wind and studying him, uncertain what heaven had in mind. A full minute passed, and still the bear stood considering, as if baffled by where the old man had come from and what his purpose could be, creeping up on him. Then at last the bear went down on all fours again, turned to where the containers for the honeycombs sat, and began—as if he had all day and had forgotten James' existence—to eat. James made for the gun and, despite the weakness of his legs, reached it. The bear turned, a low growl coming from low in his throat, then went back calmly to his business. James with wildly trembling hands raised the gun to his shoulder and aimed it at the back of the bear's head. What happened then he could not clearly remember afterward. As he was about to pull the trigger, something jerked the gun straight up—possibly, of course, his own arm. He fired at the sky, as if warning a burglar. The bear jumped three feet into the air and began shaking exactly as the old man was doing, snatched up an armload of honeycombs, and began to back off.

My analysis of the process behind this passage must of necessity be sketchy and brief. Given my tortuous way of working, revising and revising, such a passage, short as it is, may take weeks. A couple of points of background information: Throughout the novel, old man Page has more or less unconsciously associated bears with the otherworldly—with death and the possibility of divine retribution, forces no man can match; though, short of that final conflict, he has believed, stern courage like that of his earthly hero Ethan Allen can get a man through. Most of his life, James Page believed himself such a hero, but he has recently learned that his own stubborn meanness, his misapprehension of the heroic, lies behind his son's suicide and much other grief. The point of view controlling the passage is more or less omniscient, the narration moving in and out of James Page's consciousness.

Much here is simply a recording of the fictive dream (the stooped bear and man, the gun leaning against a hive, out of reach, the old bear's puzzled gaze), but language colors and helps determine events throughout. Calling the bear and man "ancient creatures" commits me to implications different from those involved in "old man and old bear": to me, a frequent teacher of courses in the epic, "ancient" summons up ancient Greece (hence in a moment Hercules will show up, bringing with him a central idea in Homer, that the gods conceive an ideal for man, an ideal revealed in the human world by the actions of a model hero like Achilles and transmitted to future generations by the epic poet, or the muses, or memory, or "epic song"); and "creatures" in its root sense (things God created) commits me to a set of ideas faintly in conflict with the first, a vision of both the old man and the seemingly mystical bear as mortal, tragically vulnerable, ultimately a view of all human heroism as illusion (hence the popular Vermont legends of Ethan Allen, almost none of them based on fact, will enter James's consciousness, specifically the legend that, dead drunk, leading a band of Indians, Ethan Allen climbed the unscalable cliff behind Ticonderoga and took the British guard by surprise). My comments on the relative uprightness of bear and man and the man's sense of helplessness come partly from a need to make the scene vivid and specific, partly from linguistic considerations. To express the tension of the situation, especially James Page's sense of panic, I need a long, rushing sentence: the rhythm appropriate to the mood helps call up phrases (looking at the picture in my mind, what can I say that will keep the sentence pounding?). Landing on the word "upright"—knowing the old man's feeling of inferiority (physical and spiritual) to the bear as he mystically understands it—I find it shades toward "righteous," as in "upright conduct," and his helplessness takes on overtones: Who can defend himself before the final judge? His sense of impotence calls up in my mind (because I'm a medievalist) the once common image of heaven as a castle or fort, which instantly becomes Fort Ticonderoga, high in its stone cliff, and, seemingly from nowhere, comes the image of that "stone man" Ethan Allen, "towering." From close recording of the fictive dream comes "the stars and gray dawn," but from deeper in the novel comes the image that follows. Throughout the novel the vivid light of October skies has been associated with the clarity and sense of doom in the mind of a man near the end of his life's season. Old man Page has been confident of his opinions, but now, understanding his guilt, knowing himself an "ordinary man," as he says, not a hero, much less a god, his mental sky is not noble though doomed, but obscene, polluted: insofar as the sky is heroic or divine, it curses him. (Partly the image comes from history, of course. Ethan Allen, gang leader and barn burner, was not a man of careful phrases.) Now, closely watching the bear, Page becomes increasingly conscious of its creature nature. If it's a Hercules—an epic model of heaven's will—it no longer remembers what message it was to bring; and, like a mortal creature encountering the unearthly, it cannot figure out where James Page came from. In the lines that follow, the bear becomes more and more a thing of nature, such a creature as James Page is.

Let me make clear, in case it's not, that I am not suggesting, by this analysis of how the passage came into being, that these subtleties of language and idea transformation are things the shrewd critic should or could point out. Many of them are private—for instance, my rapid association of Fort Ticonderoga with "stone man"—and others, like the allusion to Hercules and Homer's idea of the epic model, are of trifling significance in terms of the novel's larger meaning. I am describing only the way in which one choice of words leads to another, the way language actively influences the progress of events. When a writer finds himself stuck, it is not only because he cannot get down the fictive dream, that is, find the right words for it, but also because he's unable to go with the linguistic flow, unable to adapt what he wants to say to what his words are suggesting that he *might* say. He's like a sculptor so intent on the image in his mind that he's unwilling to compromise with—take suggestions from—the grain of the marble.

What is the writer to do? I think the answer is, given the writer's linguistic competence: *Have faith.* First, recognize that the art of writing is immensely more difficult than the beginning writer may at first believe but in the end can be mastered by anyone willing to do the work. Good writing involves the operation of many mental processes at once, and in the beginning one must deal with those many processes one at a time, breaking down the total job into its smallest segments: getting down roughly what one is trying to say; closely analyzing the words with which one has said it to see what they are saying (or refusing to say); then thinking about (*a*) how one can make the words stop saying what one does not want them to say and (*b*) how whatever it is that the words are saying might be turned to account. Second, trust that what works for other human activities will work for the activity of writing. Learning to ride a bicycle, one must learn to steer, learn to keep one's balance, learn to push the pedals, learn to stop without falling—all separate processes requiring separate focuses of concentration. Eventually they become one process.

Where does the writer get faith? Partly, as we've seen, from community support. The steady encouragement of friends makes it easier to slip into the dream and easier to endure the drudgery of learning both to control and to listen to language. And partly from the writer's selfless love of his art—a pleasure in writing, whether by other people or by himself, that makes him forget for the moment his limitations. This is why it is often helpful, when one cannot write, to read the fiction of some favorite writer. The older writer's dream world and dance of language come bursting into the mind, and one's own capacity for dreaming and playing with words comes unstuck. One starts writing, and if the dream is strong enough, and the words cooperative enough, the first-draft mistakes distract only as a fly in the corner of the room distracts, present and annoying but not overpowering as long as the writer is deeply involved in what he's doing and convinced that the result will probably justify the labor.

Since the problem of the writer unable to concentrate on the fictive dream or respond flexibly to the impulses of language is essentially a problem of inhibition, or the mind defeating itself, all of the conventional forms of breaking inhibition can be employed to get things rolling—self-hypnosis, TM, drunkenness and smoking, or falling in love. None of them are effective in the absence of hard work and occasional successes.

Let me pause to say a word here about autohypnosis, since I myself have at times found it effective (unless I'm fooling myself, which I may well be). A simple method is to sit in a chair with comfortable arms—preferably in a fairly dark, quiet room—your arms flat on the arms of the chair, and tell yourself with firm conviction (it will prove justified) that although you will not move a muscle, your hand and forearm are going to rise. Concentrate on not moving the arm, but without resisting whatever may begin to happen to the arm, and concentrate, too, on the belief that the arm will rise. You will soon begin to feel an odd lightness in the hand, and eventually, independent of conscious volition, the arm will lift. Magic. (A hypnotically raised arm can hang suspended in air for hours without discomfort. A hand raised by conscious will tires in minutes.) In this light hypnotic trance, make to yourself positive (never negative) suggestions: Tonight I will write with ease; or, tonight I'll feel no need to smoke so much. Most people discover that autohypnosis helps. Deep hypnosis by someone else, or more sophisticated forms of autohypnosis, may bring still greater benefit. If the trick doesn't work, never mind; sitting for half an hour in a dimly lit, quiet room is good for the psyche.

2

In its extreme form, the inhibition I've been describing ends in writer's block, not so much a failure of faith as a failure of will. The writer suffering writer's block can think of good plots and characters, or anyway he can think of good starts, which is all a healthy writer needs, but he can't persuade himself that they're worth writing down or developing. It's all been done before, he tells himself. And if he does, by a supreme effort, get down a few sentences, he finds the sentences disgustingly bad. In effect, a Platonic dream of what fiction ought to be has thrown its dark shadow not only over the actual rough draft the writer has begun, poisoning the writer's eye and robbing him of the strength it takes to transform the crude rough draft into a polished work of art, but over the very possibility of creating art.

Part of the writer's problem may be the wrong kind of appreciation: when he does work he knows to be less than he's capable of, his friends praise precisely those things he knows to be weak or meretricious. The writer who cannot write because nothing he writes is good enough, by his own standards, and because no one around him seems to share his standards, is in a special sort of bind: the love of good fiction that got him started in the first place makes him scornful of the flawed writing he does (nearly all first-draft writing is flawed), and his sense that nobody cares about truly good fiction robs him of motivation. This dissatisfaction is one the unusually talented writer may be especially prone to. Driven by the imperative "Make it new," he finds nothing he's written sufficiently original. In effect, he has failed to notice that originality is normally a quality achieved by diligence, not a natural condition. A glance at Hawthorne's first novel, *Fanshaw*, or any early piece by Melville, may prove instructive.

Another writer's blockage—a more serious blockage—may

arise from an excessive need for a success not actually related to good writing: an excessive need to please admirers (that is, to be loved), or prove himself vastly superior to others (that is, to be superhuman), or justify his existence against the too obstreperous cry of some old psychological wound (that is, to be redeemed). No amount of work can solve this writer's problem, because nothing he writes satisfies the actual motive behind it.

It is probably true that in some cases writer's block is incurable; but no useful purpose is served by making a great point of this, since one can never be sure whether a particular case will respond to treatment. As with all writer problems, it is usually a good idea for the writer to get as clear a notion as possible of just what is going wrong psychologically—whether on his own or with the help of someone trained in such things —and for the writer to understand that his problem, though perhaps uncommon, is not unheard of. In a given case, one or more of the following general observations may be helpful.

The writer should remind himself of how his writing went when he first began: tortuous labor and revision and gradual improvement, and first drafts at least as bad as the one he faces now—except that in those days he saw the faults less clearly, felt more excited by the possibilities, and was tricked by the exhilaration of new love. After the initial difficulties, the period of apprenticeship, writers have a tendency to think things ought to get easier. That rarely happens. As one learns more and more technical tricks, one finds oneself taking on more and more difficult projects. Instead of getting easier, one feels the work getting harder; or at any rate that's my experience. The writer impatient with his story idea, and impatient with whatever writing he can get down, has forgotten how fiction actually gets written.

Fiction, like sculpture or painting, begins with a rough sketch. One gets down the characters and their behavior any way one can, knowing the sentences will have to be revised, knowing the characters' actions may change. It makes no difference how clumsy the sketch is—sketches are not supposed to be polished and elegant. All that matters is that, going over and over the sketch as if one had all eternity for finishing one's story, one improves now this sentence, now that, noticing what changes the new sentences urge, and in the process one gets the characters and their behavior clearer in one's head, gradually discovering deeper and deeper implications of the characters' problems and hopes. Fiction does not spring into the world full grown, like Athena. It is the process of writing and rewriting that makes a fiction original and profound. One cannot judge in advance whether or not the idea of the story is worthwhile because until one has finished writing the story one does not know for sure what the idea *is;* and one cannot judge the style of a story on the basis of a first draft, because in a first draft the style of the finished story does not yet exist.

Sometimes when one cannot stand the story or novel one is working on, it helps to write something else—a different story or novel, or essays venting one's favorite peeves, or exercises aimed at passing the time and incidentally polishing up one's craft. The best way in the world for breaking a writer's block is to write a lot. Jabbering away on paper, one gets tricked into feeling interested, all at once, in something one is saying, and behold, the magic waters are flowing again. Often it helps to work on a journal, since that allows the writer to write about those things that most interest him, yet frees him of the pressure of achievement and encourages him to develop a more natural, more personal style. Almost any diversion from the overawing main job will do. I myself have kept going for years mainly by avoiding the one serious novel I mean to write someday. There it sits, five hundred rough-draft pages of it, watching me from its shelf like a skull. Nothing else I do is significant, by comparison, at least in my own mind. I am free to scatter words as an October wind scatters leaves.

Insofar as one's block comes mainly from outside oneself—

from a lack of useful appreciation, from social pressures of one kind or another, or from harsh criticism one feels to be just— there is little one can do except change one's life. The feeling that one's friends have no taste, even if it's true, is not a healthy feeling for a writer: it fills him with arrogance and self-pity, makes him a bad friend and, as a result, makes him a person plagued by secret guilt. One approach is to find a better pack of friends; another is to strive to become a more generous person. The latter way, if the writer can bring it off, will considerably enhance his odds of becoming a good writer if he ever starts working again. Occasionally, mean-spirited people have written good books, but the odds for it are long.

The best way of all for dealing with writer's block is never to get it. Some writers never do. Theoretically there's no reason one should get it, if one understands that writing, after all, is only writing, neither something one ought to feel deeply guilty about nor something one ought to be inordinately proud of. If children can build sand castles without getting sand-castle block, and if ministers can pray over the sick without getting holiness block, the writer who enjoys his work and takes measured pride in it should never be troubled by writer's block. But alas, nothing's simple. The very qualities that make one a writer in the first place contribute to block: hypersensitivity, stubbornness, insatiability, and so on. Given the general oddity of writers, no wonder there are no sure cures.

Writer's block comes from the feeling that one is doing the wrong thing or doing the right thing badly. Fiction written for the wrong reason may fail to satisfy the motive behind it and thus may block the writer, as I've said; but there is no wrong motive for writing fiction. At least in some instances, good fiction has come from the writer's wish to be loved, his wish to take revenge, his wish to work out his psychological woes, his wish for money, and so on. No motive is too low for art; finally it's the art, not the motive, that we judge.

As for writing in the wrong way, there is almost no wrong

way to write fiction; there are only ways that, for a given writer, are more efficient or less. Some respectable writers simply pour out onto paper everything that comes into their heads, then sift, edit, rearrange, and rewrite until a story of some kind emerges; others plan carefully and stick to the plan as closely as possible, so long as the characters don't object. As a general rule, highly rational writers (like Nabokov) write most comfortably in the morning, and mainly intuitive writers write most comfortably at night. Some writers compose on small cards, one sentence to a card (a crazy way to write, it seems to me, but the method is one some undeniable masters, including Nabokov, have used); and at the opposite extreme some good writers compose on typewriters fed by huge rolls of paper, so that they never have to change a page. Some writers write all day and half the night, never pausing except to keep the body functioning, shifting according to convenience from one writing implement to another, plunging into new scenes late at night when the mind's at its dreamiest, and revising in the morning, when cold-blooded intellect is at its best. Some novelists never write anything but novels, with maybe an occasional journal about a trip; others shift restlessly from form to form—now a play, now a poem, now a short story, now an article about U.S. foreign policy.

Any approach will do. But to any young novelist troubled about how or where he ought to start, I suggest something like the following: If you have trouble with novel-writing, go back for a while to short stories. In a short story it is fairly easy to work out and thus come to understand from within the basic form of storytelling. The genre is small enough that one can grasp the fundamental concepts of fiction—how one event must cause another (however the order of events may be disguised by flashbacks or by odd narrative technique); how characters' motives must be shown dramatically, not just talked about; how setting, character, and action must interpenetrate, each supporting and infusing the others; how plot must have rhythm, so that in some way it builds in intensity toward an emotional high point; how the narrative must have design, a firm structure that gives every part value but does not vulgarly call attention to itself; how style, plot, and meaning must finally be all one.

In writing short stories—as in writing novels—take one thing at a time. (For some writers, this advice I'm giving may apply best to a first draft; for others, it may hinder the flow at first but be useful when time for revision comes.) Treat a short passage of description as a complete unit and make that one small unit as perfect as you can; then turn to the next unit— a passage of dialogue, say—and make that as perfect as you can. Move to larger units, the individual scenes that together make up the plot, and work each scene until it sparkles. Like the stand-up comic who polishes each joke to its highest possible luster (gives each joke its proper accents and timing, proper eye rolls and double takes), polish each element of the total fiction so that the story is not only good as a whole but arresting from moment to moment. As class writing exercises show, almost any writer can write fairly well if he's dealing with one small problem. It's only when the writer gets confused that he begins to sound like an amateur. Break up the larger story into its components, make sure you understand the exact function of each component (a story is like a machine with numerous gears: it should contain no gear that doesn't turn something), and after each component has been carefully set in place, step back and have a look at the whole. Then rewrite until the story flows as naturally as a river, each element so blending with the rest that no one, not even yourself two years from now, can locate the separate parts. (If writing in small units bothers you, don't do it. Some writers are more comfortable pouring out page after page and only then going back to deal with problems; and some, once a draft of the story is down on paper, can rewrite only by going back to the beginning and writing straight through to the end all over again. A terrible way of

working, clearly, but all right if it's the only way you've got.)
The real message is, write in any way that works for you: write
in a tuxedo or in the shower with a raincoat or in a cave deep
in the woods.

When you write a novel, start with a plan—a careful plot
outline, some notes to yourself on characters and settings,
particular important events, and implications of meaning. In
my experience, many young writers hate this step; they'd
rather just plunge in. That's O.K., up to a point, but sooner or
later the writer has no choice but to figure out what he's doing.
Consider doing for yourself what movie people call a "treatment," a short narrative telling the whole story, introducing all
the characters and events but skipping most of the particulars,
including dialogue. Carefully studying and revising the treatment until the story has a clear inevitability, you will find
yourself understanding the story's implications more fully
than you did with just an outline, and you will save yourself
time later. For some writers it may also prove useful to write
a detailed critical explication of the text—the text that, so far,
exists only in the writer's head. The risk here is obvious: that
the resulting novel will be "workshoppy," too neat to move or
persuade.

The last step before the actual writing may be the chapter-
by-chapter breakdown of the plot. It's here that the writer
figures out in detail what information, necessary for understanding later developments, should be worked into Chapter
One, what can be slipped into Chapter Three, and so on.
Obviously one cannot begin with sixty static pages of exposition setting up the background of the story. Writing a novel
is like running grain through a hammer mill: one has to get the
central action rolling, and then feed in the background, or
sprinkle in the larger implications, whenever and wherever
one can do it without losing a finger. For some novels, working
in the background is easy; for others, it's torture. In a novel like
Grendel, all the reader needs to know in order to follow the

action is that Grendel is a monster; comes from a cave and from a mute, mindless mother; hates his sense of himself as an animal; and feels mysteriously drawn to human beings, whom he hungrily studies, longs to be friends with, and also scorns and occasionally eats. All this can easily be shown within the first chapter.

On the other hand, working in the background for the action of a novel like *Mickelsson's Ghosts* can drive a writer to the edge of despair. The novel is about a famous philosopher who, midway through his career, suddenly finds himself (as Dante did) lost. He feels he has failed his wife and family (the wife has left him), feels he has betrayed his early promise and the values of his Wisconsin Lutheran background, has lost interest in his students and has ceased to care about philosophical questions, has lost faith and hope in democracy (and owes a large sum of money to the IRS), scorns the university where he teaches and the unsophisticated town in which it's situated, and has good reason to believe he is losing his mind. He cuts himself off from his university community by buying a huge rotting house in the country, which turns out to be haunted (if he can trust his wits), and he finds himself up to the neck in evils he never before dreamt of—middle-of-the-night dumpings of poisonous wastes, witchcraft, backwoods prostitution, a mysterious string of murders, and more. (I need not here run through the whole plot and its conclusion.)

The easy way to write such a novel is to start fairly far back in time, with the breakup of the marriage, say, and then dramatize the philosopher's troubles one by one, in order. The problem is that that is not the real beginning of the story. The real beginning is the moment the philosopher, Peter Mickelsson, chooses to opt out—buy the decaying house in Pennsylvania's Endless Mountains and turn his back on all he formerly believed in or loved. What starts the novel on its dangerous course, in other words, is not Mickelsson's bad luck (that is background information which must somehow be worked in) but Mickelsson's active choice, his quest decision. If the novel is to begin where the story begins, then by the end of Chapter One Mickelsson must at least have located the house he will buy. We must know why he is hunting a house and what the hunt means to him—must understand why he hates living in town near other professors; must know, by the firm proof of dramatized scenes, why he feels superior to those around him; why even very intelligent students annoy him, as do philosophy books and lectures; why he feels himself a failure (what his family was like, what his career was like earlier, what kind of house he lived in in his days in the Ivy League); and we must understand why he's afraid he's going mad (we must see in action what it is that deeply disturbs him), and we must already in this chapter have the opportunity to observe (not just hear about from the narrator) the streak of violence in Mickelsson that enables him to cut himself off from those around him— a streak that will, later in the novel, enable him to behave in even less admirable ways—and all this must be shown without undermining Mickelsson's credibility as a brilliant man, someone who really might once have been an Ivy League professor of philosophy.

Though I knew from the beginning (more or less) the nature of the problems facing me, I cannot say I figured out the answers intellectually. I knew that, within the span of the first of the thirty- to forty-page chapters my plan of the novel allowed me (long chapters for a dense. elephantine rhythm), I could not hope to do more than introduce Mickelsson's main troubles, bringing each forward in sharp relief, then leaving its development to later chapters, wherever I could work the material in; and I knew that I would have to find a few strong scenes, sufficiently slow-moving (though dramatic and active) to allow maximum drift to Mickelsson's mind. I knew that for power, or emotional energy, I would have to depend on the force of Mickelsson's character—fuming, repressed rage and self-doubt, a deep nastiness barely reined in, and a sentimental streak always on the verge of turning repellent, saved at the last moment by Mickelsson's intelligence, the backlash of irony— a character force I would have to support by the best prose (or at least the most difficult to achieve) I'd ever written: huge, rolling sentences as dense and crackling as my weight-lifter, former-college-football-star, mad philosopher.

It depresses me to think how many versions I wrote of this first chapter and the two that followed it—working on these three in a block because they laid out all the main themes and background events to be developed, as well as, of course, advancing the present action. (By the end of the third chapter Mickelsson knows that, according to his mountain neighbors, his house is haunted.) Getting the hundred-page, three-chapter block finally right took more than a year of steady writing and revising and saw one dramatic scene after another invented, frantically polished, then discarded. In the end I settled for: (1) A large scene in which Mickelsson fumes and sweats in his overheated third-floor apartment, then walks the night streets, looking enviously at other people's large houses and imagining the lives inside, comparing them with his own lost life, hating these mediocre professors (as he thinks them) whose luck has turned out to be so much better than his own—a scene that ends with Mickelsson's killing a large black dog that threatens him on the sidewalk. (2) A scene at the university, where Mickelsson's department chairman, whom he hates, wangles out of him an undergraduate advising job (not one of Mickelsson's responsibilities) for an unpleasant young man who wants to transfer to philosophy from engineering. (3) A scene presenting Mickelsson's angry decision to look for a house in the country, then his search, concluding with his finding the ancient and eerie house in the mountains. Developed in detail, allowing space for Mickelsson's memories and ironic internal observations, this arrangement of scenes finally satisfied me, insofar as one can ever be satisfied in these matters. Together they move the story forward by a direct chain of cause and effect. The climax of the first scene, Mickelsson's killing of the dog, frightens him and gives focus to his paranoia (specifically his fear that people like his chairman are watching and judging him, suspecting the failure of which he accuses himself). The climax of the second scene, in which the unpleasant engineering student insists on enrolling in Mickelsson's own course, tips the scales of Mickelsson's increasing inclination to move as far as he can from the university without giving up his job completely. And within these sprawling scenes it is possible to place directly before the reader, in dialogue and action (sometimes in momentary flashback), the main forces that have brought Mickelsson to this moment.

As I've said, I didn't work all this out intellectually. I worked out *a* plan, did my best with it, revised it, and finally discarded it. I worked out another, and then others after that, and by muddling along, sometimes reclaiming an element or two from a scrapped approach, I finally came up with something that would do, at least for me. Except in extremely simple novels—novels almost not worth writing, in my opinion—the most careful plan in the world won't actually work. Things intended for one chapter turn out to take two, and since the overall rhythm of the novel will not allow the division, one has to overhaul the whole scheme. But an inadequate plan is better than none. Writing a novel is like heading out over the open sea in a small boat. If you have a plan and a course laid out, that's helpful. If you drift off course, checking the stars can help you find a new course. If you have no map, no course laid out, sooner or later confusion will make you check the stars.

When the tentative plan is done, maybe scrawled almost illegibly in a fat, shedding notebook, maybe tacked up neatly around the walls of your room, on butcher paper, you're ready to start the writing—if you haven't started already, turning back to the planning stage only when driven by desperation. If you have prepared yourself well, there is nothing more anyone need tell you. If you have taken the time to learn to write beautiful, rock-firm sentences, if you have mastered evocation of the vivid and continuous dream, if you are generous enough in your personal character to treat imaginary characters and readers fairly, if you have held on to your childhood virtues and have not settled for literary standards much lower than those of the fiction you admire, then the novel you write will eventually be, after the necessary labor of repeated revision, a novel to be proud of, one that almost certainly someone, sooner or later, will be glad to publish. (It may be that you can only get it published after other, later novels have proved successful.) If you do none of the things I advise in this book, then you may nevertheless, by some freak of fortune or grace, write a novel to be proud of. (The god of novelists will not be tyrannized by rules.) If, on the other hand, you miserably fail, you have only three choices: start over, or start something else, or quit.

Finally, the true novelist is the one who doesn't quit. Novel-writing is not so much a profession as a *yoga*, or "way," an alternative to ordinary life-in-the-world. Its benefits are quasi-religious—a changed quality of mind and heart, satisfactions no non-novelist can understand—and its rigors generally bring no profit except to the spirit. For those who are authentically called to the profession, spiritual profits are enough.

INDEX

ONE WRITER'S BEGINNINGS

BY EUDORA WELTY

To the memory of my parents

CHRISTIAN WEBB WELTY
1879–1931

CHESTINA ANDREWS WELTY
1883–1966

ACKNOWLEDGMENTS

The origin of this book is the set of three lectures delivered at Harvard University in April, 1983, to inaugurate the William E. Massey lecture series. I am deeply grateful to Harvard University and to the graduate program in the History of American Civilization at whose invitation I wrote and gave the lectures. Mr. David Herbert Donald, of this program, gave me the best of his firm guidance and understanding. I am grateful to Mrs. Aida D. Donald, executive editor of Harvard University Press, for her kindness and patient care during their preparation in present form. To Mr. Daniel Aaron, whose suggestion as to the direction and course the lectures might take strongly encouraged me in their writing, I wish to express particular gratitude.

Jackson, Mississippi, 1983

When I was young enough to still spend a long time buttoning my shoes in the morning, I'd listen toward the hall: Daddy upstairs was shaving in the bathroom and Mother downstairs was frying the bacon. They would begin whistling back and forth to each other up and down the stairwell. My father would whistle his phrase, my mother would try to whistle, then hum hers back. It was their duet. I drew my buttonhook in and out and listened to it—I knew it was "The Merry Widow." The difference was, their song almost floated with laughter: how different from the record, which growled from the beginning, as if the Victrola were only slowly being wound up. They kept it running between them, up and down the stairs where I was now just about ready to run clattering down and show them my shoes.

I

LISTENING

IN OUR HOUSE on North Congress Street in Jackson, Mississippi, where I was born, the oldest of three children, in 1909, we grew up to the striking of clocks. There was a mission-style oak grandfather clock standing in the hall, which sent its gong-like strokes through the living-room, diningroom, kitchen, and pantry, and up the sounding board of the stairwell. Through the night, it could find its way into our ears; sometimes, even on the sleeping porch, midnight could wake us up. My parents' bedroom had a smaller striking clock that answered it. Though the kitchen clock did nothing but show the time, the dining room clock was a cuckoo clock with weights on long chains, on one of which my baby brother, after climbing on a chair to the top of the china closet, once succeeded in suspending the cat for a moment. I don't know whether or not my father's Ohio family, in having been Swiss back in the 1700s before the first three Welty brothers came to America, had anything to do with this; but we all of us have been time-minded all our lives. This was good at least for a future fiction writer, being able to learn so penetratingly, and almost first of all, about chronology. It was one of a good many things I learned almost without knowing it; it would be there when I needed it.

My father loved all instruments that would instruct and fascinate. His place to keep things was the drawer in the "library table" where lying on top of his folded maps was a telescope with brass extensions, to find the moon and the Big Dipper after supper in our front yard, and to keep appointments with eclipses. There was a folding Kodak that was brought out for Christmas, birthdays, and trips. In the back of the drawer you could find a magnifying glass, a kaleidoscope, and a gyroscope kept in a black buckram box, which he would set dancing for us on a string pulled tight. He had also supplied himself with an assortment of puzzles composed of metal rings and intersecting links and keys chained together, impossible for the rest of us, however patiently shown, to take apart; he had an almost childlike love of the ingenious.

In time, a barometer was added to our diningroom wall; but we didn't really need it. My father had the country boy's accurate knowledge of the weather and its skies. He went out and stood on our front steps first thing in the morning and took a look at it and a sniff. He was a pretty good weather prophet.

"Well, I'm *not*," my mother would say with enormous self-satisfaction.

He told us children what to do if we were lost in a strange country. "Look for where the sky is brightest along the horizon," he said. "That reflects the nearest river. Strike out for a river and you will find habitation." Eventualities were much on his mind. In his care for us children he cautioned us to take measures against such things as being struck by lightning. He drew us all away from the windows during the severe electrical storms that are common where we live. My mother stood apart, scoffing at caution as a character failing. "Why, I always loved a storm! High winds never bothered me in West Virginia! Just listen at that! I wasn't a bit afraid of a little lightning and thunder! I'd go out on the mountain and spread my arms wide and *run* in a good big storm!"

So I developed a strong meteorological sensibility. In years ahead when I wrote stories, atmosphere took its influential role from the start. Commotion in the weather and the inner feelings aroused by such a hovering disturbance emerged connected in dramatic form. (I tried a tornado first, in a story called "The Winds.")

From our earliest Christmas times, Santa Claus brought us toys that instruct boys and girls (separately) how to build things—stone blocks cut to the castle-building style, Tinker Toys, and Erector sets. Daddy made for us himself elaborate kites that needed to be taken miles out of town to a pasture long enough (and my father was not afraid of horses and cows watching) for him to run with and get up on a long cord to which my mother held the spindle, and then we children were given it to hold, tugging like something alive at our hands. They were beautiful, sound, shapely box kites, smelling delicately of office glue for their entire short lives. And of course, as soon as the boys attained anywhere near the right age, there was an electric train, the engine with its pea-sized working headlight, its line of cars, tracks equipped with switches, semaphores, its station, its bridges, and its tunnel, which blocked off all other traffic in the upstairs hall. Even from downstairs, and through the cries of excited children, the elegant rush and click of the train could be heard through the ceiling, running around and around its figure eight.

All of this, but especially the train, represents my father's fondest beliefs—in progress, in the future. With these gifts, he was preparing his children.

And so was my mother with her different gifts.

I learned from the age of two or three that any room in our house, at any time of day, was there to read in, or to be read to. My mother read to me. She'd read to me in the big bedroom in the mornings, when we were in her rocker together, which ticked in rhythm as we rocked, as though we had a cricket accompanying the story. She'd read to me in the diningroom on winter afternoons in front of the coal fire, with our cuckoo clock ending the story with "Cuckoo," and at night when I'd got in my own bed. I must have given her no peace. Sometimes she read to me in the kitchen while she sat churning, and the churning sobbed along with *any* story. It was my ambition to have her read to me while *I* churned; once she granted my wish, but she read off my story before I brought her butter. She was an expressive reader. When she was reading "Puss in Boots," for instance, it was impossible not to know that she distrusted *all* cats.

It had been startling and disappointing to me to find out that story books had been written by *people,* that books were not natural wonders, coming up of themselves like grass. Yet regardless of where they came from, I cannot remember a time when I was not in love with them—with the books themselves, cover and binding and the paper they were printed on, with their smell and their weight and with their possession in my arms, captured and carried off to myself. Still illiterate, I was ready for them, committed to all the reading I could give them.

Neither of my parents had come from homes that could afford to buy many books, but though it must have been something of a strain on his salary, as the youngest officer in a young insurance company, my father was all the while carefully selecting and ordering away for what he and Mother thought we children should grow up with. They bought first for the future.

Besides the bookcase in the livingroom, which was always called "the library," there were the encyclopedia tables and dictionary stand under windows in our diningroom. Here to help us grow up arguing around the diningroom table were the Unabridged Webster, the Columbia Encyclopedia, Compton's Pictured Encyclopedia, the Lincoln Library of Information, and later the Book of Knowledge. And the year we moved into our new house, there was room to celebrate it with the new 1925 edition of the Britannica, which my father, his face always deliberately turned toward the future, was of course disposed to think better than any previous edition.

In "the library," inside the mission-style bookcase with its three diamond-latticed glass doors, with my father's Morris chair and the glass-shaded lamp on its table beside it, were books I could soon begin on—and I did, reading them all alike and as they came, straight down their rows, top shelf to bottom. There was the set of Stoddard's Lectures, in all its late nineteenth-century vocabulary and vignettes of peasant life and quaint beliefs and customs, with matching halftone illustrations: Vesuvius erupting, Venice by moonlight, gypsies glimpsed by their campfires. I didn't know then the clue they were to my father's longing to see the rest of the world. I read straight through his other love-from-afar: the Victrola Book of the Opera, with opera after opera in synopsis, with portraits in costume of Melba, Caruso, Galli-Curci, and Geraldine Farrar, some of whose voices we could listen to on our Red Seal records.

My mother read secondarily for information; she sank as a hedonist into novels. She read Dickens in the spirit in which she would have eloped with him. The novels of her girlhood that had stayed on in her imagination, besides those of Dickens and Scott and Robert Louis Stevenson, were *Jane Eyre, Trilby, The Woman in White, Green Mansions, King Solomon's Mines*. Marie Corelli's name would crop up but I understood she had gone out of favor with my mother, who had only kept *Ardath* out of loyalty. In time she absorbed herself in Galsworthy, Edith Wharton, above all in Thomas Mann of the *Joseph* volumes.

St. Elmo was not in our house; I saw it often in other houses. This wildly popular Southern novel is where all the Edna Earles in our population started coming from. They're all named for the heroine, who succeeded in bringing a dissolute, sinning roué and atheist of a lover (St. Elmo) to his knees. My mother was able to forgo it. But she remembered the classic advice given to rose growers on how to water their bushes long enough: "Take a chair and *St. Elmo*."

7

To both my parents I owe my early acquaintance with a beloved Mark Twain. There was a full set of Mark Twain and a short set of Ring Lardner in our bookcase, and those were the volumes that in time united us all, parents and children.

Reading everything that stood before me was how I came upon a worn old book without a back that had belonged to my father as a child. It was called *Sanford and Merton*. Is there anyone left who recognizes it, I wonder? It is the famous moral tale written by Thomas Day in the 1780s, but of him no mention is made on the title page of *this* book; here it is *Sanford and Merton in Words of One Syllable* by Mary Godolphin. Here are the rich boy and the poor boy and Mr. Barlow, their teacher and interlocutor, in long discourses alternating with dramatic scenes—danger and rescue allotted to the rich and the poor respectively. It may have only words of one syllable, but one of them is "quoth." It ends with not one but two morals, both engraved on rings: "Do what you ought, come what may," and "If we would be great, we must first learn to be good."

This book was lacking its front cover, the back held on by strips of pasted paper, now turned golden, in several layers, and the pages stained, flecked, and tattered around the edges; its garish illustrations had come unattached but were preserved, laid in. I had the feeling even in my heedless childhood that this was the only book my father as a little boy had had of his own. He had held onto it, and might have gone to sleep on its coverless face: he had lost his mother when he was seven. My father had never made any mention to his own children of the book, but he had brought it along with him from Ohio to our house and shelved it in our bookcase.

My mother had brought from West Virginia that set of Dickens; those books looked sad, too—they had been through fire and water before I was born, she told me, and there they were, lined up—as I later realized, waiting for *me*.

I was presented, from as early as I can remember, with books of my own, which appeared on my birthday and Christmas morning. Indeed, my parents could not give me books enough. They must have sacrificed to give me on my sixth or seventh birthday—it was after I became a reader for myself—the ten-volume set of Our Wonder World. These were beautifully made, heavy books I would lie down with on the floor in front of the diningroom hearth, and more often than the rest volume 5, *Every Child's Story Book*, was under my eyes. There were the fairy tales—Grimm, Andersen, the English, the French, "Ali Baba and the Forty Thieves"; and there was Aesop and Reynard the Fox; there were the myths and legends, Robin Hood, King Arthur, and St. George and the Dragon, even the history of Joan of Arc; a whack of *Pilgrim's Progress* and a long piece of *Gulliver*. They all carried their classic illustrations. I located myself in these pages and could go straight to the stories and pictures I loved; very often "The Yellow Dwarf" was first choice, with Walter Crane's Yellow Dwarf in full color making his terrifying appearance flanked by turkeys. Now that volume is as worn and backless and hanging apart as my father's poor *Sanford and Merton*. The precious page with Edward Lear's "Jumblies" on it has been in danger of slipping out for all these years. One measure of my love for Our Wonder World was that for a long time I wondered if I would go through fire and water for it as my mother had done for Charles Dickens; and the only comfort was to think I could ask my mother to do it for me.

I believe I'm the only child I know of who grew up with this treasure in the house. I used to ask others, "Did you have Our Wonder World?" I'd have to tell them The Book of Knowledge could not hold a candle to it.

I live in gratitude to my parents for initiating me—and as early as I begged for it, without keeping me waiting—

into knowledge of the word, into reading and spelling, by way of the alphabet. They taught it to me at home in time for me to begin to read before starting to school. I believe the alphabet is no longer considered an essential piece of equipment for traveling through life. In my day it was the keystone to knowledge. You learned the alphabet as you learned to count to ten, as you learned "Now I lay me" and the Lord's Prayer and your father's and mother's name and address and telephone number, all in case you were lost.

My love for the alphabet, which endures, grew out of reciting it but, before that, out of seeing the letters on the page. In my own story books, before I could read them for myself, I fell in love with various winding, enchanted-looking initials drawn by Walter Crane at the heads of fairy tales. In "Once upon a time," an "O" had a rabbit running it as a treadmill, his feet upon flowers. When the day came, years later, for me to see the Book of Kells, all the wizardry of letter, initial, and word swept over me a thousand times over, and the illumination, the gold, seemed a part of the word's beauty and holiness that had been there from the start.

LEARNING stamps you with its moments. Childhood's learning is made up of moments. It isn't steady. It's a pulse.

In a children's art class, we sat in a ring on kindergarten chairs and drew three daffodils that had just been picked out of the yard; and while I was drawing, my sharpened yellow pencil and the cup of the yellow daffodils gave off whiffs just alike. That the pencil doing the drawing should give off the same smell as the flower it drew seemed part of the art lesson—as shouldn't it be? Children, like animals, use all their senses to discover the world. Then artists come along and discover it the same way, all over again. Here and there, it's the same world. Or now and then we'll hear from an artist who's never lost it.

In my sensory education I include my physical awareness of the *word*. Of a certain word, that is; the connection
it has with what it stands for. At around age six, perhaps, I
was standing by myself in our front yard waiting for supper,
just at that hour in a late summer day when the sun is already below the horizon and the risen full moon in the visible sky stops being chalky and begins to take on light.
There comes the moment, and I saw it then, when the
moon goes from flat to round. For the first time it met my
eyes as a globe. The word "moon" came into my mouth as
though fed to me out of a silver spoon. Held in my mouth
the moon became a word. It had the roundness of a Con-
cord grape Grandpa took off his vine and gave me to suck
out of its skin and swallow whole, in Ohio.

This love did not prevent me from living for years in
foolish error about the moon. The new moon just appearing
in the west was the rising moon to me. The new should be
rising. And in early childhood the sun and moon, those opposite reigning powers, I just as easily assumed rose in east
and west respectively in their opposite sides of the sky, and
like partners in a reel they advanced, sun from the east,
moon from the west, crossed over (when I wasn't looking)
and went down on the other side. My father couldn't have
known I believed that when, bending behind me and guiding my shoulder, he positioned me at our telescope in the
front yard and, with careful adjustment of the focus,
brought the moon close to me.

The night sky over my childhood Jackson was velvety
black. I could see the full constellations in it and call their
names; when I could read, I knew their myths. Though I
was always waked for eclipses, and indeed carried to the
window as an infant in arms and shown Halley's Comet in
my sleep, and though I'd been taught at our diningroom
table about the solar system and knew the earth revolved
around the sun, and our moon around us, I never found out

11

the moon didn't come up in the west until I was a writer and Herschel Brickell, the literary critic, told me after I misplaced it in a story. He said valuable words to me about my new profession: "Always be sure you get your moon in the right part of the sky."

MY MOTHER always sang to her children. Her voice came out just a little bit in the minor key. "Wee Willie Winkie's" song was wonderfully sad when she sang the lullabies.

"Oh, but now there's a record. She could have her own record to listen to," my father would have said. For there came a Victrola record of "Bobby Shafftoe" and "Rock-a-Bye Baby," all of Mother's lullabies, which could be played to take her place. Soon I was able to play her my own lullabies all day long.

Our Victrola stood in the diningroom. I was allowed to climb onto the seat of a diningroom chair to wind it, start the record turning, and set the needle playing. In a second I'd jumped to the floor, to spin or march around the table as the music called for—now there were all the other records I could play too. I skinned back onto the chair just in time to lift the needle at the end, stop the record and turn it over, then change the needle. That brass receptacle with a hole in the lid gave off a metallic smell like human sweat, from all the hot needles that were fed it. Winding up, dancing, being cocked to start and stop the record, was of course all in one the act of *listening*—to "Overture to *Daughter of the Regiment*," "Selections from *The Fortune Teller*," "Kiss Me Again," "Gypsy Dance from *Carmen*," "Stars and Stripes Forever," "When the Midnight Choo-Choo Leaves for Alabam," or whatever came next. Movement must be at the very heart of listening.

Ever since I was first read to, then started reading to myself, there has never been a line read that I didn't *hear*. As my eyes followed the sentence, a voice was saying it silently to me. It isn't my mother's voice, or the voice of any person I can identify, certainly not my own. It is human, but inward, and it is inwardly that I listen to it. It is to me the voice of the story or the poem itself. The cadence, whatever it is that asks you to believe, the feeling that resides in the printed word, reaches me through the reader-voice. I have supposed, but never found out, that this is the case with all readers—to read as listeners—and with all writers, to write as listeners. It may be part of the desire to write. The sound of what falls on the page begins the process of testing it for truth, for me. Whether I am right to trust so far I don't know. By now I don't know whether I could do either one, reading or writing, without the other.

My own words, when I am at work on a story, I hear too as they go, in the same voice that I hear when I read in books. When I write and the sound of it comes back to my ears, then I act to make my changes. I have always trusted this voice.

IN THAT vanished time in small-town Jackson, most of the ladies I was familiar with, the mothers of my friends in the neighborhood, were busiest when they were sociable. In the afternoons there was regular visiting up and down the little grid of residential streets. Everybody had calling cards, even certain children; and newborn babies themselves were properly announced by sending out their tiny engraved calling cards attached with a pink or blue bow to those of their parents. Graduation presents to high-school pupils were often "card cases." On the hall table in every house the first thing you saw was a silver tray waiting to receive more calling cards on top of the stack already piled up like jackstraws; they were never thrown away.

My mother let none of this idling, as she saw it, pertain to her; she went her own way with or without her calling cards, and though she was fond of her friends and they were

13

fond of her, she had little time for small talk. At first, I hadn't known what I'd missed.

When we at length bought our first automobile, one of our neighbors was often invited to go with us on the family Sunday afternoon ride. In Jackson it was counted an affront to the neighbors to start out for anywhere with an empty seat in the car. My mother sat in the back with her friend, and I'm told that as a small child I would ask to sit in the middle, and say as we started off, "Now *talk.*"

There was dialogue throughout the lady's accounts to my mother. "I said" ... "He said" ... "And I'm told she very plainly said" ... "It was midnight before they finally heard, and what do you think it *was?*"

What I loved about her stories was that everything happened in *scenes.* I might not catch on to what the root of the trouble was in all that happened, but my ear told me it was dramatic. Often she said, "The crisis had come!"

This same lady was one of Mother's callers on the telephone who always talked a long time. I knew who it was when my mother would only reply, now and then, "Well, I declare," or "You don't say so," or "Surely not." She'd be standing at the wall telephone, listening against her will, and I'd sit on the stairs close by her. Our telephone had a little bar set into the handle which had to be pressed and held down to keep the connection open, and when her friend had said goodbye, my mother needed me to prize her fingers loose from the little bar; her grip had become paralyzed. "What did she say?" I asked.

"She wasn't *saying* a thing in this world," sighed my mother. "She was just ready to talk, that's all."

My mother was right. Years later, beginning with my story "Why I Live at the P.O.," I wrote reasonably often in the form of a monologue that takes possession of the speaker. How much more gets told besides!

This lady told everything in her sweet, marveling

voice, and meant every word of it kindly. She enjoyed my company perhaps even more than my mother's. She invited me to catch her doodlebugs; under the trees in her backyard were dozens of their holes. When you stuck a broom straw down one and called, "Doodlebug, doodlebug, your house is on fire and all your children are burning up," she believed this is why the doodlebug came running out of the hole. This was why I loved to call up her doodlebugs instead of ours.

My mother could never have told me her stories, and I think I knew why even then: my mother didn't believe them. But I could listen to this murmuring lady all day. She believed everything she heard, like the doodlebug. And so did I.

This was a day when ladies' and children's clothes were very often made at home. My mother cut out all the dresses and her little boys' rompers, and a sewing woman would come and spend the day upstairs in the sewing room fitting and stitching them all. This was Fannie. This old black sewing woman, along with her speed and dexterity, brought along a great provision of up-to-the-minute news. She spent her life going from family to family in town and worked right in its bosom, and nothing could stop her. My mother would try, while I stood being pinned up. "Fannie, I'd rather Eudora didn't hear that." "That" would be just what I was longing to hear, whatever it was. "I don't want her exposed to gossip"—as if gossip were measles and I could catch it. I did catch some of it but not enough. "Mrs. O'Neil's oldest daughter she had her wedding dress *tried on,* and all her fine underclothes featherstitched and ribbon run in and then—" "I think that will do, Fannie," said my mother. It was tantalizing never to be exposed long enough to hear the end.

Fannie was the worldliest old woman to be imagined. She could do whatever her hands were doing without having to stop talking; and she could speak in a wonderfully derogatory way with any number of pins stuck in her mouth. Her hands steadied me like claws as she stumped on her knees around me, tacking me together. The gist of her tale would be lost on me, but Fannie didn't bother about the ear she was telling it to; she just liked telling. She was like an author. In fact, for a good deal of what she said, I daresay she *was* the author.

Long before I wrote stories, I listened for stories. Listening *for* them is something more acute than listening *to* them. I suppose it's an early form of participation in what goes on. Listening children know stories are *there*. When their elders sit and begin, children are just waiting and hoping for one to come out, like a mouse from its hole.

It was taken entirely for granted that there wasn't any lying in our family, and I was advanced in adolescence before I realized that in plenty of homes where I played with schoolmates and went to their parties, children lied to their parents and parents lied to their children and to each other. It took me a long time to realize that these very same everyday lies, and the stratagems and jokes and tricks and dares that went with them, were in fact the basis of the *scenes* I so well loved to hear about and hoped for and treasured in the conversation of adults.

My instinct—the dramatic instinct—was to lead me, eventually, on the right track for a storyteller: the *scene* was full of hints, pointers, suggestions, and promises of things to find out and know about human beings. I had to grow up and learn to listen for the unspoken as well as the spoken—and to know a truth, I also had to recognize a lie.

IT WAS when my mother came out onto the sleeping porch to tell me goodnight that her trial came. The sudden silence in the double bed meant my younger brothers had both keeled over in sleep, and I in the single bed at my end of the porch would be lying electrified, waiting for this to be the night when she'd tell me what she'd promised for so long. Just as she bent to kiss me I grabbed her and asked: "Where do babies come from?"

My poor mother! But something saved her every time. Almost any night I put the baby question to her, suddenly, as if the whole outdoors exploded, Professor Holt would start to sing. The Holts lived next door; he taught penmanship (the Palmer Method), typing, bookkeeping and shorthand at the high school. His excitable voice traveled out of their diningroom windows across the two driveways between our houses, and up to our upstairs sleeping porch. His wife, usually so quiet and gentle, was his uncannily spirited accompanist at the piano. "High-ho! Come to the Fair!" he'd sing, unless he sang "Oho ye oho ye, who's bound for the ferry, the briar's in bud and the sun's going down!"

"Dear, this isn't a very good time for you to hear Mother, is it?"

She couldn't get started. As soon as she'd whisper something, Professor Holt galloped into the chorus, "And 'tis but a penny to Twickenham town!" "Isn't that enough?" she'd ask me. She'd told me that the mother and the father had to both *want* the baby. This couldn't be enough. I knew she was not trying to fib to me, for she never did fib, but also I could not help but know she was not really *telling* me. And more than that, I was afraid of what I was going to hear next. This was partly because she wanted to tell me in the dark. I thought *she* might be afraid. In something like childish hopelessness I thought she probably *couldn't* tell, just as she *couldn't* lie.

On the night we came the closest to having it over with, she started to tell me without being asked, and I ruined it by yelling, "Mother, look at the lightning bugs!"

In those days, the dark was dark. And all the dark out

17

there was filled with the soft, near lights of lightning bugs. They were everywhere, flashing on the slow, horizontal move, on the upswings, rising and subsiding in the soundless dark. Lightning bugs signaled and answered back without a stop, from down below all the way to the top of our sycamore tree. My mother just gave me a businesslike kiss and went on back to Daddy in their room at the front of the house. Distracted by lightning bugs, I had missed my chance. The fact is she never did tell me.

I doubt that any child I knew ever was told by her mother any more than I was about babies. In fact, I doubt that her own mother ever told her any more than she told me, though there were five brothers who were born after Mother, one after the other, and she was taking care of babies all her childhood.

Not being able to bring herself to open that door to reveal its secret, one of those days, she opened another door.

In my mother's bottom bureau drawer in her bedroom she kept treasures of hers in boxes, and had given me permission to play with one of them—a switch of her own chestnut-colored hair, kept in a heavy bright braid that coiled around like a snake inside a cardboard box. I hung it from her doorknob and unplaited it; it fell in ripples nearly to the floor, and it satisfied the Rapunzel in me to comb it out. But one day I noticed in the same drawer a small white cardboard box such as her engraved calling cards came in from the printing house. It was tightly closed, but I opened it, to find to my puzzlement and covetousness two polished buffalo nickels, embedded in white cotton. I rushed with this opened box to my mother and asked if I could run out and spend the nickels.

"No!" she exclaimed in a most passionate way. She seized the box into her own hands. I begged her; somehow I had started to cry. Then she sat down, drew me to her, and told me that I had had a little brother who had come before

I did, and who had died as a baby before I was born. And these two nickels that I'd wanted to claim as my find were his. They had lain on his eyelids, for a purpose untold and unimaginable. "He was a fine little baby, my first baby, and he shouldn't have died. But he did. It was because your mother almost died at the same time," she told me. "In looking after me, they too nearly forgot about the little baby."

She'd told me the wrong secret—not how babies could come but how they could die, how they could be forgotten about.

I wondered in after years: how could my mother have kept those two coins? Yet how could someone like herself have disposed of them in any way at all? She suffered from a morbid streak which in all the life of the family reached out on occasions—the worst occasions—and touched us, clung around us, making it worse for her; her unbearable moments could find nowhere to go.

The future story writer in the child I was must have taken unconscious note and stored it away then: one secret is liable to be revealed in the place of another that is harder to tell, and the substitute secret when nakedly exposed is often the more appalling.

Perhaps telling me what she did was made easier for my mother by the two secrets, told and still not told, being connected in her deepest feeling, more intimately than anyone ever knew, perhaps even herself. So far as I remember now, this is the only time this baby was ever mentioned in my presence. So far as I can remember, and I've tried, he was never mentioned in the presence of my father, for whom he had been named. I am only certain that my father, who could never bear pain very well, would not have been able to bear it.

It was my father (my mother told me at some later date) who saved her own life, after that baby was born. She had in fact been given up by the doctor, as she had long been unable to take any nourishment. (That was the illness when they'd cut her hair, which formed the switch in the same bureau drawer.) What had struck her was septicemia, in those days nearly always fatal. What my father did was to try champagne.

I once wondered where he, who'd come not very long before from an Ohio farm, had ever heard of such a remedy, such a measure. Or perhaps as far as he was concerned he invented it, out of the strength of desperation. It would have been desperation augmented because champagne couldn't be bought in Jackson. But somehow he knew what to do about that too. He telephoned to Canton, forty miles north, to an Italian orchard grower, Mr. Trolio, told him the necessity, and asked, begged, that he put a bottle of his wine on Number 3, which was due in a few minutes to stop in Canton to "take on water" (my father knew everything about train schedules). My father would be waiting to meet the train in Jackson. Mr. Trolio did—he sent the bottle in a bucket of ice and my father snatched it off the baggage car. He offered my mother a glass of chilled champagne and she drank it and kept it down. She was to live, after all.

Now, her hair was long again, it would reach in a braid down her back, and now I was her child. She hadn't died. And when I came, I hadn't died either. Would she ever? Would I ever? I couldn't face *ever*. I must have rushed into her lap, demanding her like a baby. And she had to put her first-born aside again, for me.

OF COURSE it's easy to see why they both overprotected me, why my father, before I could wear a new pair of shoes for the first time, made me wait while he took out his thin silver pocket knife and with the point of the blade scored the polished soles all over, carefully, in a diamond pattern, to prevent me from sliding on the polished floor when I ran.

As I was to learn over and over again, my mother's mind was a mass of associations. Whatever happened would be forever paired for her with something that had happened before it, to one of us or to her. It became a private anniversary. Every time any possible harm came near me, she thought of how she lost her first child. When a Roman candle at Christmas backfired up my sleeve, she rushed to smother the blaze with the first thing she could grab, which was a dish towel hanging in the kitchen, and the burn on my arm became infected. I was nothing but proud of my sling, for I could wear it to school, and her repeated blaming of herself—for even my sling—puzzled and troubled me.

When my mother would tell me that she wanted me to have something because she as a child had never had it, I wanted, or I partly wanted, to give it back. All my life I continued to feel that bliss for me would have to imply my mother's deprivation or sacrifice. I don't think it would have occurred to her what a double emotion I felt, and indeed I know that it was being unfair to her, for what she said was simply the truth.

"I'm going to let you go to the Century Theatre with your father tonight on my ticket. I'd rather you saw *Blossom Time* than go myself."

In the Century first-row balcony, where their seats always were, I'd be sitting beside my father at this hour beyond my bedtime carried totally away by the performance, and then suddenly the thought of my mother staying home with my sleeping younger brothers, missing the spectacle at this moment before my eyes, and doing without all the excitement and wonder that filled my being, would arrest me and I could hardly bear my pleasure for my guilt.

There is no wonder that a passion for independence sprang up in me at the earliest age. It took me a long time to manage the independence, for I loved those who protected me—and I wanted inevitably to protect them back. I have never managed to handle the guilt. In the act and the course of writing stories, these are two of the springs, one bright, one dark, that feed the stream.

WHEN I was six or seven, I was taken out of school and put to bed for several months for an ailment the doctor described as "fast-beating heart." I felt all right—perhaps I felt too good. It was the feeling of suspense. At any rate, I was allowed to occupy all day my parents' double bed in the front upstairs bedroom.

I was supposed to rest, and the little children didn't get to run in and excite me often. Davis School was as close as across the street. I could keep up with it from the window beside me, hear the principal ring her bell, see which children were tardy, watch my classmates eat together at recess: I knew their sandwiches. I was homesick for school; my mother made time for teaching me arithmetic and hearing my spelling.

An opulence of story books covered my bed; it was the "Land of Counterpane." As I read away, I was Rapunzel, or the Goose Girl, or the Princess Labam in one of the *Thousand and One Nights* who mounted the roof of her palace every night and of her own radiance faithfully lighted the whole city just by reposing there, and I daydreamed I could light Davis School from across the street.

But I never dreamed I could learn as long as I was away from the schoolroom, and that bits of enlightenment far-reaching in my life went on as ever in their own good time. After they'd told me goodnight and tucked me in—although I knew that after I'd finally fallen asleep they'd pick me up and carry me away—my parents draped the lampshade with a sheet of the daily paper, which was tilted, like a hatbrim, so that they could sit in their rockers in a lighted part of the room and I could supposedly go to sleep in the protected dark of the bed. They sat talking. What was thus dramatically made a present of to me was the secure sense of the hidden observer. As long as I could make myself keep awake, I was free to listen to every word my parents said between them.

I don't remember that any secrets were revealed to me, nor do I remember any avid curiosity on my part to learn something I wasn't supposed to—perhaps I was too young to know what to listen for. But I was present in the room with the chief secret there was—the two of them, father and mother, sitting there as one. I was conscious of this secret and of my fast-beating heart in step together, as I lay in the slant-shaded light of the room, with a brown, pear-shaped scorch in the newspaper shade where it had become overheated once.

What they talked about I have no idea, and the subject was not what mattered to me. It was no doubt whatever a young married couple spending their first time privately in each other's company in the long, probably harried day would talk about. It was the murmur of their voices, the back-and-forth, the unnoticed stretching away of time between my bedtime and theirs, that made me bask there at my distance. What I felt was not that I was excluded from them but that I was included, in—and because of—what I could hear of their voices and what I could see of their faces in the cone of yellow light under the brown-scorched shade.

I suppose I was exercising as early as then the turn of mind, the nature of temperament, of a privileged observer; and owing to the way I became so, it turned out that I became the loving kind.

A conscious act grew out of this by the time I began to write stories: getting my distance, a prerequisite of my understanding of human events, is the way I begin work. Just as, of course, it was an initial step when, in my first journalism job, I stumbled into making pictures with a camera. Frame, proportion, perspective, the values of light and shade, all are determined by the distance of the observing eye.

I have always been shy physically. This in part tended to keep me from rushing into things, including relationships, headlong. Not rushing headlong, though I may have wanted to, but beginning to write stories about people, I drew near slowly; noting and guessing, apprehending, hoping, drawing my eventual conclusions out of my own heart, I *did* venture closer to where I wanted to go. As time and my imagination led me on, I did plunge.

FROM the first I was clamorous to learn—I wanted to know and begged to be told not so much what, or how, or why, or where, as when. How soon?

Pear tree by the garden gate,
How much longer must I wait?

This rhyme from one of my nursery books was the one that spoke for me. But I lived not at all unhappily in this craving, for my wild curiosity was in large part suspense, which carries its own secret pleasure. And so one of the godmothers of fiction was already bending over me.

When I was five years old, I knew the alphabet, I'd been vaccinated (for smallpox), and I could read. So my mother walked across the street to Jefferson Davis Grammar School and asked the principal if she would allow me to enter the first grade after Christmas.

"Oh, all right," said Miss Duling. "Probably the best thing you could do with her."

Miss Duling, a lifelong subscriber to perfection, was a figure of authority, the most whole-souled I have ever come to know. She was a dedicated schoolteacher who denied herself all she might have done or whatever other way she might have lived (this possibility was the last that could have occurred to us, her subjects in school). I believe she came of well-off people, well-educated, in Kentucky, and certainly old photographs show she was a beautiful, high-spirited-looking young lady—and came down to Jackson to its new grammar school that was going begging for a principal. She must have earned next to nothing; Mississippi then as now was the nation's lowest-ranking state economically, and our legislature has always shown a painfully loud reluctance to give money to public education. That challenge *brought* her.

In the long run she came into touch, as teacher or principal, with three generations of Jacksonians. My parents had not, but everybody else's parents had gone to school to her. She'd taught most of our leaders somewhere along the line. When she wanted something done—some civic oversight corrected, some injustice made right overnight, or even a tree spared that the fool telephone people were about to cut down—she telephoned the mayor, or the chief of police, or the president of the power company, or the head doctor at the hospital, or the judge in charge of a case, or whoever, and calling them by their first names, *told* them. It is impossible to imagine her meeting with anything less than compliance. The ringing of her brass bell from their days at Davis School would still be in their ears. She also proposed a spelling match between the fourth grade at Davis School and the Mississippi Legislature, who went through with it; and that told the Legislature.

Her standards were very high and of course inflexible, her authority was total; why *wouldn't* this carry with it a brass bell that could be heard ringing for a block in all directions? That bell belonged to the figure of Miss Duling as though it grew directly out of her right arm, as wings grew

25

out of an angel or a tail out of the devil. When we entered, marching, into her school, by strictest teaching, surveillance, and order we learned grammar, arithmetic, spelling, reading, writing, and geography; and she, not the teachers, I believe, wrote out the examinations: need I tell you, they were "hard."

She's not the only teacher who has influenced me, but Miss Duling, in some fictional shape or form, has stridden into a larger part of my work than I'd realized until now. She emerges in my perhaps inordinate number of schoolteacher characters. I loved those characters in the writing. But I did not, in life, love Miss Duling. I was afraid of her high-arched bony nose, her eyebrows lifted in half-circles above her hooded, brilliant eyes, and of the Kentucky R's in her speech, and the long steps she took in her hightop shoes. I did nothing but fear her bearing-down authority, and did not connect this (as of course we were meant to) with our own need or desire to learn, perhaps because I already had this wish, and did not need to be driven.

She was impervious to lies or foolish excuses or the insufferable plea of not knowing any better. She wasn't going to have any frills, either, at Davis School. When a new governor moved into the mansion, he sent his daughter to Davis School; her name was Lady Rachel Conner. Miss Duling at once called the governor to the telephone and told him, "She'll be plain Rachel here."

Miss Duling dressed as plainly as a Pilgrim on a Thanksgiving poster we made in the schoolroom, in a longish black-and-white checked gingham dress, a bright thick wool sweater the red of a railroad lantern—she'd knitted it herself—black stockings and her narrow elegant feet in black hightop shoes with heels you could hear coming, rhythmical as a parade drum down the hall. Her silky black curly hair was drawn back out of curl, fastened by high combs, and knotted behind. She carried her spectacles on a gold chain hung around her neck. Her gaze was in general sweeping, then suddenly at the point of concentration upon you. With a swing of her bell that took her whole right arm and shoulder, she rang it, militant and impartial, from the head of the front steps of Davis School when it was time for us all to line up, girls on one side, boys on the other. We were to march past her into the school building, while the fourth-grader she nabbed played time on the piano, mostly to a tune we could have skipped to, but we didn't skip into Davis School.

Little recess (open-air exercises) and big recess (lunch-boxes from home opened and eaten on the grass, on the girls' side and the boys' side of the yard) and dismissal were also regulated by Miss Duling's bell. The bell was also used to catch us off guard with fire drill.

It was examinations that drove my wits away, as all emergencies do. Being expected to measure up was paralysing. I failed to make 100 on my spelling exam because I missed one word and that word was "uncle." Mother, as I knew she would, took it personally. "You couldn't spell *uncle?* When you've got those five perfectly splendid uncles in West Virginia? What would *they* say to that?"

It was never that Mother wanted me to beat my classmates in grades; what she wanted was for me to have my answers right. It was unclouded perfection I was up against.

My father was much more tolerant of possible error. He only said, as he steeply and impeccably sharpened my pencils on examination morning, "Now just keep remembering: the examinations were made out for the *average* student to pass. That's the majority. And if the majority can pass, think how much better *you* can do."

I looked to my mother, who had her own opinions about the majority. My father wished to treat it with respect, she didn't. I'd been born left-handed, but the habit was broken when I entered the first grade in Davis School.

My father had insisted. He pointed out that everything in life had been made for the convenience of right-handed people, because they were the majority, and he often used "what the majority wants" as a criterion for what was for the best. My mother said she could not promise him, could not promise him at all, that I wouldn't stutter as a consequence. Mother had been born left-handed too; her family consisted of five left-handed brothers, a left-handed mother, and a father who could write with both hands at the same time, also backwards and forwards and upside down, different words with each hand. She had been broken of it when she was young, and she said she used to stutter.

"But you still stutter," I'd remind her, only to hear her say loftily, "You should have heard me when I was your age."

In my childhood days, a great deal of stock was put, in general, in the value of doing well in school. Both daily newspapers in Jackson saw the honor roll as news and published the lists, and the grades, of all the honor students. The city fathers gave the children who made the honor roll free season tickets to the baseball games down at the grandstand. We all attended and all worshiped some player on the Jackson Senators: I offered up my 100's in arithmetic and spelling, reading and writing, attendance and, yes, deportment—I must have been a prig!—to Red McDermott, the third baseman. And our happiness matched that of knowing Miss Duling was on her summer vacation, far, far away in Kentucky.

EVERY school week, visiting teachers came on their days for special lessons. On Mondays, the singing teacher blew into the room fresh from the early outdoors, singing in her high soprano "How do you do?" to do-mi-sol-do, and we responded in chorus from our desks, "I'm ve-ry well" to do-sol-mi-do. Miss Johnson taught us rounds—"Row row row your boat gently down the stream"—and "Little Sir Echo," with half the room singing the words and the other half being the echo, a competition. She was from the North, and she was the one who wanted us all to stop the Christmas carols and see snow. The snow falling that morning outside the window was the first most of us had ever seen, and Miss Johnson threw up the window and held out wide her own black cape and caught flakes on it and ran, as fast as she could go, up and down the aisles to show us the real thing before it melted.

Thursday was Miss Eyrich and Miss Eyrich was Thursday. She came to give us physical training. She wasted no time on nonsense. Without greeting, we were marched straight outside and summarily divided into teams (no choosing sides), put on the mark, and ordered to get set for a relay race. Miss Eyrich cracked out "Go!" Dread rose in my throat. My head swam. Here was my turn, nearly upon me. (Wait, have I been touched—was that slap the touch? Go on! Do I go on without our passing a word? What word? Now am I racing too fast to turn around? Now I'm nearly home, but where is the hand waiting for mine to touch? Am I too late? Have I lost the whole race for our side?) I lost the relay race for our side before I started, through living ahead of myself, dreading to make my start, feeling too late prematurely, and standing transfixed by emergency, trying to think of a password. Thursdays still can make me hear Miss Eyrich's voice. "On your mark—get set—GO!"

Very composedly and very slowly, the art teacher, who visited each room on Fridays, paced the aisle and looked down over your shoulder at what you were drawing for her. This was Miss Ascher. Coming from behind you, her deep, resonant voice reached you without being a word at all, but a sort of purr. It was much the sound given out by our family doctor when he read the thermometer and found you were running a slight fever: "Um-hm. Um-hm." Both alike, they let you go right ahead with it.

THE SCHOOL toilets were in the boys' and girls' respective basements. After Miss Duling had rung to dismiss school, a friend and I were making our plans for Saturday from adjoining cubicles. "Can you come spend the day with me?" I called out, and she called back, "I might could."

"Who—said—MIGHT—COULD?" It sounded like "Fe Fi Fo Fum!"

We both were petrified, for we knew whose deep measured words those were that came from just outside our doors. That was the voice of Mrs. McWillie, who taught the other fourth grade across the hall from ours. She was not even our teacher, but a very heavy, stern lady who dressed entirely in widow's weeds with a pleated black shirtwaist with a high net collar and velvet ribbon, and a black skirt to her ankles, with black circles under her eyes and a mournful, Presbyterian expression. We children took her to be a hundred years old. We held still.

"You might as well tell me," continued Mrs. McWillie. "I'm going to plant myself right here and wait till you come out. Then I'll see who it was I heard saying 'MIGHT-COULD.' "

If Elizabeth wouldn't go out, of course I wouldn't either. We knew her to be a teacher who would not flinch from standing there in the basement all afternoon, perhaps even all day Saturday. So we surrendered and came out. I priggishly hoped Elizabeth would clear it up which child it was—it wasn't me.

"So it's you." She regarded us as a brace, made no distinction: whoever didn't say it was guilty by association. "If I ever catch you down here one more time saying 'MIGHT-COULD,' I'm going to carry it to Miss Duling. You'll be kept in every day for a week! I hope you're both sufficiently ashamed of yourselves?" Saying "might-could" was bad, but saying it in the basement made bad grammar a sin. I knew Presbyterians believed that you could go to Hell.

Mrs. McWillie never scared us into grammar, of course. It was my first-year Latin teacher in high school who made me discover I'd fallen in love with it. It took Latin to thrust me into bona fide alliance with words in their true meaning. Learning Latin (once I was free of Caesar) fed my love for words upon words, words in continuation and modification, and the beautiful, sober, accretion of a sentence. I could see the achieved sentence finally standing there, as real, intact, and built to stay as the Mississippi State Capitol at the top of my street, where I could walk through it on my way to school and hear underfoot the echo of its marble floor, and over me the bell of its rotunda.

On winter's rainy days, the schoolrooms would grow so dark that sometimes you couldn't see the figures on the blackboard. At that point, Mrs. McWillie, that stern fourth-grade teacher, would let her children close their books, and she would move, broad in widow's weeds like darkness itself, to the window and by what light there was she would stand and read aloud "The King of the Golden River." But I was excluded—in the other fourth grade, across the hall. Miss Louella Varnado, my teacher, didn't copy Mrs. McWillie; we had a spelling match: you could spell in the dark. I did not then suspect that there was any other way I could learn the story of "The King of the Golden River" than to have been assigned in the beginning to Mrs. McWillie's cowering fourth grade, then wait for her to treat you to it on the rainy day of her choice. I only now realize how much the treat depended, too, on there not having been money enough to put electric lights in Davis School. John Ruskin had to come in through courtesy of darkness. When in time I found the story in a book and read it to myself, it didn't seem to live up to my longings for a story with that name; as indeed, how could it?

JACKSON'S Carnegie Library was on the same street where our house was, on the other side of the State Capitol. "Through the Capitol" was the way to go to the Library. You could glide through it on your bicycle or even coast through on roller skates, though without family permission.

I never knew anyone who'd grown up in Jackson without being afraid of Mrs. Calloway, our librarian. She ran the Library absolutely by herself, from the desk where she sat with her back to the books and facing the stairs, her dragon eye on the front door, where who knew what kind of person might come in from the public? SILENCE in big black letters was on signs tacked up everywhere. She herself spoke in her normally commanding voice; every word could be heard all over the Library above a steady seething sound coming from her electric fan; it was the only fan in the Library and stood on her desk, turned directly onto her streaming face.

As you came in from the bright outside, if you were a girl, she sent her strong eyes down the stairway to test you; if she could see through your skirt she sent you straight back home: you could just put on another petticoat if you wanted a book that badly from the public library. I was willing; I would do anything to read.

My mother was not afraid of Mrs. Calloway. She wished me to have my own library card to check out books for myself. She took me in to introduce me and I saw I had met a witch. "Eudora is nine years old and has my permission to read any book she wants from the shelves, children or adult," Mother said. "With the exception of *Elsie Dinsmore*," she added. Later she explained to me that she'd made this rule because Elsie the heroine, being made by her father to practice too long and hard at the piano, fainted and fell off the piano stool. "You're too impressionable, dear," she told me. "You'd read that and the very first thing you'd do, you'd fall off the piano stool." "Impressionable" was a new word. I never hear it yet without the image that comes with it of falling straight off the piano stool.

Mrs. Calloway made her own rules about books. You could not take back a book to the Library on the same day you'd taken it out; it made no difference to her that you'd read every word in it and needed another to start. You could take out two books at a time and two only; this applied as long as you were a child and also for the rest of your life, to my mother as severely as to me. So two by two, I read library books as fast as I could go, rushing them home in the basket of my bicycle. From the minute I reached our house, I started to read. Every book I seized on, from *Bunny Brown and His Sister Sue at Camp Rest-a-While* to *Twenty Thousand Leagues under the Sea,* stood for the devouring wish to read being instantly granted. I knew this was bliss, knew it at the time. Taste isn't nearly so important; it comes in its own time. I wanted to read *immediately.* The only fear was that of books coming to an end.

My mother was very sharing of this feeling of insatiability. Now, I think of her as reading so much of the time while doing something else. In my mind's eye *The Origin of Species* is lying on the shelf in the pantry under a light dusting of flour—my mother was a bread maker; she'd pick it up, sit by the kitchen window and find her place, with one eye on the oven. I remember her picking up *The Man in Lower Ten* while my hair got dry enough to unroll from a load of kid curlers trying to make me like my idol, Mary Pickford. A generation later, when my brother Walter was away in the Navy and his two little girls often spent the day in our house, I remember Mother reading the new issue of *Time* magazine while taking the part of the Wolf in a game

33

of "Little Red Riding Hood" with the children. She'd just look up at the right time, long enough to answer—in character—"The better to eat you with, my dear," and go back to her place in the war news.

BOTH our parents had grown up in religious households. In our own family, we children were christened as babies, and were taught our prayers to say at night, and sent as we were growing up to Sunday school, but ours was never a churchgoing family. At home we did not, like Grandpa Welty, say grace at table. In this way we were variously different from most of the families we knew. On Sundays, Presbyterians were not allowed to eat hot food or read the funnypapers or travel the shortest journey; parents believed in Hell and believed tiny babies could go there. Baptists were not supposed to know, up until their dying day, how to play cards or dance. And so on. We went to the Methodist Episcopal Church South Sunday School, and of course we never saw anything strange about Methodists.

But we grew up in a religious-minded society. Even in high school, pupils were used to answering the history teacher's roll call with a perfectly recited verse from the Bible. (No fair "Jesus wept.")

In the primary department of Sunday school, we little girls rose up in taffeta dresses and hot white gloves, with a nickel for collection embedded inside our palms, and while elastic bands from our Madge Evans hats sawed us under the chin, we sang songs led and exhorted by Miss Hattie. This little lady was a wonder of animation, also dressed up, and she stood next to the piano making wild chopping motions with both arms together, a chairleg off one of our Sunday school chairs in her hand to beat time with, and no matter how loudly we sang, we could always hear her even louder: "Bring them in! Bring them in! Bring them in from the fields of sin! Bring the little ones to Jesus!" Those favorite Methodist hymns all sounded happy and pleased with the world, even though the words ran quite the other way. "Throw out the lifeline! Throw out the lifeline! Someone is sinking today!" went to a cheering tune. "I was sinking deep in sin, Far from the peaceful shore, Very deeply stained within, Sinking to rise no more" made you want to dance, and the chorus—"Love lifted me! Love lifted me! When nothing else would help, Love lifted me!"—would send you leaping. Those hymns set your feet moving like the march played on the piano for us to enter Davis School— "Dorothy, an Old English Dance" was the name of that, and of course so many of the Protestant hymns reached down to us from the same place; they *were* old English rounds and dance tunes, and Charles Wesley and the rest had—no wonder—taken them over.

EVANGELISTS visited Jackson then; along with the Redpath Chautauqua and political speakings, they seemed to be part of August. Gypsy Smith was a great local favorite. He was an evangelist, but the term meant nothing like what it stands for today. He had no "team," no organization, no big business, no public address system; he wasn't a showman. Billy Sunday, a little later on, who preached with the athletics of a baseball player, threw off his coat when he got going, and in his shirt-sleeves and red suspenders, he wound up and pitched his punchlines into the audience.

Gypsy Smith was a real Gypsy; in this may have lain part of his magnetism, though he spoke with sincerity too. He was so persuasive that, as night after night went by, he saved "everybody in Jackson," saved all the well-known businessmen on Capitol Street. They might well have been churchgoers already, but they never had been saved by Gypsy Smith. While amalgamated Jackson church choirs sang "Softly and Tenderly Jesus Is Calling" and "Just as I Am," Gypsy Smith called, and being saved—standing up and coming forward—swept Jackson like an epidemic. Most spectacular of all, the firebrand editor of the evening newspaper rose up and came forward one night. It made him lastingly righteous so that he knew just what to say in the *Jackson Daily News* when one of our fellow Mississippians had the unmitigated gall to publish, and expect other Mississippians to read, a book like *Sanctuary*.

Gypsy Smith may have been a Methodist; I don't know. At any rate, our Sunday school class was expected to attend, but I did not go up to be saved. Though all my life susceptible to anyone on a stage, I never would have been able to hold up my hand in front of the crowd at the City Auditorium and "come forward" while the choir leaned out singing "Come home! Come home! All God's children, come home, come home!" And I never felt anything like the pang of secular longing that I'd felt as a much younger child to go up onto the stage at the Century Theatre when the magician dazzlingly called for the valuable assistance of a child from the audience in the performance of his next feat of magic.

Neither was my father among the businessmen who were saved. As if the whole town were simply going through a temperamental meteorological disturbance, he remained calm and at home on Congress Street.

My mother did too. She liked reading her Bible in her own rocking chair, and while she rocked. She considered herself something of a student. "Run get me my Concordance," she'd say, referring to a little book bound in thin leather, falling apart. She liked to correct herself. Then from time to time her lips would twitch in the stern books of the Bible, such as Romans, providing her as they did with memories of her Grandfather Carden who had been a Baptist preacher in the days when she grew up in West Virginia. She liked to try in retrospect to correct Grandpa too.

I painlessly came to realize that the reverence I felt for

the holiness of life is not ever likely to be entirely at home in organized religion. It was later, when I was able to travel farther, that the presence of holiness and mystery seemed, as far as my vision was able to see, to descend into the windows of Chartres, the stone peasant figures in the capitals of Autun, the tall sheets of gold on the walls of Torcello that reflected the light of the sea; in the frescoes of Piero, of Giotto; in the shell of a church wall in Ireland still standing on a floor of sheep-cropped grass with no ceiling other than the changing sky.

I'm grateful that, from my mother's example, I had found the base for this worship—that I had found a love of sitting and reading the Bible for myself and looking up things in it.

How many of us, the South's writers-to-be of my generation, were blessed in one way or another, if not blessed alike, in not having gone deprived of the King James Version of the Bible. Its cadence entered into our ears and our memories for good. The evidence, or the ghost of it, lingers in all our books.

"In the beginning was the Word."

AFTER Sunday school, Daddy might take us children to visit his office. The Lamar Life was in those days housed in a little one-story four-columned Greek temple, next door to the Pythian Castle—a building with crenellations and a high roof that looked as though Douglas Fairbanks might come swinging out of the top window on a rope. On Sunday, nobody else was in Daddy's building, and the water in the cooler was dead quiet too, warm and flat. There was a low mahogany fence around his office with a little gate for people to enter by, and he let us swing on his gate and bounce on the leather davenport while he went over his mail. He put the earphones over my ears to let me discover what I could hear on his dictaphone (I believe he had the

37

first in Jackson). I heard his voice speaking to Miss Montgomery; this was his secretary, who always wore her hair in stylish puffs over her ears, and I had seen her seated at her typewriter while wearing these earphones right on top of her puffs.

He allowed us all our turns to peck at the typewriter. We used the Lamar Life stationery, which carried on its letterhead an oval portrait of Lucius Quintus Cincinnatus Lamar, for whom the Company had been named: a Mississippian who had been a member of Congress, Secretary of the Interior under Cleveland, and a U.S. Supreme Court Justice, a powerful orator who had pressed for the better reconciliation of North and South after the Civil War. Under his bearded portrait we all wrote letters to Mother.

She kept one of Walter's. There wasn't much of it he could spell, but it said, to help her guess who had written it, "Dear Mrs. C. W. Welty. I think you know me. I think you like me."

I CAN'T think I had much of a sense of humor as long as I remained the only child. When my brother Edward came along after I was three, we both became comics, making each other laugh. We set each other off, as we did for life, from the minute he learned to talk. A sense of the absurd was communicated between us probably before that.

Though he hated to see me reading to myself, he accepted my reading to him as long as it made him laugh. We read the same things over and over, chapters from *Alice,* stretches from *Tom Sawyer,* Edward Lear's "Story of the Four Little Children Who Went Around the World." Whenever we came to the names of the four little children we rang them out in unison—"Violet, Slingsby, Guy, and Lionel!" And fell over. We kept this up at mealtimes, screaming nonsense at each other. My mother would warn us that we were *acting* the fool and would very shortly be asked to leave the table. She wouldn't call one of us a fool, or allow us to do it either. "He who calleth his brother a fool," she'd interrupt us, "is in danger of hell fire." I think she never in her life called anyone a fool, though she never bore one gladly, but she *would* say, "Well, it appears to me that Mrs. So-and-So is the least bit *limited*."

Walter, three years again younger than Edward, was soberer than we. In his long baby dress he looked like a judge. I snatched up his baby bathtub and got behind it and danced for him, to hear him really crow. On the pink bottom of his tub I'd drawn a face with crayons, and all he could see of anybody's being there was my legs prancing under it. Walter wore a little kimono when he was up from acidosis, and, another way of adoring him, Edward tried to teach him to fly off Daddy's chair in his kimono, spreading the sleeves, then cried on the floor with him. Walter grew up to be the most serious in his expression of the three of us, and remained the calmest—the one who most took after our father.

When one of us caught measles or whooping cough and we were isolated in bed upstairs, we wrote notes to each other perhaps on the hour. Our devoted mother would pass them for us, after first running them in a hot oven to kill the germs. They came into our hands curled up and warm, sometimes scorched, like toast. Edward replied to my funny notes with his funny drawings. He was a born cartoonist.

In the Spanish influenza epidemic, when Edward had high fever in one room and I high fever in another, I shot him off a jingle about the little boy down our street who was in bed with the same thing: "There was a little boy and his name was Lindsey. He went to Heaven with the influenzy." My mother, horrified, told me to be ashamed of myself and refused to deliver it. So I saw we were all pretty sick, though a proper horror, on finding out what heedless written words of mine have really said, had to come later, as it has. But Edward and I and Lindsey all three got well, and so did Mother, who had much the worst case.

ALL CHILDREN in those small-town, unhurried days had a vast inner life going on in the movies. Whole families attended together in the evenings, at least once a week, and children were allowed to go without chaperone in the long summer afternoons—schoolmates with their best friends, pairs of little girls trotting on foot the short distance through the park to town under their Japanese parasols.

In devotion to Buster Keaton, Charlie Chaplin, Ben Blue, and the Keystone Kops, my brother Edward and I collapsed in laughter. My sense of making fictional comedy undoubtedly caught its first spark from the antic pantomime of the silent screen, and from having a kindred soul to laugh with.

The silent movies were a source also of words that you might never have learned anywhere else. You read them in the captions. "Jeopardy," for example, I got to know from *Drums of Jeopardy* with Alice Brady, who was wearing a leopard skin, a verbal connection I shall never forget. *The Cabinet of Dr. Caligari* turned up by some strange fluke in place of the Saturday western on the screen of the Istrione Theatre (known as the Eyestrain) where it was seen by an attendance consisting entirely of children. I learned "somnambulist" in terror, a word I still never hear or read without seeing again Conrad Veidt in black tights and bangs, making his way at night alongside a high leaning wall with eyes closed, one arm reaching high, seeing with his fingers. But of course all of us together in the movie had screamed with laughter, laughing at what terrified us, exactly as if it were funny, and exactly as grown-up audiences do today.

Events that weren't quite clear in meaning, things we children were shielded from, seemed to have their own routes, their own streets in town, and you might hear them coming near but then they never came, like the organ grinder with his monkey—surely you'd see him, but then the music went down the other street, and the monkey couldn't find you, though you waited with your penny.

In Davis School days, there lived a little boy two or three streets over from ours who was home sick in bed, and when the circus came to town that year, someone got the parade to march up a different street from the usual way to the Fairgrounds, to go past his house. He was carried to the window to watch it go by. Just for him the ponderous elephants, the plumes, the spangles, the acrobats, the clowns, the caged lion, the band playing, the steam calliope, the whole thing! When not long after that he disappeared forever from our view, having died of what had given him his special privilege, none of this at all was acceptable to the rest of us children. He had been tricked, not celebrated, by the parade's brazen marching up his street with the band playing, and we had somehow been tricked by envying him—betrayed into it.

It is not for nothing that an ominous feeling often attaches itself to a procession. This was when I learned it. "The Pied Piper of Hamelin" had done more than just hint at this. In films and stories we see spectacles forming in the street and parades coming from around the corner, and we know to greet them with distrust and apprehension: their intent is still to be revealed. (Think what it was in "My Kinsman, Major Molineux.")

I never resisted it when, in almost every story I ever wrote, some parade or procession, impromptu or ceremonious, comic or mocking or funereal, has risen up to mark some stage of the story's unfolding. They've started from far back.

WE ALL had something like the same sense of humor. It was in losing our tempers that we were wide apart. Our tempers were all strong and intense. When we children quarreled, my brother Edward, in the terrible position of having to hit either a girl or a baby, yelled the loudest in outrage and was driven to bite. Walter, resourceful and practical in his childish fury as in everything else, was locked into the basement once by Edward who had grown tired of being followed around; but our little brother found the ax and made a good start on chopping himself a hole through the bottom of the door before rescue came.

I didn't hit other people or hit purposefully, I just hit. Some object would be at fault. In one case it was a pin-oak tree in the park which I had climbed all the way up and now couldn't get down. So I screamed and hit it with my head, the only part I could spare, and did my best to have a tantrum, while my family stood below making fun and arguing that nobody could bring me down but me. My anger was at myself, every time, all vanity. As an adolescent I was a slammer of drawers and a packer of suitcases. I was responsible for scenes.

Control came imperfectly to all of us: we reached it at different times of life, frustrated, shot into indignation, by different things—some that are grown out of, and others not.

"I don't understand where you children *get* it," said my mother. "I never lose my temper. I just get hurt." (But that was it.)

One time, and one time only, she told us in a voice that opens a subject to close it, "I believe your father himself had a terrible temper once. But he learned to control his, a long time ago."

We tried to imagine Daddy swinging our ax. We could not, even our precious Walter, who had done it.

Of all my strong emotions, anger is the one least responsible for any of my work. I don't write out of anger. For one thing, simply as a fiction writer, I am minus an adversary—except, of course, that of time—and for another thing, the act of writing in itself brings me happiness.

There was one story that anger certainly lit the fuse of. In the 1960s, in my home town of Jackson, the civil rights leader Medgar Evers was murdered one night in darkness, and I wrote a story that same night about the murderer (his identity then unknown) called "Where Is the Voice Coming From?" But all that absorbed me, though it started as outrage, was the necessity I felt for entering into the mind and inside the skin of a character who could hardly have been more alien or repugnant to me. Trying for my utmost, I wrote it in the first person. I was wholly vaunting the prerogative of the short-story writer. It is always vaunting, of course, to imagine yourself inside another person, but it is what a story writer does in every piece of work; it is his first step, and his last too, I suppose. I'm not sure this story was brought off; and I don't believe that my anger showed me anything about human character that my sympathy and rapport never had.

EVEN as we grew up, my mother could not help imposing herself between her children and whatever it was they might take it in mind to reach out for in the world. For she would get it for them, if it was good enough for them—she would have to be very sure—and give it to them, at whatever cost to herself: valiance was in her very fibre. She stood always prepared in herself to challenge the world in our place. She did indeed tend to make the world look dangerous, and so it had been to her. A way had to be found around her love sometimes, without challenging *that,* and at the same time cherishing it in its unassailable strength. Each of us children did, sooner or later, in part at least, solve this in a different, respectful, complicated way.

But I think she was relieved when I chose to be a writer of stories, for she thought writing was safe.

II

LEARNING
TO SEE

WHEN we set out in our five-passenger Oakland touring car on our summer trip to Ohio and West Virginia to visit the two families, my mother was the navigator. She sat at the alert all the way at Daddy's side as he drove, correlating the AAA Blue Book and the speedometer, often with the baby on her lap. She'd call out, "All right, Daddy: '86-point-2, crossroads. Jog right, past white church. Gravel ends.'—And there's the church!" she'd say, as though we had scored. Our road always became her adversary. "This doesn't surprise me at all," she'd say as Daddy backed up a mile or so into our own dust on a road that had petered out. "I could've told you a road that looked like that had little intention of going anywhere."

"It was the first one we'd seen all day going in the right direction," he'd say. His sense of direction was unassailable, and every mile of our distance was familiar to my father by rail. But the way we set out to go was popularly known as "through the country."

My mother's hat rode in the back with the children, suspended over our heads in a pillowcase. It rose and fell with us when we hit the bumps, thumped our heads and batted our ears in an authoritative manner when sometimes we bounced as high as the ceiling. This was 1917 or 1918; a lady couldn't expect to travel without a hat.

Edward and I rode with our legs straight out in front of us over some suitcases. The rest of the suitcases rode just outside the doors, strapped on the running boards. Cars weren't made with trunks. The tools were kept under the back seat and were heard from in syncopation with the bumps; we'd jump out of the car so Daddy could get them out and jack up the car to patch and vulcanize a tire, or haul out the tow rope or the tire chains. If it rained so hard we couldn't see the road in front of us, we waited it out, snapped in behind the rain curtains and playing "Twenty Questions."

My mother was not naturally observant, but she could scrutinize; when she gave the surroundings her attention, it was to verify something—the truth or a mistake, hers or another's. My father kept his eyes on the road, with glances toward the horizon and overhead. My brother Edward periodically stood up in the back seat with his eyelids fluttering while he played the harmonica, "Old Macdonald had a farm" and "Abdul the Bulbul Amir," and the baby slept in Mother's lap and only woke up when we crossed some rattling old bridge. *"There's* a river!" he'd crow to us all. "Why, it certainly *is,"* my mother would reassure him, patting him back to sleep. I rode as a hypnotic, with my set gaze on the landscape that vibrated past at twenty-five miles an hour. We were all wrapped by the long ride into some cocoon of our own.

The journey took about a week each way, and each day had my parents both in its grip. Riding behind my father I could see that the road had him by the shoulders, by the hair under his driving cap. It took my mother to make him stop. I inherited his nervous energy in the way I can't stop writing on a story. It makes me understand how Ohio had him around the heart, as West Virginia had my mother. Writers and travelers are mesmerized alike by knowing of their destinations.

And all the time that we think we're getting there so fast, how slowly we do move. In the days of our first car trip, Mother proudly entered in her log, "Mileage today: 161!" with an exclamation mark.

"A Detroit car passed us yesterday." She always kept those logs, with times, miles, routes of the day's progress, and expenses totaled up.

That kind of travel made you conscious of borders; you

Eudora, 1929 University of Wisconsin.

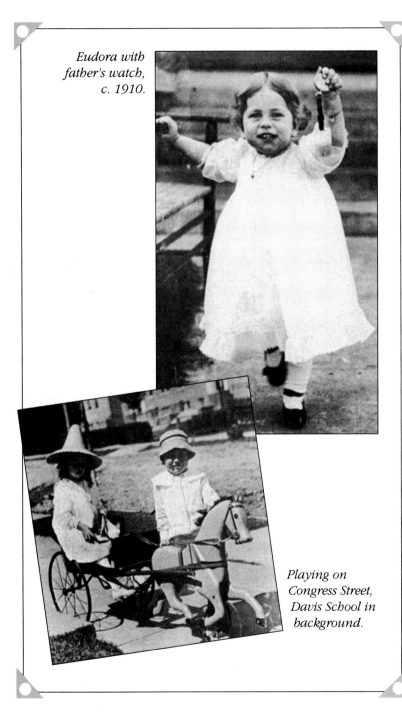

*Eudora with
father's watch,
c. 1910.*

*Playing on
Congress Street,
Davis School in
background.*

With my father,
Christian Welty.

Christina Andrews Welty.

My grandmother, Eudora Carden Andrews, seated in the chair, with five of her six children: my mother and, left to right, John, Moses, Carl, and Edward Columbus (Bus). At their mountain-top home near clay, West Virginia.

Our summer trip. A road through the Mississippi Delta, c. 1917.

Ferrying the Kentucky (?), family car trip to West Virginia and Ohio, in the Oakland car.

Grandpa Jefferson Welty, on the farm near Logan, Ohio, with Edward, Walter, Eudora, c. 1917.

Eudora and Edward, c. 1913.

Eudora, Edward, Mother, Walter, c. 1917.

Christina Andrews and Christian Welty in West Virginia, in courtship days, c. 1903.

My mother's mother, Eudora Carden Andrews. Photograph of a tintype made by Edward Raboteau Andrews, in West Virginia, c. 1882.

Edward Raboteau Andrews, my mother's father.

My mother coming down the stairs at 741 North Congress Street, Jackson. (My father took all these photos.)

Eudora, 1936, at the time of publication of first story, "Death of a Traveling Salesman."

Eudora, 1941, at the time of first book, A Curtain of Green, *in the backyard on Pinehurst Street.*

rode ready for them. Crossing a river, crossing a county line, crossing a state line—especially crossing the line you couldn't see but knew was there, between the South and the North—you could draw a breath and feel the difference.

The Blue Book warned you of the times for the ferries to run; sometimes there were waits of an hour between. With rivers and roads alike winding, you had to cross some rivers three times to be done with them. Lying on the water at the foot of a river bank would be a ferry no bigger than somebody's back porch. When our car had been driven on board—often it was down a roadless bank, through sliding stones and runaway gravel, with Daddy simply aiming at the two-plank gangway—father and older children got out of the car to enjoy the trip. My brother and I got barefooted to stand on wet, sun-warm boards that, weighted with your car, seemed exactly on the level with the water; our feet were the same as in the river. Some of these ferries were operated by a single man pulling hand over hand on a rope bleached and frazzled as if made from cornshucks.

I watched the frayed rope running through his hands. I thought it would break before we could reach the other side.

"No, it's not going to break," said my father. "It's never broken before, has it?" he asked the ferry man.

"No sirree."

"You see? If it never broke before, it's not going to break this time."

His general belief in life's well-being worked either way. If you had a pain, it was "Have you ever had it before? You have? It's not going to kill you, then. If you've had the same thing before, you'll be all right in the morning."

My mother couldn't have more profoundly disagreed with that.

"You're such an optimist, dear," she often said with a sigh, as she did now on the ferry.

"You're a good deal of a pessimist, sweetheart."

"I certainly *am.*"

And yet I was well aware as I stood between them with the water running over my toes, he the optimist was the one who was prepared for the worst, and she the pessimist was the daredevil: he the one who on our trip carried chains and a coil of rope and an ax all upstairs to our hotel bedroom every night in case of fire, and she the one—before I was born—when there *was* a fire, had broken loose from all hands and run back—on crutches, too—into the burning house to rescue her set of Dickens which she flung, all twenty-four volumes, from the window before she jumped out after them, all for Daddy to catch.

"I make no secret of my lifelong fear of the water," said my mother, who on ferry boats remained inside the car, clasping the baby to her—my brother Walter, who was destined to prowl the waters of the Pacific Ocean in a mine-sweeper.

As soon as the sun was beginning to go down, we went more slowly. My father would drive sizing up the towns, inspecting the hotel in each, deciding where we could safely spend the night. Towns little or big had beginnings and ends, they reached to an edge and stopped, where the country began again as though they hadn't happened. They were intact and to themselves. You could see a town lying ahead in its whole, as definitely formed as a plate on a table. And your road entered and ran straight through the heart of it; you could see it all, laid out for your passage through. Towns, like people, had clear identities and your imagination could go out to meet them. You saw houses, yards, fields, and people busy in them, the people that had a life where they were. You could hear their bank clocks striking, you could smell their bakeries. You would know those towns again, recognize the salient detail, seen so close up. Nothing was blurred, and in passing along Main Street, slowed down from twenty-five to twenty miles an hour, you didn't miss anything on either side. Going somewhere "through the country" acquainted you with the whole way there and back.

My mother never fully gave in to her pleasure in our trip—for pleasure every bit of it was to us all—because she knew we were traveling with a loaded pistol in the pocket on the door of the car on Daddy's side. I doubt if my father fired off any kind of gun in his life, but he could not have carried his family from Jackson, Mississippi to West Virginia and Ohio through the country, unprotected.

THIS was not the first time I'd been brought here to visit Grandma in West Virginia, but the first visit I barely remembered. Where I stood now was inside the house where my mother had been born and where she grew up. It was a low, gray-weathered wooden house with a broad hall through the middle of it with the light of day at each end, the house that Ned Andrews, her father, had built to stand on the very top of the highest mountain he could find.

"And here's where I first began to read my Dickens," Mother said, pointing. "Under that very bed. Hiding my candle. To keep them from knowing what I was up to all night."

"But where did it all *come* from?" I asked her at last. "All that Dickens?"

"Why, Papa gave me that set of Dickens for agreeing to let them cut off my hair," she said, as if surprised that a reason like that wouldn't have occurred to me. "In those days, they thought very long thick hair like mine would sap a child's strength. I said *No!* I wanted my hair left the very way it was. They offered me gold earrings first—in those days little girls often developed a wish to have their ears pierced and fitted with little gold rings. I said *No!* I'd rather keep my hair. Then Papa said, 'What about books? I'll have

51

them send a whole set of Charles Dickens to you, right up the river from Baltimore, in a barrel.' I agreed."

Ned Andrews had been the county's youngest member of the bar. He quickly made a name for himself on the side as an orator. When he gave the dedicatory address for the opening of a new courthouse in Nicholas County, West Virginia, my mother put away a copy. He is praising the architecture of the building: "The student turns with a sigh of relief from the crumbling pillars and columns of Athens and Alexandria to the symmetrical and colossal temples of the New World. As time eats from the tombstones of the past the epitaphs of primeval greatness, and covers the pyramids with the moss of forgetfulness, she directs the eye to the new temples of art and progress that make America the monumental beacon-light of the world."

People may have expected the highfalutin in oratory in those days, but they might not have expected Ned's courtroom flair. There was a murder trial of a woman given to fortunetelling. She had been overheard reading in an old man's cards that his days were numbered. When, the very next day, this old man had been found in his bed dead from a gunshot wound, it appeared to the public that that fortuneteller might have known too much about it. She was put on trial for murder. Ned Andrews' defense centered on the well-known fact that the old man kept his loaded gun mounted at all times over the head of his bed. This was the gun that had shot him. The old man could have discharged it perfectly easily himself, Ned argued, by carelessly bouncing on the bed a little bit. He proposed to prove it, and invited the jury of dubious mountaineers to watch him do it. Leading them all the way up the mountain to the old man's cabin, he mounted the gun in place on its rests, having first loaded it with blank shells, and while they watched he mimicked the old man and made a running jump onto the bed. The gun jarred loose, tumbled down, and fired at him. He rested his case. The fortuneteller was without any more ado declared not guilty.

He was brim full of talents. He'd attended Trinity College (later, Duke University) where he organized a literary society; he'd been a journalist and a photographer in Norfolk, Virginia, and in West Virginia where he'd run away to, to seek adventure, he'd turned into a lawyer. He seems to have been a legendary fisherman in those mountain streams, is still now and then referred to in local sportsmen's tales. Ned was impervious to the sting of bees and could always be summoned to capture a wild swarm. Ned was the one they sent for when someone fell down an empty well, because he was not afraid to harness himself and be lowered into the deathly gasses at the bottom and bring the unconscious victim up again.

Yet the human failings Mother could least forgive in other people, she regarded with only tenderness in him. I gathered—slowly and over the years I gathered—that sometimes he drank. He told tall tales to his wife, Eudora Carden. He told one to begin with, in order to marry her, saying he was of age to do so, when he was nineteen and four years younger than she. She was superstitious; he loved to tease her with tricks, to stage elaborate charades with the connivance of one of his little boys, that preyed on her fear of ghosts. He shocked her with a tale—Mother said there was nothing to prove it wasn't a fact—that one of the Andrews ancestors had been hanged in Ireland. Eudora Carden came from the home of a strongly dedicated Baptist preacher, and about all preachers he was irreverent and irrepressible. I have seen photographs he took of her—tintypes; it's clear that he took them with great care to show how beautiful he found her. In one she is standing up behind a chair, with her long hands crossed at the wrist over the back of it; she is dressed in her best, with her dark hair drawn high above her oval face and tucked with a flower that looks like a wild rose. She is very young. She has long gray eyes over high cheekbones; she is gazing to the front, looking straight at him. Her mouth is sensitive, her lips youthfully full. She told her daughter Chessie years later that she was objecting to his taking this picture because she was pregnant at the time, and the pose—the crossed hands on the back of a chair—had been to hide that. (With my mother herself, I wondered, her first child?) When she came back from the well on cold mornings, her hands would be bleeding from breaking the ice on it: this is what my mother would remember when she looked at those soft hands in the tintypes.

I don't know from whom it came or to whom it was passed, but at one time an old, home-made drawing of the Andrews family tree came into my mother's hands. It was rolled up; if unrolled it was capable of rattling shut the next instant. The tree was drawn as a living tree, spreading from a rooted trunk, every branch, twig, and leaf in clear outline, all with names and dates on them in a copperplate hand-writing. The most riveting feature was the thick branch stemming from near the base of the main trunk: it was bro-ken off short to a jagged end, branchless and leafless, and la-beled "Joseph, Killed by lightning."

It had been executed with the finest possible pen in ink grown very pale, as if it had been drawn in watered maple syrup. The leaves weren't stiffly drawn or conventional ellip-ses, all alike, but each one daintily fashioned with a pointed tip and turned on its stem this way or that, as if this family tree were tossed by a slight breeze. The massed whole had the look, at that time to me, of a children's puzzle in which you were supposed to find your mother. I found mine— only a tiny leaf on a twig of a branch near the top, hardly big enough to hold her tiny name.

The Andrews branch my mother came from represents the mix most usual in the Southeast—English, Scottish,

Irish, with a dash of French Huguenot. The first American one, Isham, who fought in the Revolutionary War, was born in Virginia and moved to Georgia, where succeeding generations lived. The Andrewses were not a rural clan, like the Weltys; they lived in towns, were educators and preachers, with some Methodist circuit riders; one cousin of Ned's (Walter Hines Page) was an ambassador to England. Trinity College educated some of them, including, for an impatient time, young Ned. By the time my mother's father, Edward Raboteau Andrews (Ned) was born in 1862, the family had returned to Virginia. He broke from the mold and at eighteen ran away from a home of parents, grandparents, sisters, brothers, and aunts in Norfolk to become the first West Virginian.

Here in the center of the Andrews kitchen, at the same long table where the family always ate, not too far from where Grandma seemed to be always busy at the warm stove, Ned had sat and worked up his cases for the defense in Clay Courthouse, far below and out of sight straight down the mountain. Mother remembered him transposing band music there, too; he had sent off for the instruments, got together a band, and proceeded to teach them to play in concert, lined up on the courthouse lawn: he had a strong need of music. His children had an instrument to learn to play too: he assigned my mother the cornet. (When I think back to how she sang "Blessed Assurance" while washing the dishes, I realize she flatted her high notes just where a child's cornet might.)

It was in the quilted bed in the front room of this house where he lay in so much pain (probably from the affliction that brought on his death, an infected appendix) that he once told Mother, a little girl, to bring the kitchen knife and plunge it into his side; she, hypnotized, almost believed she must obey. It was from that door that later she went with him on the frozen winter night when it was clear he had to get, somehow, to a hospital. The mountain roads were impassable, there was ice in the Elk River: but a neighbor vowed he could make way by raft. She was fifteen. Leaving her mother and the five little brothers at home, Chessie went with him. Her father lay on the raft, on which a fire had been lit to warm him, Chessie beside him. The neighbor managed to pole the raft through the icy river and eventually across it to a railroad. They flagged the train. (It seems likely that the place they flagged it was the same as where my mother and I were let off that train when I was three, arriving on that nearly forgotten visit. It was an early summer dawn; everything was a cloud of mist—we were standing on the bank of a river and I didn't know it. When my mother pulled the rope of an iron bell, we watched a boat come out of the mist to meet us, with her five brothers all inside.)

Mother had to return by herself from Baltimore, her father's body in a coffin on the same train. He had died on the operating table in Johns Hopkins, of a ruptured appendix, at thirty-seven years of age. The last lucid remark he'd made to my mother was "If you let them tie me down, I'll die." (The surgeon had come out where she stood waiting in the hall. "Little girl," he'd said, "you'd better get in touch now with somebody in Baltimore." "Sir, I don't know anybody in Baltimore," she said, and what she never forgot was his astounded reply: "You don't know anybody in *Baltimore?*")

It was from this house that my mother very soon after that piled up her hair and went out to teach in a one-room school, mountain children little and big alike. The first day, some fathers came along to see if she could whip their children, some who were older than she. She told the children that she did intend to whip them if they became unruly and refused to learn, and invited the fathers to stay if they liked and she'd be able to whip them too. Having been thus tried out, she was a great success with them after that. She left home every day on her horse; since she had the river to cross, a little brother rode on her horse behind her, to ride him home, while she rowed across the river in a boat. And he would be there to meet her with her horse again at evening. All this way, to pass the time, she told me, she recited the poems in McGuffey's Readers out loud.

She could still recite them in full when she was lying helpless and nearly blind, in her bed, an old lady. Reciting, her voice took on resonance and firmness, it rang with the old fervor, with ferocity even. She was teaching me one more, almost her last, lesson: emotions do not grow old. I knew that I would feel as she did, and I do.

TEACHING, my mother earned, little by little, money enough to go to nearby Marshall College in the summers and in time was graduated. Her mind was filled with *Paradise Lost*, she told me later, showing me the notebook she still kept with its diagrams. It was as a schoolteacher she'd met my father, Christian Welty, a young man from Ohio, who had come to work that summer in the office of a lumber company in the vicinity. While they courted, they used to take long walks up and down the railroad tracks, which I imagine my father found in themselves romantic—they took snapshots of each other, my father with one foot on a milepost, my mother sitting on a stile with an open book and wearing a "fascinator" over her hair. My father had her snap his picture standing on a moving sidecar, his hand at the lever. It was in leaving this house that she married him and set off for a new life and a new part of the world for both of them, in Jackson, Mississippi.

Mother's brothers were called "the boys." Their long-necked banjos hung on pegs along the wide hall, as casually as hats and coats. Coming in from outdoors, Carl and Mose lifted their banjos off the wall and sat down side by side and struck in. This was what I remembered from my early visit;

I had till now forgotten. They played together like soul-mates. At age three, I'd cried "Two Carls!" They sang in the same perfect beat, perfect unison, "Frog Went A-Courting and He Did Ride."

That effortless, drumlike rhythm, heard in double, too, would have put a claim on any child. They had a repertoire of ballads and country songs and rousing hymns. My mother would tell her brothers, plead with them, to stop—I didn't want to go to bed. "Aw, Sister, let Girlie have her one more song," and one song could keep going without loss of a beat into still one more.

The boys liked to sing together too, all five, without accompaniment. Gus, the heaviest, with his broad chest, dominated the others with a bass down to his toes. Those old hymns they'd grown up with, coming out chorus after chorus, sounded more and more uproarious, especially sung outdoors. "Roll, Jordan, Roll" would fill the air around them and roll back on them from the next mountain in echoes, as if the mountain were full of singers like black-birds in a pie, just waiting for the song to let them out.

I don't suppose now that my mother ever thought of her father in any other light than the one she saw him in when she was a little girl—for he didn't live much beyond then. All I was given to know of him myself is her same childlike vision, uncorrectable—half of it adoring dream, half brutal memory of his death, the part of his story that she, all by herself, was the one able to tell. Her brothers were all too little to have kept a clear memory of him at all; they remembered his songs best, remembered him when *they* sang, and told how he made up more and more verses to "Where Have You Been, Billy Boy?" putting his own ram-bunctious words to the tune. What they remember is what the stories tell about him, and what they could see lay in their mother.

What did my father, Christian Welty, think of all

these stories of her father my mother told? I never knew. My father was his very opposite, all that was stable, reticent, self-contained, willing to be patient if need be, and, in all *he* said, factual. Before the birth of my brothers, when my mother and I went up on the train alone, my father would come at the end of our visit to shepherd us home. Perhaps I remembered this without too much understanding, but I was not too much of a baby to notice and remember how different it was when my father arrived on the scene./A difference came over whatever we were doing, like a change in the wind.

The fact was my mother and I were the only ones really dying to see him come. Of course he was older than they, the brothers—four years older than Chessie, their older sister—and he was a Yankee, but I came to realize later what must have been the real reason for the polite distance they put into their welcome: ever since he'd first come courting, they'd known he was only here to take their sister away from them.

It was in this house they saw their sister married. Mother's brothers never in my memory called my father other than "Mr. Welty," and certainly they didn't then, on their wedding day; Moses, the youngest, went out and "cried on the ground." The newlyweds left on the train for the World's Fair and Louisiana Purchase Centennial Exposition that had opened (a year late) in St. Louis. It was October 1904. They would then go on to Jackson, Mississippi, and the future. My mother thought it was ill-becoming to brag about your courage; the nearest she came was to say, "Yes, I expect I was pretty venturesome."

It must have seemed to her family behind her that she had been cut off from them forever. They never really got over her absence from home.

I don't think she ever really got over it either. I think she could listen sometimes and hear the mountain's voice—

the delayed echo of the unseen and distant old man—"just an old hermit," said Grandma—chopping wood with his ax and calling on God in alternation, in answering blows; the prattling of the Queen's Shoals in Elk river somewhere below, equally out of sight, which I believed I could hear from Grandma's front-yard rocking chair, though I was told that I must be listening to something else; the loss and recovery of traveling sound, the *carrying* of the voice that called as if on long threads the hand could hold to, so I would keep asking who that was, who was still out of sight but calling in the mountains as he neared us, as we brought him near.

I think when my mother came to Jackson she brought West Virginia with her. Of course, I brought some of it with me too.

For as long as she lived, letters went back and forth every day between my grandmother and my mother. Grandma always had to concern herself with her letters getting carried down the mountain to the Court House to make the train.

Dear Chessie, I wrote to you last night but did not give it to Gus this morning as I thought Carl would be sure to go to the C.H. and as he had letters of his own to mail would not be likely to forget. He had his overcoat on to go before dinner but I told him that dinner was ready and after we had started to eat Moses came in and said the dog was after a fox and all of the boys left as soon as they were through dinner and here is my letter and I hear the train now so it will not go. It stopped raining last night and today it has been snowing part of the time and blowing nearly all of the time and so dark and gloomy looking that I only sit by the fire. I wish you had a half dozen of my chickens. I killed three last week for the boys to take to school. I do wish I could step in a while and see you and as I cannot I think I will take a nap. With lots of love from Mother.

and

... Carl is writing letters to different ones that he thinks might come to school, Gus and Moses are playing on their banjoes as Eudora would say, I do not know what John is doing, he is in the other room ... Say, do you believe that two pigeons could be sent from here to Eudora say in April or do you think they could not go without some one being along to take care of them. She would like them for they would fly all around her and eat out of her hand if she would let them. We are all well and do hope you are all well, with lots of love from Mother, and kiss Baby.

and one on a November 4:

My dear child, I received no letter yesterday but had expected to start one to you this morning but failed. I had thought I would walk to the C.H. and started to get ready. It is a beautiful day overhead, you cannot see a cloud and yet the wind is fearful. I have nearly finished my looming [?], scrubbed the dining room and kitchen, picked up three or four bushels of walnuts, I washed yesterday and found two hen's nests with sixteen eggs in them. I told Gus I had saved 75¢ or a dollar and made a quarter, as eggs are 25¢ a dozen ... The boys have started to school and I believe they will learn, they both seem pleased with their Teacher. Maggie Keeney's fourth sister is teaching the lower room. Maggie Cora and Mattie as you may know are married, that leaves Hester and this one to teach. Gus said last night that one of Clay's teachers died yesterday, a bright young man. I wish I was able to do with my hands as fast as I find jobs to do, and maybe I could set

61

things straight but I cannot do that. I am lonely enough but if you and baby could walk in sometime to see Grandma I would do all right but I hope both and all three of you keep well, with a heart full of love from Mother.

This is a letter she wrote to me:

My dear Eudora Alice, I do wish I could go on the choo choo train and see you and be at your little party, I would bring you two pretty little pigeons, for I know both you and your little friends would enjoy having them, but as I cannot go nor send the little pigeons, I am going to the Court House this morning and see if I can send you a little cup of sugar you can eat and think of Grandma. I hope you will have a nice time and be well. With lots of love from Grandma. P.S. Tell your Ma I will write to her next time.

Such were my mother's component parts.

Grandma had thought my agitation and apprehension of her over-familiar pigeons was love. I can see now that perhaps she was right.

That summer, lying in the long grass with my head propped against the back of a saddle, with the zenith above me and the drop of distance below, I listened to the mountain silence until I could hear as far into it as the faintest clink of a cowbell. In the mountains, what might be out of sight had never really gone away. Like the mountain, that distant bell would always be there. It would keep reminding.

IT TOOK the mountain top, it seems to me now, to give me the sensation of independence. It was as if I'd discovered something I'd never tasted before in my short life. Or rediscovered it—for I associated it with the taste of the water that came out of the well, accompanied with the ring of that long metal sleeve against the sides of the living mountain, as from deep down it was wound up to view brimming and streaming long drops behind it like bright stars on a ribbon. It thrilled me to drink from the common dipper. The coldness, the far, unseen, unheard springs of what was in my mouth now, the iron strength of its flavor that drew my cheeks in, its fern-laced smell, all said mountain mountain mountain as I swallowed. Every swallow was making me a part of being here, sealing me in place, with my bare feet planted on the mountain and sprinkled with my rapturous spills. What I felt I'd come here to do was something on my own.

My mother adored her brothers, "the boys," and she was their heart. One day she and the boys, taking me along, were dawdling down the mountain path and talking family together. I thought I'd take off on a superior track I saw for myself, and the next moment I was flying down it, straight down, then falling, rolling and tumbling, gathering dust and leaves in my clothes and hair, and I could hear a long rip coming in my skirt without being able to stop until some bush caught hold of me. I got to my feet and looked back up. It wasn't far, but my mother and the boys might have been standing over the rim of the moon: they were laughing at me, my mother along with the boys, helplessly laughing. One of my uncles dropped down to me and carried me up again. I went back with them, riding on his shoulders. The boys, though not my mother now, were still teasing, and I was aloft up there, hanging my head or holding it up—I can't be sure now.

"Well, now Girlie's learned what a log chute is," said Uncle Carl, putting me down in front of Grandma as if to let her in on the family joke. Her gesture then was the last other thing I remembered from being here before: with her forefinger she pushed my hair behind my ears and bared my face to hers. She looked seriously right into my eyes. Hadn't we come right to the point of our both being named Eudora?

"Run take that little dress of yours off, and Grandma'll sew up the hole in it right quick," she said. Then she looked from me to my mother and back. I learned on our trip what that look meant: it was matching family faces.

THE CARDENS had been in West Virginia for a while— I believe were there before West Virginia was a state. Eudora Carden's own mother had been Eudora Ayres, of an Orange County, Virginia, family, the daughter of a Huguenot mother and an English father. He was a planter, fairly well-to-do. Eudora Ayres married another young Virginian, William Carden, who was poor and called a "dreamer"; and when these two innocents went to start life in the wild mountainous country, in the unknown part that had separated itself from Virginia, among his possessions he brought his leather-covered Latin dictionary and grammar, and she brought her father's wedding present of five slaves. The dictionary was forever kept in the tiny farmhouse and the slaves were let go. One of the stark facts of their lives in Enon is that during the Civil War Great-Grandfather Carden was taken prisoner and incarcerated in Ohio on suspicion of being, as a Virginian, a Confederate sympathizer, and lost his eyesight in confinement.

Their son, Mother's Grandpa Carden, was a Baptist preacher. Enon-near-Gilboa was the name of his church— taken from the Bible, of course; Gilboa, on the mountain as in the Bible, was the older church it was near to. This was where Eudora Carden and four brothers were born, and where later the Andrews children spent a great deal of their time. He was an enormously strict and vigorous-minded old man.

When his first wife died, leaving him a young man

with little children, Grandpa did what so many did then: he sent back to Virginia for her sister. Then, after an interval, he married her. My mother, at a young and knowing age, once praised her to her face for her unselfishness in coming from Virginia and marrying Grandpa for the sake of his motherless children, and the old lady replied tartly, "Who says that's why I married him?"

My mother and the boys spent a lot of time visiting Grandpa and Grandma Carden. This good old man liked to retire to the barn to say his bedtime prayers, where he could thunder them up as he pleased, to the rafters. Mother's little brothers used to delight in hiding in the hay where they could listen to Grandpa pray, and he on his side would be sure to get all their names in when he was asking for forgiveness and beg the Lord to be patient with them, whatever had been their sinful ways, and lead them into righteousness *before it was too late.*

Sometimes at our house, when my mother read the Bible in her rocking chair by the fire, she'd hail a passage to read out oratorically. "I'm just so strongly reminded of Grandpa Carden when I come to Romans," she'd say.

She'd been pretty lively toward Grandpa in her own youth. "I don't agree with Saint Paul," she'd told him once: it was in connection with the rule of wearing a hat to church.

In our picture of Grandpa Carden, his long beard and side whiskers are pure white, and seem to be stirred by some mountain wind. His large black hat is resting upside-down on his knee as he sits on a straight-back bench. His right hand is holding, straight up and down and thin as a rod, his staff; it looks four or five feet tall. The photograph is inscribed across the back in a strict hand, "To Chessie, if she will have it."

Those had been early days. I tend to think that it had been Ned Andrews who saw himself in West Virginia as some original pioneer; he was the lone romantic in this story. He might have delighted in imagining the figure he'd cut to them back in Tidewater Virginia. (They *did* wonder at him: I grew to know the Virginia kin, his remarkable mother and his sisters who, when they knew, rallied around young Chessie and all Ned's family.)

His fine-grained wife lived on as a woman of unceasing courage and of considerable grace, with a great deal to make the best of. In the eyes of all their devoted children, and in every word I ever heard them say, it appeared that neither of their parents could ever have done conscious wrong or made an irretrievable mistake in their lives. When their mother died, the boys came down from the mountain. They married and made their own lives—except for John, who died of pneumonia after enlisting in the Army in 1918—in teaching, banking, civic or business affairs below. Carl became mayor of Charleston. They never let go of the home place. It was kept up as a family retreat, a camp for hunting and fishing. My mother and her brothers were able to visit each other, not only in times of trouble or crisis. It became comparatively easy, one day, after all.

IT SEEMS likely to me now that the very element in my character that took possession of me there on top of the mountain, the fierce independence that was suddenly mine, to remain inside me no matter how it scared me when I tumbled, was an inheritance. Indeed it was my chief inheritance from my mother, who was braver. Yet, while she knew that independent spirit so well, it was what she so agonizingly tried to protect me from, in effect to warn me against. It was what we shared, it made the strongest bond between us and the strongest tension. To grow up is to fight for it, to grow old is to lose it after having possessed it. For her, too, it was most deeply connected to the mountains.

When she was old, widowed, ill, and losing her sight,

my mother one day announced to me she would be very glad to have the piano back in our house. It was the Steinway upright she had bought for me when I was nine, so far beyond her means, and had paid for herself out of the housekeeping money, which she added to by buying a Jersey cow, milking her, and selling part of the milk to the neighbors on our street, in quart bottles which I delivered on my bicycle. While I sat on the piano stool practicing my scales, I imagined my mother sitting on her stool in the cowshed, her fingers just as rhythmically pulling the teats of Daisy.

Two of her children had played this piano, I practicing my lessons and my brother Edward all along playing better by ear. When her grand-daughters came along, the piano was sent to their house to practice their lessons on. Now, all those years later, Mother wanted it under her roof again. Right now! It was brought and, the same day, tuned. She asked me to go directly to it and play for her "The West Virginia Hills."

I sat down and remembered how it went, and as I played I heard her singing it—singing it to herself, just as she used to while washing the dishes after supper:

O the West Virginia hills!
How my heart with rapture thrills ...
O the hills! Beautiful hills! ...

This one moment seemed to satisfy her. Once from her wheelchair, afterwards, she tried to pick it out herself, laying her finger slowly down on keys she couldn't really see. "A mountaineer," she announced to me proudly, as though she had never told me this before and now I had better remember it, "always will be *free.*"

''OH YES, we're in the North now," said my mother after we'd crossed the state line from West Virginia into Ohio. "The barns are all bigger than the houses. They care more about the horses and cows than they do about—" She forbore to say.

The farm my father grew up on, where Grandpa Welty and Grandma lived, was in southern Ohio in the rolling hills of Hocking County, near the small town of Logan. It was one of the neat, narrow-porched, two-story farmhouses, painted white, of the Pennsylvania-German country. Across its front grew feathery cosmos and barrel-sized peony bushes with stripy heavy-scented blooms pushing out of the leaves. There was a springhouse to one side, down a little walk only one brick in width, and an old apple orchard in front, the barn and the pasture and fields of corn and wheat behind. Periodically there came sounds from the barn, and you could hear the crows, but everything else was still.

In the house it was solid stillness, it seemed to me, at almost any hour, all day, except for dinnertime. Whoever was in the house seemed to remain invisible, but this was because they were all busy. I think in retrospect that my father had set our visit in time to help with the harvest, and certainly he was very busy outside all day. He let my brother Edward go with him.

My mother, in the way she had, never put aside her *first* impression of Grandpa Welty. She was hurt when he had met the train in the spring wagon, not the buggy. All the way home to the farm, he never started a conversation with her. "But that was his *custom*," years later she explained to me. "He never brought out much to say till I was ready to go. Then on my last day, on the long ride to the station, he never stopped talking at all. He talked up one blue streak." They took to each other enormously.

Throughout our visit, as long as the daylight held, he was out stirring about the barn or moving through the fields. He was a quiet, gentle man, with a flourishing mustache, with not much to say to the women and children in his house; when he did sit down, it would be in his wooden platform swing outside, usually with his pipe and holding one of the farm kittens on his knee. Now and then he held me there, and then I could hold the kitten.

My grandmother Welty was my father's stepmother. My mother would remark, "There's one thing I will have to say about Mother Welty: she makes the best *bread* I ever put in my mouth." It really is the only thing I can remember she ever said about Grandma Welty, though she did feel often compelled to repeat it, and never said anything different after the old lady died.

Grandma Welty, with each work day in the week set firmly aside for a single task, was not very expectant of conversation either. Of course I remember Friday best—baking day. Her pies, enough for a week, were set to cool when done on the kitchen windowsills, side by side like so many cheeky faces telling us "One at a time!"

Like the hub that would make the dinner table go round, if it ever could start, was a tulip-shaped glass in the center in which the bright-polished teaspoons, all the largest family could ever need, stood facing in with their backs turned. I don't believe this spoonholder ever left the table. Even in the dark diningroom at midnight in the sleeping house, it would stand ready there. The smell of all those loaves of bread and the row of pies didn't easily go away either. And in the parlor where the blinds were drawn, the smell of being unvisited would pervade, pervade, pervade.

Compared to the Andrews clan, the Welty family at the time of the first visit I remember was very scarce in the way of uncles and cousins and kin of an older generation. Grandpa, Jefferson Welty, had been the youngest of thirteen children, but he is the only one I ever saw; his parents were Christian and Salome Welty, early settlers in Marion Township, Hocking County. The Weltys were originally German Swiss; the first ones to come to this country, back before the Revolutionary War here, were three brothers, and the whole family is descended from them, I understand—it seems to hark back to German fairy-tale tradition.

My father is not the one who told me this: he never happened to tell us a single family story; could it have been because he'd heard so many of the Andrews stories? I think it was rather because, as he said, he had no interest in ancient history—only the future, he said, should count. At the same time, he was exceedingly devoted to his father, went to see him whenever he could, and wrote to him regularly from his desk at home; I grew up familiar with seeing the long envelopes being addressed in my father's clear, careful hand: Jefferson Welty, Esquire. It was the only use my father made of the word; he saved it for his father. I took "Esquire" for a term of reverence, and I think it stood for that with him; we were always aware that Daddy loved him.

An English Welti, who spelled his name thus with an *i*, wrote to me once from Kent, in curiosity, after an early book of mine had appeared over there; he asked me about my name. My father, who had never told us anything, had died, and this was before my mother set herself as she did later to looking into records. Mr. Welti knew about the whole throng of them, from medieval times on, and the three brothers who set forth to the New World from German Switzerland and settled from Virginia westward over Pennsylvania, Ohio, and Indiana before the Revolutionary War. "I expect you know," wrote the British Mr. Welti, "that one unfortunate Welty fell at Saratoga."

The only part of his letter that would have interested my father is that about the St. Gotthard Tunnel and the Welty who pushed it through. The fact that this same Welty had been President of Switzerland seven times running would have caused him to say "Pshaw!", his strongest expletive. (That my mother's strongest exclamation was

70

"Pshaw!" too rather took away some of its force for both of them.)

In Grandpa and Grandma's parlor stood the organ, which, my mother had whispered to me, they preferred not to hear played. I tiptoed around it as if it were asleep. There were steep, uphill pedals; the flowered carpet continued right on up them as if they were part of the floor. When opened, the organ gave off a smell sharp as an exclamation, as if opening it were a mistake in company manners, which I already knew. I chilled my finger by touching a key. The key did not yield. The whole keyboard withstood me as if it had been a kitchen table; I suppose the organ had to be pumped.

But either I had been told, or I got the feeling there and then that this organ had belonged to my father's real mother, who had died when he was a little boy. But when I was named Eudora for my Andrews grandmother, I had been named for this grandmother too. Alice was my middle name. Her name had been Allie. Too late, after I was already christened, it came out that Allie stood for not Alice but Almira. Her name had been remembered wrong. I imagined what that would have done to her. It seemed to me to have made her an orphan. That was worse to me than if I had been able to imagine dying.

Barefooted on the slick brick walk I rushed to where I could breathe in the cool breath from the interior of the springhouse. On a cold bubbling spring, covered dishes and crocks and pitchers of butter and milk and so on floated in a circle in the mild whirlpool, like horses on a merry-go-round, in the water that smelled of the mint that grew close by.

Or I ran to the barn where all you touched was warm. Grandpa's barn *was* bigger than his house. The doors had to be rolled back. It had a plank floor like a bridge that came to an end at the wall and another door. The barn was fuller of furnishings than the house, with barrels and tubs and crates and sacks piled on top of one another, odorous of all the different things they held. There was more to see, more to smell, more to climb on; nothing appeared to be forbidden. At times when the animals were down in the pasture, I could hear the dry seedcorn I let run through my fingers in the waiting stillness. After the animals had been led inside, now and then a horse's head would appear looking over the door of his stall. Then I played nearby, to give the head a chance to speak to me, like Falada the white horse's head nailed above the gate in the fairy tale. Falada says to the Goose Girl driving her geese, "Princess, Princess, passing by, / Alas, alas, if thy mother knew it, / Sadly, sadly her heart would rue it." Up in the loft, jumping wild in the new hay, I skinned through the hole in the floor, the way it went down when it was tossed to the trough below, and the trough caught me neatly. My brother Edward, not missing a jump overhead, didn't even know I'd gone.

There was an old buggy being used for hens to nest in, standing in the shadows of the barn. The shiny black buggy next to it, with a fringe on top, was the one in which Grandpa drove us to church. He allowed me to stand between his knees and hold the reins, even though I could not see over the horse's too-busy tail where we were going. But standing up on the back seat, I could see, squinting through the peephole window at the back, where the narrow wheels on a rainy Sunday sliced the road to chocolate ribbons. I got to hear Grandpa's voice on Sunday more than in all the rest of the week, because he sang in the choir; indeed, Grandpa led the choir.

AT the end of the day at Grandpa's house, there wasn't much talking and no tales were told, even for the first time. Sometimes we all sat listening to a music box play.

There was a rack pulled out from inside the music box; we could see it holding shining metal discs as large as silver waiters, with teeth around the edges, and pierced with tiny holes in the shape of triangles or stars, like the tissue-paper patterns by which my mother cut out cloth for my dresses. When the discs began to turn, taking hold by their little teeth, a strange, chimelike music came about.

Its sounds had no kinship with those of "His Master's Voice" that we could listen to at home. They were thin and metallic, not exactly keeping to time—rather as if the spoons in the spoonholder had started a quiet fretting among themselves. Whatever song it was was slow and halting and remote, as if the music box were playing something I knew as well as "Believe Me If All Those Endearing Young Charms" but did not intend me to recognize. It seemed to be reaching the parlor from far away. It might even have been the sound going through the rooms and up and down the stairs of our house in Jackson at night while all of us were here in Ohio, too far from home even to hear the clock striking from the downstairs hall. While we listened, there at the open window, the moonflowers opened little by little, and the song continued like a wire spring allowing itself slowly, slowly to uncoil, then just stopped trying. Music and moonflower might have been geared to move together.

Then, in my father's grown-up presence, I could not imagine him as a child in this house, the sober way he looked in the little daguerreotype, motherless in his fair bangs and heavy little shoes, sitting on one foot. Now I look back, or listen back, in the same desire to imagine, and it seems possible that the sound of that sparse music, so faint and unearthly to my childhood ears, was the sound he'd had to speak to him in all that country silence among so many elders where he was the only child. To me it was a sound of unspeakable loneliness that I did not know how to run away from. I was there in its company, watching the moonflower open.

I NEVER saw until after he was dead a small keepsake book given to my father in his early childhood. On one page was a message of one sentence written to him by his mother on April 15, 1886. The date is the day of her death. "My dearest Webbie: I want you to be a good boy and to meet me in heaven. Your loving Mother." Webb was his middle name—her maiden name. She always called him by it. He was seven years old, her only child.

He had other messages in his little book to keep and read over to himself. "May your life, though short, be pleasant / As a warm and melting day" is from "Dr. Armstrong," and as it follows his mother's message may have been entered on the same day. Another entry reads: "Dear Webbie, If God send thee a cross, take it up willingly and follow Him. If it be light, slight it not. If it be heavy, murmur not. After the cross is the crown. Your aunt, Nina Welty." This is dated earlier—he was then three years old. The cover of the little book is red and embossed with baby ducklings falling out of a basket entwined with morning glories. It is very rubbed and worn. It had been given him to keep and he had kept it; he had brought it among his possessions to Mississippi when he married; my mother had put it away.

In the farmhouse, the staircase was not in sight until evening prayers were over—it was time to go to bed then, and a door in the kitchen wall was opened and there were the stairs, as if kept put away in a closet. They went up like a ladder, steep and narrow, that we climbed on the way to bed. Step by step became visible as I reached it, by the climbing yellow light of the oil lamp that Grandpa himself carried behind me.

* * *

BACK on Congress Street, when my father unlocked the door of our closed-up, waiting house, I rushed ahead into the airless hall and stormed up the stairs, pounding the carpet of each step with both hands ahead of me, and putting my face right down into the cloud of the dear dust of our long absence. I was welcoming ourselves back. Doing likewise, more methodically, my father was going from room to room re-starting all the clocks.

I think now, in looking back on these summer trips— this one and a number later, made in the car and on the train—that another element in them must have been influencing my mind. The trips were wholes unto themselves. They were stories. Not only in form, but in their taking on direction, movement, development, change. They changed something in my life: each trip made its particular revelation, though I could not have found words for it. But with the passage of time, I could look back on them and see them bringing me news, discoveries, premonitions, promises—I still can; they still do. When I did begin to write, the short story was a shape that had already formed itself and stood waiting in the back of my mind. Nor is it surprising to me that when I made my first attempt at a novel, I entered its world—that of the mysterious Yazoo-Mississippi Delta—as a child riding there on a train: "From the warm windowsill the endless fields glowed like a hearth in firelight, and Laura, looking out, leaning on her elbows with her head between her hands, felt what an arriver in a land feels—that slow hard pounding in the breast."

The events in our lives happen in a sequence in time, but in their significance to ourselves they find their own order, a timetable not necessarily—perhaps not possibly— chronological. The time as we know it subjectively is often the chronology that stories and novels follow: it is the continuous thread of revelation.

III

FINDING A
VOICE

I HAD the window seat. Beside me, my father checked the progress of our train by moving his finger down the timetable and springing open his pocket watch. He explained to me what the position of the arms of the semaphore meant; before we were to pass through a switch we would watch the signal lights change. Along our track, the mileposts could be read; he read them. Right on time by Daddy's watch, the next town sprang into view, and just as quickly was gone.

Side by side and separately, we each lost ourselves in the experience of not missing anything, of seeing everything, of knowing each time what the blows of the whistle meant. But of course it was not the same experience: what was new to me, not older than ten, was a landmark to him. My father knew our way mile by mile; by day or by night, he knew where we were. Everything that changed under our eyes, in the flying countryside, was the known world to him, the imagination to me. Each in our own way, we hungered for all of this: my father and I were in no other respect or situation so congenial.

In Daddy's leather grip was his traveler's drinking cup, collapsible; a lid to fit over it had a ring to carry it by; it traveled in a round leather box. This treasure would be brought out at my request, for me to bear to the water cooler at the end of the Pullman car, fill to the brim, and bear back to my seat, to drink water over its smooth lip. The taste of silver could almost be relied on to shock your teeth.

After dinner in the sparkling dining car, my father and I walked back to the open-air observation platform at the end of the train and sat on the folding chairs placed at the railing. We watched the sparks we made fly behind us into the night. Fast as our speed was, it gave us time enough to see the rose-red cinders turn to ash, each one, and disappear from sight. Sometimes a house far back in the empty hills showed a light no bigger than a star. The sleeping countryside seemed itself to open a way through for our passage, then close again behind us.

The swaying porter would be making ready our berths for the night, pulling the shade down just so, drawing the green fishnet hammock across the window so the clothes you took off could ride along beside you, turning down the tight-made bed, standing up the two snowy pillows as high as they were wide, switching on the eye of the reading lamp, starting the tiny electric fan—you suddenly saw its blades turn into gauze and heard its insect murmur; and drawing across it all the pair of thick green theaterlike curtains—billowing, smelling of cigar smoke—between which you would crawl or dive headfirst to button them together with yourself inside, to be seen no more that night.

When you lay enclosed and enwrapped, your head on a pillow parallel to the track, the rhythm of the rail clicks pressed closer to your body as if it might be your heart beating, but the sound of the engine seemed to come from farther away than when it carried you in daylight. The whistle was almost too far away to be heard, its sound wavering back from the engine over the roofs of the cars. What you listened for was the different sound that ran under you when your own car crossed on a trestle, then another sound on an iron bridge; a low or a high bridge—each had its pitch, or drumbeat, for your car.

Riding in the sleeper rhythmically lulled me and waked me. From time to time, waked suddenly, I raised my window shade and looked out at my own strip of the night. Sometimes there was unexpected moonlight out there. Sometimes the perfect shadow of our train, with our car, with me invisibly included, ran deep below, crossing a river with us by the light of the moon. Sometimes the encroaching walls of mountains woke me by clapping at my ears. The tunnels made the train's passage resound like the "loud" pedal of a piano, a roar that seemed to last as long as a giant's temper tantrum.

But my father put it all into the frame of regularity, predictability, that was his fatherly gift in the course of our journey. I saw it going by, the outside world, in a flash. I dreamed over what I could see as it passed, as well as over what I couldn't. Part of the dream was what lay beyond, where the path wandered off through the pasture, the red clay road climbed and went over the hill or made a turn and was hidden in trees, or toward a river whose bridge I could see but whose name I'd never know. A house back at its distance at night showing a light from an open doorway, the morning faces of the children who stopped still in what they were doing, perhaps picking blackberries or wild plums, and watched us go by—I never saw with the thought of their continuing to be there just the same after we were out of sight. For now, and for a long while to come, I was proceeding in fantasy.

I LEARNED much later—after he was dead, in fact, the time when we so often learn fundamental things about our parents—how well indeed he knew the journey, and how he happened to do so. He fell in love with my mother, and she with him, in West Virginia when she was a teacher in the mountain schools near her home and he was a young man from Ohio who'd gone over to West Virginia to work in the office of a lumber construction company. When they decided to marry, they saw it as part of the adventure of starting a new life to go to a place far away and new to both of them, and that turned out to be Jackson, Mississippi. From rural Ohio and rural West Virginia, that must have seemed, in 1904, as far away as Bangkok might possibly seem to young people today. My father went down and got a job in a new insurance company being formed in Jackson. This was the Lamar Life. He was promoted almost at once, made secretary and one of the directors, and he was to stay with the company for the rest of his life. He set about first thing finding a house in Jackson, then a town of six or eight thousand people, for them to live in until they could build a house of their own. So during the engagement, he went the thousand miles to see her when he could afford it. The rest of the time—every day, sometimes twice a day—the two of them sent letters back and forth by this same train.

Their letters had all been kept by that great keeper, my mother; they were in one of the trunks in the attic—the trunk that used to go on the train with us to West Virginia and Ohio on summer trips. I didn't in the end feel like a trespasser when I came to open the letters: they brought my parents before me for the first time as young, as inexperienced, consumed with the strength of their hopes and desires, as *living* on these letters. I would have known my mother's voice in her letters anywhere. But I wouldn't have so quickly known my father's. Annihilating those miles between them—the miles I came along to travel with him, that first time on the train—those miles he knew nearly altogether by heart, he wrote more often than only once a day, and mailed his letters directly onto the mail car—letters that are so ardent, so direct and tender in expression, so urgent, that they seemed to bare, along with his love, the rest of his whole life to me.

On the train I saw that world passing my window. It was when I came to see it was *I* who was passing that my self-centered childhood was over. But it was not until I began to write, as I seriously did only when I reached my twenties, that I found the world out there revealing, because (as with my father now) *memory* had become attached to seeing, love had added itself to discovery, and because I recognized in my own continuing longing to keep going, the need I carried inside myself to know—the apprehension, first, and then the passion, to connect myself to it. Through travel I first became aware of the outside world; it was through travel that I found my own introspective way into becoming a part of it.

This is, of course, simply saying that the outside world is the vital component of my inner life. My work, in the terms in which I see it, is as dearly matched to the world as its secret sharer. My imagination takes its strength and guides its direction from what I see and hear and learn and feel and remember of my living world. But I was to learn slowly that both these worlds, outer and inner, were different from what they seemed to me in the beginning.

THE BEST college in the state was very possibly the private liberal-arts one right here in Jackson, but I was filled with desire to go somewhere away and enter a school I'd never passed on the street. My parents thought that I was too young at sixteen to live for my first year too far from home. Mississippi State College for Women was well enough accredited and two hundred miles to the north.

There I landed in a world to itself, and indeed it was all new to me. It was surging with twelve hundred girls. They came from every nook and corner of the state, from the Delta, the piney woods, the Gulf Coast, the black prairie, the red clay hills, and Jackson—as the capital city and the only sizeable town, a region to itself. All were clearly differentiated sections, at that time, and though we were all put into uniforms of navy blue so as to unify us, it could have been told by the girls' accents, by their bearings, the way they came into the classroom and the way they ate, where they'd grown up. This was my first chance to learn what the body of us were like and what differences in background, persuasion of mind, and resources of character there

83

were among Mississippians—at that, among only half of us, for we were all white. I missed the significance of both what was in, and what was out of, our well-enclosed but vibrantly alive society. What was never there was money enough provided by our Legislature for education, and what was always there was a faculty accomplishing that education as a *feat*. Mississippi State College for Women, the oldest institution of its kind in America, poverty-stricken, enormously overcrowded, keeping within the tradition we were all used to in Mississippi, was conscientiously and, on the average, well taught by a dedicated faculty remaining and growing old there.

It was life in a crowd. We'd fight to get our mail in the basement post office, on rainy mornings, surrounded by other girls doing the Three Graces, where the gym teacher would have had to bring her first-period class indoors to practice. Even a gym piano, in competition with girls screaming over their letters and opening the food packages from home, was almost defeated. When we all had to crowd into compulsory chapel, one or two little frail undernourished students would faint sometimes—we had a fifteen-minute long Alma Mater to sing.

Old Main, the dormitory where I lived, had been built in 1860. It was packed to the roof with freshmen, three, four, or a half-dozen sometimes to the room, rising up four steep flights of wooden stairs. The chapel clock striking the hour very close by would shake our beds under us. It was the practice to use the fire escape to go to class, and at night to slip outside for a few minutes before going to bed.

It was the iron standpipe kind of fire escape, with a tin chute running down through it—all corkscrew turns from top to bottom, with holes along its passage where girls at fire drill could pour out of the different floors, and a hole at the bottom to pitch you out onto the ground, head still whirling.

It seemed impossible to be alone. Only music students had a good way. On a spring night you might hear one of them alone in a practice room of the Music Building, playing her heart out at an open window. It would be something like "Pale Hands I Loved Beside the Shalimar (Where Are You Now?)"—she'd be imagining of course that what she sent floating in the air was from someone else singing this song to *her*. At other times, when some strange song with low guttural notes and dragging movement, dramatically working up to a crescendo, was heard later still through that same open window, we freshmen told one another that was Miss Pohl, the spectacular gym teacher with the flying gray hair, who was, we had heard and believed, a Russian by birth, who'd been crossed, long years ago, in love. She may have indeed been crossed in love, but she was a Mississippian, just like us.

A time could be seized, close to bedtime, when it was possible to slip down the fire escape and, before the doors were all locked against my getting back, walk to an iron fountain on the campus and around it, with poetry running through my head. I'd bought the first book for my shelf from the college bookstore, *In April Once,* by William Alexander Percy, our chief Mississippi poet. Its first poem was one written from New York City, entitled "Home."

> *I have a need of silence and of stars.*
> *Too much is said too loudly. I am dazed.*
> *The silken sound of whirled infinity*
> *Is lost in voices shouting to be heard . . .*

Where I walked at that moment, within the little town of Columbus, and further within the iron gates of the campus of a girls' college at night, now everywhere going to bed, and while I said the poem to myself, around me was nothing *but* silence and stars. This did not impinge upon my longing. In the beautiful spring night, I was dedicated to *wanting* a beautiful spring night. To be *transported* to it was what I wanted. Whatever a poem was about—that it could be called "Home" didn't matter—it was about somewhere else, somewhere distant and far.

I was lucky enough to have found for myself, at the very beginning, an outside shell, that of freshman reporter on our college newspaper, *The Spectator*. I became a wit and humorist of the parochial kind, and the amount I was able to show off in print must have been a great comfort to me. (I saw *The Bat* and wrote "The Gnat," laid in MSCW. The Gnat assumes the disguise of our gym uniform—navy blue serge one-piece with pleated bloomers reaching below the knee, and white tennis shoes—and enters through the College Library, after hours; our librarian starts screaming at his opening line, "Beulah Culbertson, I have come for those fines.") I'd been a devoted reader of S. J. Perelman, Corey Ford, and other humorists who appeared in *Judge* magazine, and I'd imagined that with these as a springboard, I could swim.

After great floods struck the state and Columbus had been overflowed by the Tombigbee River, I contributed an editorial to *The Spectator* for its April Fool issue. This lamented that five of our freshman class got drowned when the waters rose, but by this Act of God, it went on, there was that much more room now for the rest of us. Years later, a Columbus newspaperman, on whose press our paper was printed, told me that H. L. Mencken had picked up this chirp out of me for *The American Mercury* as sample thinking from the Bible Belt. But by chance, in the home of a town student, I had just met my first intellectual. Within a few moments he had lent me *Candide!* It was just published, the first Modern Library book (I believe the very first)— that thin little book with leatherlike covers that heated up, while you read, warmer than your hand. Voltaire, too, I could call on.

But I learned my vital lesson in the classroom.

Mr. Lawrence Painter, the only man teacher in the college, spent his life conducting the MSCW girls in their sophomore year through English Survey, from "Summer is y-comen in" to "I have a rendezvous with Death." In my time a handsome, learned, sandy-haired man—wildly popular, of course, on campus—he got instant silence when he would throw open the book and begin to read aloud to us.

In high-school freshman English, we had committed to memory "Whan that Aprille with his shoures soote . . ." which as poetry was not less remote to our ears than "Arma virumque cano . . ." I had come unprepared for the immediacy of poetry.

I felt the shock closest to this a year later at the University of Wisconsin when I walked into my art class and saw, in place of the bowl of fruit and the glass bottle and ginger jar of the still life I used to draw at MSCW, a live human being. As we sat at our easels, a model, a young woman, lightly dropped her robe and stood, before us and a little above us, holding herself perfectly contained, in her full self and naked. Often that year in Survey Course, as Mr. Painter read, poetry came into the room where we could see it and all around it, free-standing poetry. As we listened, Mr. Painter's, too, was a life class.

After I transferred, in my junior year, to the University of Wisconsin, I made in this far, new place a discovery for myself that has fed my life ever since. I express a little of my experience in a story, one fairly recent and not yet completed. It's the story of a middle-aged man who'd come from a farm in the Middle West, who's taciturn and unhappy as a teacher of linguistics and now has reached a critical point in his life. The scene is New Orleans; he and a woman are walking at night (they are really saying goodbye) and he speaks of himself without reserve to her for the first time.

87

He'd put himself through the University of Wisconsin, he tells her:

"And I happened to discover Yeats, reading through some of the stacks in the library. I read the early and then the later poems all in the same one afternoon, standing up, by the window ... I read 'Sailing to Byzantium,' standing up in the stacks, read it by the light of falling snow. It seemed to me that if I could stir, if I could move to take the next step, I could go out into the poem the way I could go out into that snow. That it would be falling on my shoulders. That it would pelt me on its way down—that I could move in it, live in it—that I could die in it, maybe. So after that I had to *learn* it," he said. "And I told myself that I would. That I accepted the invitation."

The experience I describe in the story had indeed been my own, snow and all; the poem that smote me first was "The Song of Wandering Aengus"; it was the poem that turned up, fifteen years or so later, in my stories of *The Golden Apples* and runs all through that book.

At length too, at Wisconsin, I learned the word for the nature of what I had come upon in reading Yeats. Mr. Riccardo Quintana lecturing to his class on Swift and Donne used it in its true meaning and import. The word is *passion*.

IT WAS my mother who emotionally and imaginatively supported me in my wish to become a writer. It was my father who gave me the first dictionary of my own, a Webster's Collegiate, inscribed on the flyleaf with my full name (he always included Alice, my middle name, after his mother) and the date, 1925. I still consult it. It was also he who expressed his reservations that I wouldn't achieve financial success by becoming a writer, a sensible fear; nevertheless he fitted me out with my first typewriter, my little red Royal Portable, which I carried off to the University of Wisconsin. It was also he who advised me, after I'd told him I still meant to try writing, even though I didn't expect to sell my stories to *The Saturday Evening Post* which paid well, to go ahead and try myself—but to prepare to earn my living some other way. My supportive parents had already very willingly agreed that I go farther from home for my last two years of college and sent me to Wisconsin—my father's choice for its high liberal-arts reputation. Now that I'd been graduated from there, they sent me to my first choice of a place to prepare for a job: New York City, at Columbia University Graduate School of Business. (As certain as I was of wanting to be a writer, I was certain of *not* wanting to be a teacher. I lacked the instructing turn of mind, the selflessness, the patience for teaching, and I had the unreasoning feeling that I'd be trapped. The odd thing is that when I did come to write my stories, the longest list of my characters turns out to be schoolteachers. They are to a great extent my heroines.)

My father did not bring it up, but of course I knew that he had another reason to worry about my decision to write. Though he was a reader, he was not a lover of fiction, because fiction is not true, and for that flaw it was forever inferior to fact. If reading fiction was a waste of time, so was the writing of it. (Why is it, I wonder, that humor didn't count? Wodehouse, for one, whom both of us loved, was a flawless fiction writer.)

But I was not to be in time to show him what I could do, to hear what he thought, on the evidence, of where I was headed.

MY FATHER had given immense study to the erection of the new Lamar Life home office building on Capitol Street, which was completed in 1925—"Jackson's first skyscraper." It is a delicately imposing Gothic building of white marble, thirteen stories high with a clock tower at the top. It had been designed, as my father had asked of the Fort Worth architect, to be congenial with the Episcopal parish church that stood next door to it and with the fine Governor's Mansion that faced it from across the street. The architect pleased him with his gargoyles: the stone decorations of the main entrance took the form of alligators, which related it as well to Mississippi.

At every stage of the building, Daddy took his family to see as much as we could climb over, usually on Sunday mornings. At last we could climb by the fire escape to reach the top. We stood on the roof, with the not-yet-working clock towering at our backs, and viewed all Jackson below, spread to its seeable limits, its green rim, where the still river-like Pearl River and the still-unpaved-over Town Creek meandered and joined together in their unmolested swamp, with "the country" beyond. We were located where we stood there—part of our own map.

At the grand opening, the whole of the new building was lighted from top to bottom and the Company—its business now expanded into other Southern states—had a public reception. My father made a statement at the time: "Not a dollar was borrowed nor a security sold for the erection of this new building, and it is all paid for. The building will stand, now and always, free from all debt, as a most valuable asset to policy-holders."

It was a crowning year of his life. At the same time that the new building was going up, so was our new house, designed by the same architect. The house was on a slight hill (my mother never could see the hill) covered with its original forest pines, on a gravel road then a little out from town, and was built in a style very much of its day, of stucco and brick and beams in the Tudor style. We had moved in, and Mother was laying out the garden.

Six years later, my father was dead.

The Lamar Life tower is overshadowed now, and you can no longer read the time on its clocktower from all over town, as he'd wanted to be possible always, but the building's grace and good proportion contrast tellingly with the overpowering, sometimes brutal, character of some of the structures that rise above it. Renovators have sandblasted away the alligators that graced the entrance. But the Company still has its home there, and my father is remembered.

My father's enthusiasm for business was not the part of him that he passed on to his children. But his imaginative conception of the building, and his pride in seeing it go up and his love of working in his tenth-floor office with the windows open to the view on three sides, may well have entered into his son Edward. He went on to become an architect, especially gifted in design, who had a hand in a number of public buildings and private houses to be seen today in Jackson. Walter was a more literal kind of inheritor; after taking his master's degree in mathematics he went into the office of an insurance company—not the Lamar Life, but another.

Plans for the Company had included the launching of a radio station, and its office was a cubbyhole installed in the base of the tower. After my father was dead and the Great Depression remained with us, I got a part-time job there. My first paid work was in communications: Mississippi's first radio station, operating there under the big clock, to which he would have given his nod of approval.

MY FIRST full-time job was rewarding to me in a way I could never have foreseen in those early days of my writing. I went to work for the state office of the Works Progress Administration as junior publicity agent. (This was of course one of President Roosevelt's national measures to combat the Great Depression.) Traveling over the whole of Mississippi, writing news stories for county papers, taking

91

pictures, I saw my home state at close hand, really for the first time.

With the accretion of years, the hundreds of photographs—life as I found it, all unposed—constitute a record of that desolate period; but most of what I learned for myself came right at the time and directly out of the *taking* of the pictures. The camera was a hand-held auxiliary of wanting-to-know.

It had more than information and accuracy to teach me. I learned in the doing how *ready* I had to be. Life doesn't hold still. A good snapshot stopped a moment from running away. Photography taught me that to be able to capture transience, by being ready to click the shutter at the crucial moment, was the greatest need I had. Making pictures of people in all sorts of situations, I learned that every feeling waits upon its gesture; and I had to be prepared to recognize this moment when I saw it. These were things a story writer needed to know. And I felt the need to hold transient life in *words*—there's so much more of life that only words can convey—strongly enough to last me as long as I lived. The direction my mind took was a writer's direction from the start, not a photographer's, or a recorder's.

Along Mississippi roads you'd now and then see bottle trees; you'd see them alone or in crowds in the front yard of remote farmhouses. I photographed one—a bare crape myrtle tree with every branch of it ending in the mouth of a colored glass bottle—a blue Milk of Magnesia or an orange or green pop bottle; reflecting the light, flashing its colors in the sun, it stood as the centerpiece in a little thicket of peach trees in bloom. Later, I wrote a story called "Livvie" about youth and old age: the death of an old, proud, possessive man and the coming into flower, after dormant years, of his young wife—a spring story. Numbered among old Solomon's proud possessions is this bottle tree.

I know that the actual bottle tree, from the time of my

actual sight of it, was the origin of my story. I know equally well that the bottle tree appearing in the story is a projection from my imagination; it isn't the real one except in that it is corrected by reality. The fictional eye sees in, through, and around what is really there. In "Livvie," old Solomon's bottle tree stands bright with dramatic significance, it stands vulnerable, ready for invading youth to sail a stone into the bottles and shatter them, as Livvie is claimed by love in the bursting light of spring. This I saw could be brought into being in the form of a story.

I WAS always my own teacher. The earliest story I kept a copy of was, I had thought, sophisticated, for I'd had the inspiration to lay it in Paris. I wrote it on my new typewriter, and its opening sentence was, "Monsieur Boule inserted a delicate dagger into Mademoiselle's left side and departed with a poised immediacy." I'm afraid it was a perfect example of what my father thought "fiction" mostly was. I was ten years older before I redeemed that in my first published story, "Death of a Traveling Salesman." I backslid, for I found it hard to save myself from starting stories to show off what I could write.

In "Acrobats in a Park," though I laid the story in my home town, I was writing about Europeans, acrobats, adultery, and the Roman Catholic Church (seen from across the street), in all of which I was equally ignorant. In real life I fell easily under the spell of all traveling artists. En route to New Orleans, entertainments of many kinds would stop over in those days for a single performance in Jackson's Century Theatre. Galli-Curci came, so did Blackstone the Magician, so did Paderewski, so did *The Cat and the Canary* and the extravaganza *Chu Chin Chow*. Our family attended them all. My stories from the first drew visiting performers in, beginning modestly with a ladies' trio of the Redpath Chatauqua in "The Winds" and going so far as Segovia in

"Music from Spain." Then, as now, my imagination was magnetized toward transient artists—toward the transience as much as the artists.

I must have seen "Acrobats in a Park" at the time I wrote the story as exotic, free of any experience as I knew it. And yet in the simplest way it isn't unrelated. The acrobats I led in procession into Smith Park in Jackson, Mississippi, were a *family*. They sat down in our family park, eating their lunch under a pin-oak tree I knew intimately. A father, a mother, and their children made up the troupe. At the center of the little story is the Zorros' act: the feat of erecting a structure of their bodies that holds together, interlocked, and stands like a wall, the Zorro Wall. Writing about the family act, I was writing about the family itself, its strength as a unit, testing its frailty under stress. I treated it in an artificial and oddly formal way; the stronghold of the family is put on public view as a structure built each night; on the night before the story opens, the Wall has come down when the most vulnerable member slips, and the act is done for. But from various points within it and from outside it, I've been writing about the structure of the family in stories and novels ever since. In spite of my unpromising approach to it, my fundamental story form might have been trying to announce itself to me.

My first good story began spontaneously, in a remark repeated to me by a traveling man—our neighbor—to whom it had been spoken while he was on a trip into North Mississippi: "He's gone to borry some fire." The words, which carried such lyrical and mythological and dramatic overtones, were real and actual—their hearer repeated them to me.

As usual, I began writing from a distance, but "Death of a Traveling Salesman" led me closer. It drew me toward what was at the center of it, to a cabin back in the red clay hills—perhaps just such a house as I used to see from far off on a train at night, with the firelight or lamplight showing yellow from its open doorway. In writing the story I approached and went inside with my traveling salesman, and had him, pressed by imminent death, figure out what was there:

> Bowman could not speak. He was shocked with knowing what was really in this house. A marriage, a fruitful marriage. That simple thing. Anyone could have had that.

Writing "Death of a Traveling Salesman" opened my eyes. And I had received the shock of having touched, for the first time, on my real subject: human relationships. Daydreaming had started me on the way; but story writing, once I was truly in its grip, took me and shook me awake.

My TEMPERAMENT and my instinct had told me alike that the author, who writes at his own emergency, remains and needs to remain at his private remove. I wished to be, not effaced, but invisible—actually a powerful position. Perspective, the line of vision, the frame of vision—these set a distance.

An early story called "A Memory" is a discovery in the making. This is how it begins:

> One summer morning when I was a child I lay on the sand after swimming in the small lake in the park. The sun beat down—it was almost noon. The water shone like steel, motionless except for the feathery curl behind a distant swimmer. From my position I was looking at a rectangle brightly lit, actually glaring at me, with sun, sand, water, a little pavilion, a few solitary people in fixed attitudes, and around it all a border of dark rounded oak trees, like the engraved thunderclouds surrounding illustrations in the Bible. Ever

since I had begun taking painting lessons, I had made small frames with my fingers, to look out at everything.

Since this was a weekday morning, the only persons who were at liberty to be in the park were either children, who had nothing to occupy them, or those older people whose lives are obscure, irregular, and consciously of no worth to anything: this I put down as my observation at that time. I was at an age when I formed a judgment upon every person and every event which came under my eye, although I was easily frightened. When a person, or a happening, seemed to me not in keeping with my opinion, or even my hope or expectation, I was terrified by a vision of abandonment and wildness which tore my heart with a kind of sorrow. My father and mother, who believed that I saw nothing in the world which was not strictly coaxed into place like a vine on our garden trellis to be presented to my eyes, would have been badly concerned if they had guessed how often the weak and inferior and strangely turned examples of what was to come showed themselves to me.

I do not know even now what it was that I was waiting to see; but in those days I was convinced that I almost saw it at every turn. To watch everything about me I regarded grimly and possessively as a *need*. All through this summer I had lain on the sand beside the small lake, with my hands squared over my eyes, finger tips touching, looking out by this device to see everything: which appeared as a kind of projection. It did not matter to me what I looked at; from any observation I would conclude that a secret of life had been revealed to me—for I was obsessed with notions about concealment, and from the smallest gesture of a stranger I would wrest what was to me a communication or a presentiment.

This is not, on reaching its end, an observer's story. The tableau discovered through the young girl's framing hands is unwelcome realism. How can she accommodate the existence of this view to the dream of love, which she carried already inside her? Amorphous and tender, from now on it will have to remain hidden, her own secret imagining. The frame only raises the question of the vision. It has something of my own dreaming at the train window. But now the dreamer has stopped to look. After that, dreaming or awake, she will be drawn in.

"A Still Moment"—another early story—was a fantasy, in which the separate interior visions guiding three highly individual and widely differing men marvelously meet and converge upon the same single exterior object. All my characters were actual persons who had lived at the same time, who would have been strangers to one another, but whose lives had actually taken them at some point to the same neighborhood. The scene was in the Mississippi wilderness in the historic year 1811—"*anno mirabilis*," the year the stars fell on Alabama and lemmings, or squirrels perhaps, rushed straight down the continent and plunged into the Gulf of Mexico, and an earthquake made the Mississippi River run backwards and New Madrid, Missouri, tumbled in and disappeared. My real characters were Lorenzo Dow the New England evangelist, Murrell the outlaw bandit and murderer on the Natchez Trace, and Audubon the painter; and the exterior object on which they all at the same moment set their eyes is a small heron, feeding.

I never wrote another such story as that, but other sorts of vision, dream, illusion, hallucination, obsession, and that most wonderful interior vision which is memory, have all gone to make up my stories, to form and to project them, to impel them.

The frame through which I viewed the world changed too, with time. Greater than scene, I came to see, is situation. Greater than situation is implication. Greater than all of these is a single, entire human being, who will never be confined in any frame.

WRITING a story or a novel is one way of discovering *sequence* in experience, of stumbling upon cause and effect in the happenings of a writer's own life. This has been the case with me. Connections slowly emerge. Like distant landmarks you are approaching, cause and effect begin to align themselves, draw closer together. Experiences too indefinite of outline in themselves to be recognized for themselves connect and are identified as a larger shape. And suddenly a light is thrown back, as when your train makes a curve, showing that there has been a mountain of meaning rising behind you on the way you've come, is rising there still, proven now through retrospect.

It seems to me, writing of my parents now in my seventies, that I see continuities in their lives that weren't visible to me when they were living. Even at the times that have left me my most vivid memories of them, there were connections between them that escaped me. Could it be because I can better see their lives—or any lives I know—today because I'm a fiction writer? See them not as fiction, certainly—see them, perhaps, as even greater mysteries than I knew. Writing fiction has developed in me an abiding respect for the unknown in a human lifetime and a sense of where to look for the threads, how to follow, how to connect, find in the thick of the tangle what clear line persists. The strands are all there: to the memory nothing is ever really lost.

The little keepsake book given to my father so long

ago, of which I never heard a word spoken by anybody, has grown in eloquence to me. The messages that were meant to "go with him"—and which did—the farewell from his mother on the day of her death; and the doctor's following words that the child's own life would be short; the admonition from his Aunt Penina to bear his cross and murmur not—made a sum that he had been left to ponder over from the time he had learned to read. It seems to me that my father's choosing life insurance as his work, and indeed he exhausted his life for it, must have always had a deeper reason behind it than his conviction, strong as it was, in which he joined the majority in the twenties, that success in business was the solution to most of the problems of living—security of the family, their ongoing comfort and welfare, and especially the certainty of education for the children. This was partly why the past had no interest for him. He saw life in terms of the future, and he worked to provide that future for his children.

Right along with the energetic practice of optimism, and deeper than this, was an abiding awareness of mortality itself—most of all the mortality of a parent. This care, this caution, that ruled his life in the family, and in the business he chose and succeeded in expanding so far, began very possibly when he was seven years old, when his mother, asking him with perhaps literally her last words to be a good boy and meet her in heaven, died and left him alone.

Strangely enough, what Ned Andrews had extolled too, in all his rhetoric, was the future works of man and the leaving of the past behind. No two characters could have been wider apart than those of Ned Andrews and Christian Welty, or more different in their self-expression. They never knew each other, and the only thing they had in common was my mother's love. Who knows but that this ambition for the betterment of mankind in the attainable future was the quality in them both that she loved first? She would have responded to the ardency of their beliefs. I'm not sure she succeeded in having faith in their predictions. Neither got to live their lives out; the hurt she felt in this was part of her love for both.

My father of course liberally insured his own life for the future provision of his family, and had cause to believe that all was safe ahead. Then the Great Depression arrived. And in 1931 a disease that up to then even he had never heard of, leukemia, caused his death in a matter of weeks, at the age of fifty-two.

I BELIEVE the guiding emotion in my mother's life was pity. It encompassed the world. During the war (World War II), she heard on a radio broadcast that the Chinese, fearing their great library would be destroyed, took the books up in their hands and put them onto their backs and carried all of them, on foot, over long mountain paths, away to safety. Mother cried for them, and for their books. Almost more than eventual disaster, brave hope that it could be averted undid her. She had had so many of those brave hopes herself. Crying for the old Chinese scholars carrying their precious books over the mountain gave her a way too of crying for herself, with her youngest child, who was serving with the Navy at the battle of Okinawa.

She suffered perhaps more than an ordinary number of blows in her long life. We her children, like our father before us, had to learn the lesson that we never would be able to console her for any of them; especially could we not console her for what happened to ourselves.

Her strongest habit of thought was association. There is no way to help that.

When my father was dying in the hospital, there was a desperate last decision to try a blood transfusion. How much was known about compatibility of blood types then, or about the procedure itself, I'm unable to say. All I know is that there was no question in my mother's mind as to who the donor was to be.

I was present when it was done; my two brothers were in school. Both my parents were lying on cots, my father had been brought in on one and my mother lay on the other. Then a tube was simply run from her arm to his.

My father, I believe, was unconscious. My mother was looking at him. I could see her fervent face: there was no doubt as to what she was thinking. This time, *she* would save *his* life, as he'd saved hers so long ago, when she was dying of septicemia. What he'd done for her in giving her the champagne, she would be able to do for him now in giving him her own blood.

All at once his face turned dusky red all over. The doctor made a disparaging sound with his lips, the kind a woman knitting makes when she drops a stitch. What the doctor meant by it was that my father had died.

My mother never recovered emotionally. Though she lived for over thirty years more, and suffered other bitter losses, she never stopped blaming herself. She saw this as her failure to save his life.

AS THE New York train pulled, close to midnight, out of the station at home, your friends stood waving as though they'd never see you again. Your last view of Jackson from your window was an old dark wooden building by the tracks topped by a hand-painted sign under an arc light: "Where Will YOU Spend Eternity?" This sign was also the first thing you saw in the dawn when the train brought you back home again.

As the train picked up speed, rolled faster out of town, I would lie back with an iron cage around my chest of guilt.

In the later times of the Depression, I saved all I could from my part-time or temporary jobs in Jackson to go to New York. I hoped to show my stories and the photographs I'd taken over Mississippi in the Depression to an editor who would like them—either or both—enough to publish them. A two-week stay in the City, which I'd proved could be managed for $100 then—and that included the theatre—seemed long enough to me for a decision; but I would have to come away without knowing. It didn't at all occur to me how many times over my own manuscripts were multiplied on an editor's desk. It was the *encouraging* responses that took so long to come—a year sometimes; the editors who gave me an extraordinary amount of understanding and hope, and praise too, had so far found they still had to say no in the end. All this would go on the train with me, up there and back. It was part of my flying landscape.

I knew that even as I was moving farther away from Jackson, my mother was already writing to me at her desk, telling me she missed me but only wanted what was best for me. She would not leave the house till she had my wire, sent from Penn Station the third day from now, that I had arrived safely. I was not to worry about her or things at home, about how she was getting along. She anxiously awaited my letter after I had tried my stories on the publishers.

I knew this was how she must have waited when my father had left on one of his business trips, and I thought I could guess how he, the train lover, the trip lover, must have felt too while he remained away. I thought of the big box of Fanny May Chocolates he brought back from Chicago, the sheet music to "I Want to Be Happy" from *No, No, Nanette* that would tell us all about the show he'd so much enjoyed and wished we had seen with him. Taking trips tore all of us up inside, for they seemed, each journey away from home, something that might have been less selfishly undertaken, or something that would test us, or something that had better be momentous, to justify such a leap into the dark. The torment and guilt—the torment of having the loved one go, the guilt of being the loved one gone—comes into my fiction as it did and does into my life. And most of all the guilt then was because it was true: I had left to arrive at some future and secret joy, at what was unknown, and what was now in New York, waiting to be discovered. My joy was connected with writing; that was as much as I knew.

In Meridian (I had only gone ninety miles from Jackson) there was a wait of hours for the train that went from New Orleans to New York. The ceiling lights in the station were so lofty that you couldn't see to read. Long after midnight, the first signal came from the blackness outside—the whistle blowing for the curve south of town. The ancient and familiar figure of the black lady who for the last two hours had carried around coffee in a black iron pot as large as a churn would be at your side as you woke up. She was the sole attendant. Now she proceeded to call the stations. Her white frilled bonnet and starched white apron only made her look official at 2 A.M. in Meridian. She shouted out the whole list of destinations exactly as she must have done for fifty years under the echoing vault of the grand railroad station of its day. Above the thunder of the approaching engine, and then a bell heard ringing, rising in pitch as it rang nearer, and its alarm right at our ears now, and over the clanging and banging of arrival at the platform and the shriek of vented steam, one human voice recited the roster of our destination. Slowly and from deep-down inside her each name came measured out to us like words in a church: "Birmingham ... Chattanooga ... Bristol ... Lynchburg ... Washington ... Baltimore ... Philadelphia ... and New York." And changing herself one more time—now into the porter—she would start loading her arms and shoulders with all our suitcases, as many as she could carry at one time, and herd us down the platform to our daycoach, getting rid of us herself to make sure we were gone. She appears as herself in one story I wrote, "The Demonstrators," but she's there in spirit in many more. She was to me the very Angel of Departure, and I thought how often, parked over there insensible in the sleeping car waiting for the same connection, in those earlier times, I'd slept through her.

The trip to New York meant two nights and parts of three days sitting up and changing trains several times. This cost only $17.50 each way, cheaper if I could run into an excursion rate out of Washington. We spent all one day crossing the width of Tennessee, then peacefully rural. I came to know the layout of any given town we went through, the name of the hardware store, where to look for a bank clock that kept good time. I knew where the shade patches came at mid-afternoon in upland pastures, and remembered to look for the pony among the horses gathered there. The same little dogs from summer to summer would always chase our train past the gates of certain farms. We went through the mountains by night; you could only hear your passage, not see. If I were asleep and a stop awakened me at dawn, I'd look out the window instinctively knowing I'd see the station where the fat, simpleminded boy would be skipping down the sidewalk at the drugstore corner, just in time to greet the train. I could have prophesied I'd see the same man and woman standing on ladders every time we went around a certain long curve, endlessly re-painting their greenhouse.

Yet those were the last years when there seemed to be timetables, schedules, in operation. With the approach of the War, on crowded and ill-maintained trains, the kind never running on time and often breaking down, the route itself retraced the same country as in those earlier days; landmarks were slower then to fade away. But the train often stopped for no discernible reason in the open country and stood without sound or motion, like a becalmed ship. My father would have been right out there, finding out the trouble from the brakeman or the engineer, taking out his watch, as concerned as they were. You had to expect to stop dead where the track reached a three-way meeting of branchlines in perfectly empty country; a tiny shed-like station carried the name "Ooltewah." Was this "Waterloo" said backwards? But nothing, it seemed to me, ever did happen at this prolonged stop. We met no other train; no train came to pass us. Destination, when the train isn't moving, seems only a forgotten dream.

Once, when my train came to one of those inexplicable stops in open country, this happened: Out there was spread around us a long, high valley, a green peaceful stretch of Tennessee with distant farmhouses and, threading off toward planted fields, a little foot path. It was sunset. Presently, without a word, a soldier sitting opposite me rose and stepped off the halted train. He hadn't spoken to anybody for the whole day and now, taking nothing with him and not stopping to put on his cap, he just left us. We saw him walking right away from the track, into the green valley, making a long shadow and never looking back. The train in time proceeded, and as we left him back there in the landscape, I felt *us* going out of sight for *him,* diminishing and soon to be forgotten.

Eventually, without stirring a mile from home, I fell into the safest possible hands. After I had written enough stories that were the best I could make them, my future literary agent Diarmuid Russell and my future editors, who became my friends for life, found *me.* (John Woodburn, an editor who came through Jackson scouting for his publisher, wrote when he'd persuaded the house to take my first book, "I knew when I tasted your mother's waffles everything would turn out all right.")

TRAVEL itself is part of some longer continuity.

Just this past summer, in some effects of my father's, I came across photographic negatives I'd never seen—even their size was different from all those he made of our family. I had them printed and found before me scenes of unfamiliar places—city streets and buildings and tram cars and docksides, public parks with running children who seemed in costume; young ladies sitting in boats or strolling in long skirts and straw hats; ships, flags, stretches of sea or some wide river—and all at once Niagara Falls, no mistake about that, by day and by night, lit up. On the other hand, there was a frozen waterfall with a man in overcoat and hat posing beside it, holding to one long icicle as to a lady's hand in an opera-length white glove. I was mystified until at a later time this same summer I ran across by chance a railway timetable with ferry-boat schedules and hours for band concerts, and excursion prices from Halifax, for a given week in August, 1903. That was my father's, all right—he would have taken every one of those offers. And the date I recognized now as the summer before the year he married my mother. In those snapshots I was looking at the festival scenes of his last fling.

No, I was looking at more than that. It came back to me that my mother had said he'd offered her a choice between the Thousand Islands and Jackson, Mississippi, as their future home, and she'd chosen Jackson, Mississippi; we had her to thank. But I could see now that of course he would have gone up there to look over the Thousand Islands and ridden the train or sailed the St. Lawrence from Ontario to Halifax, stopping off for Niagara Falls, and taken those pictures to bring her, before he'd say a rash thing like that to Chessie Andrews. And here they were, the choice she didn't take. She'd chosen the other place, and here was I now, one of the results, in it, with pictures of the other choice now turning up in my hand.

Along with the ferry timetable and the schedule of excursions and the souvenir book of the Thousand Islands, I came across a sizeable commercial photograph taken of my father. A slim figure in a light business suit, he is standing, with one foot up on a rock, apparently right in the rapids of Niagara Falls. His usual expression of kind regard is on his face. He'd probably had this trick photograph made just to present to my mother. It made me remember what countless times he tried by joking means to make her laugh. When he did, it took *him* with delighted surprise, too—a triumph for both of them. I could imagine her being handed this picture of her fiancé standing in the rapids above Niagara Falls with his hat in his hand, and saying to him, "I don't see the humor in that." He *knew* how terrified she was of the water!

W H A T discoveries I've made in the course of writing stories all begin with the particular, never the general. They are mostly hindsight: arrows that I now find I myself have left behind me, which have shown me some right, or wrong, way I have come. What one story may have pointed out to me is of no avail in the writing of another. But "avail" is not what I want; freedom ahead is what each story promises—beginning anew. And all the while, as further hindsight has told me, certain patterns in my work repeat themselves without my realizing. There would be no way to know this, for during the writing of any single story, there is no other existing. Each writer must find out for himself, I imagine, on what strange basis he lives with his own stories.

I had been writing a number of stories, more or less one after the other, before it belatedly dawned on me that some of the characters in one story were, and had been all the time, the same charactèrs who had appeared already in another story. Only I'd written about them originally under different names, at different periods in their lives, in situations not yet interlocking but ready for it. They touched on every side. These stories were all related (and the fact was buried in their inceptions) by the strongest ties—identities, kinships, relationships, or affinities already known or remembered or foreshadowed. From story to story, connections between the characters' lives, through their motives or actions, sometimes their dreams, already existed: there to be found. Now the whole assembly—some of it still in the future—fell, by stages, into place in one location already evoked, which I saw now was a focusing point for all the stories. What had drawn the characters together there was one strong strand in them all: they lived in one way or another in a dream or in romantic aspiration, or under an illusion of what their lives were coming to, about the meaning of their (now) related lives.

The stories were connected most provocatively of all to me, perhaps, through the entry into my story-telling mind of another sort of tie—a shadowing of Greek mythological figures, gods and heroes that wander in various guises, at various times, in and out, emblems of the characters' heady dreams.

Writing these stories, which eventually appeared joined together in the book called *The Golden Apples,* was an experience in a writer's own discovery of affinities. In writing, as in life, the connections of all sorts of relationships and kinds lie in wait of discovery, and give out their signals to the Geiger counter of the charged imagination, once it is drawn into the right field.

The characters who go to make up my stories and novels are not portraits. Characters I invent along with the story that carries them. Attached to them are what I've borrowed, perhaps unconsciously, bit by bit, of persons I have seen or noticed or remembered in the flesh—a cast of countenance here, a manner of walking there, that jump to the visualizing mind when a story is underway. (Elizabeth Bowen said, "Physical detail cannot be invented." It can only be chosen.) I don't write by invasion into the life of a real person: my own sense of privacy is too strong for that; and I also know instinctively that living people to whom you are close—those known to you in ways too deep, too overflowing, ever to be plumbed outside love—do not yield to, could never fit into, the demands of a story. On the other hand, what I do make my stories out of is the *whole* fund of my feelings, my responses to the real experiences of my own life, to the relationships that formed and changed it, that I have given most of myself to, and so learned my way toward a dramatic counterpart. Characters take on life sometimes by luck, but I suspect it is when you can write most entirely out of yourself, inside the skin, heart, mind, and soul of a person who is not yourself, that a character becomes in his own right another human being on the page.

It was not my intention—it never was—to invent a character who should speak for me, the author, in person. A character is in a story to fill a role there, and the character's life along with its expression of life is defined by that surrounding—indeed is created by his own story. Yet, it seems to me now, years after I wrote *The Golden Apples,* that I did bring forth a character with whom I came to feel oddly in touch. This is Miss Eckhart, a woman who has come from away to give piano lessons to the young of Morgana. She is formidable and eccentric in the eyes of everyone, is scarcely accepted in the town. But she persisted with me, as she persisted in spite of herself with the other characters in the stories.

Where did the character of Miss Eckhart come from?

There was my own real-life piano teacher, "eligible" to the extent that she swatted my hands at the keyboard with a fly-swatter if I made a mistake; and when she wrote "Practice" on my page of sheet music she made her "P" as Miss Eckhart did—a cat's face with a long tail. She did indeed hold a recital of her pupils every June that was a fair model for Miss Eckhart's, and of many another as well, I suppose. But the character of Miss Eckhart was miles away from that of the teacher I knew as a child, or from that of anybody I did know. Nor was she like other teacher-characters I was responsible for: my stories and novels suddenly appear to me to be full of teachers, with Miss Eckhart different from them all.

What the story "June Recital" most acutely shows the reader lies in her inner life. I haven't the slightest idea what my real teacher's life was like inside. But I knew what Miss Eckhart's was, for it protruded itself well enough into the story.

As I looked longer and longer for the origins of this passionate and strange character, at last I realized that Miss Eckhart came from me. There wasn't any resemblance in her outward identity: I am not musical, not a teacher, nor foreign in birth; not humorless or ridiculed or missing out in love; nor have I yet let the world around me slip from my recognition. But none of that counts. What counts is only what lies at the solitary core. She derived from what I already knew for myself, even felt I had always known. What I have put into her is my passion for my own life work, my own art. Exposing yourself to risk is a truth Miss Eckhart and I had in common. What animates and possesses me is what drives Miss Eckhart, the love of her art and the love of giving it, the desire to give it until there is no more left. Even in the small and literal way, what I had done in assembling and connecting all the stories in *The Golden*

Apples, and bringing them off as one, was not too unlike the June recital itself.

Not in Miss Eckhart as she stands solidly and almost opaquely in the surround of her story, but in the making of her character out of my most inward and most deeply feeling self, I would say I have found my voice in my fiction.

Of course any writer is in part all of his characters. How otherwise would they be known to him, occur to him, become what they are? I was also part Cassie in that same story, the girl who hung back, and indeed part of most of the main characters in the connected stories into whose minds I go. Except for Virgie, the heroine. She is right outside me. She is powerfully like Miss Eckhart, her co-equal in stubborn and passionate feeling, while more expressive of it—but fully apart from me. And as Miss Eckhart's powers shrink and fade away, the young Virgie grows up more rampant, and struggles into some sort of life independent from all the rest.

If somewhere in its course your work seems to you to have come into a life of its own, and you can stand back from it and leave it be, you are looking then at your subject—so I feel. This is how I came to regard the character of Virgie in *The Golden Apples.* She comes into her own in the last of the stories, "The Wanderers." Passionate, recalcitrant, stubbornly undefeated by failure or hurt or disgrace or bereavement, all the while heedlessly wasting of her gifts, she knows to the last that there is a world that remains out there, a world living and mysterious, and that she is of it.

Inasmuch as Miss Eckhart might have been said to come from me, the author, Virgie, at her moments, might have always been my subject.

THROUGH learning at my later date things I hadn't known, or had escaped or possibly feared realizing, about my parents—and myself—I glimpse our whole family life as if it were freed of that clock time which spaces us apart so inhibitingly, divides young and old, keeps our living through the same experiences at separate distances.

It is our inward journey that leads us through time—forward or back, seldom in a straight line, most often spiraling. Each of us is moving, changing, with respect to others. As we discover, we remember; remembering, we discover; and most intensely do we experience this when our separate journeys converge. Our living experience at those meeting points is one of the charged dramatic fields of fiction.

I'm prepared now to use the wonderful word *confluence,* which of itself exists as a reality and a symbol in one. It is the only kind of symbol that for me as a writer has any weight, testifying to the pattern, one of the chief patterns, of human experience.

Here I am leading to the last scenes in my novel, *The Optimist's Daughter:*

She had slept in the chair, like a passenger who had come on an emergency journey in a train. But she had rested deeply.

She had dreamed that she *was* a passenger, and riding with Phil. They had ridden together over a long bridge.

Awake, she recognized it: it was a dream of something that had really happened. When she and Phil were coming down from Chicago to Mount Salus to be married in the Presbyterian Church, they came on the train. Laurel, when she travelled back and forth between Mount Salus and Chicago, had always taken the sleeper. She and Phil followed the route on the day train, and she saw it for the first time.

When they were climbing the long approach to a bridge after leaving Cairo, rising slowly higher until

they rode above the tops of bare trees, she looked down
and saw the pale light widening and the river bottoms
opening out, and then the water appearing, reflecting
the low, early sun. There were two rivers. Here was
where they came together. This was the confluence of
the waters, the Ohio and the Mississippi.

They were looking down from a great elevation and
all they saw was at the point of coming together, the
bare trees marching in from the horizon, the rivers
moving into one, and as he touched her arm she
looked up with him and saw the long, ragged, pencil-
faint line of birds within the crystal of the zenith, flying in a V of their own, following the same course
down. All they could see was sky, water, birds, light,
and confluence. It was the whole morning world.

And they themselves were a part of the confluence.
Their own joint act of faith had brought them here at
the very moment and matched its occurrence, and proceeded as it proceeded. Direction itself was made beautiful, momentous. They were riding as one with it,
right up front. It's our turn! she'd thought exultantly.
And we're going to live forever.

Left bodiless and graveless of a death made of water
and fire in a year long gone, Phil could still tell her of
her life. For her life, any life, she had to believe, was
nothing but the continuity of its love.

She believed it just as she believed that the confluence of the waters was still happening at Cairo. It
would be there the same as it ever was when she went
flying over it today on her way back—out of sight, for
her, this time, thousands of feet below, but with nothing in between except thin air.

Of course the greatest confluence of all is that which
makes up the human memory—the individual human mem-

ory. My own is the treasure most dearly regarded by me, in my life and in my work as a writer. Here time, also, is subject to confluence. The memory is a living thing—it too is in transit. But during its moment, all that is remembered joins, and lives—the old and the young, the past and the present, the living and the dead.

As you have seen, I am a writer who came of a sheltered life. A sheltered life can be a daring life as well. For all serious daring starts from within.